A CUP

OF COLD

WATER IN

.... 60 ways to care for the needy

HIS NAME

A Cup of Cold Water in His Name: 60 Ways to Help the Needy
© 2012 by Lorie Newman

Discovery House is affiliated with RBC Ministries, Grand Rapids, Michigan.

Requests for permission to quote from this book should be directed to: Permissions Department, Discovery House Publishers, P.O. Box 3566, Grand Rapids, MI 49501, or contact us by e-mail at permissionsdept@dhp.org

Scripture taken from the *Holy Bible,* New Living Translation, copyright © 1996, 2004. Used by permission of Tyndale House Publishers, Inc., Wheaton, Illinois 60189. All rights reserved.

Names and personal stories in this book have been used with permission. To protect the privacy of individuals, some names have been changed.

Cover design: Tim Green, Faceout Studio
Interior design: Paul Nielsen, Faceout Studio

ISBN 978-1-57293-512-9

Library of Congress Cataloging-in-Publication Data
Newman, Lorie.
A cup of cold water in His name : 60 ways to help the needy / Lorie Newman.
    p. cm.
ISBN 978-1-57293-512-9
1. Church work. I. Title.
BV4400.N49 2012
253—dc23
                    2011044414

Printed in the United States of America

Second printing in 2013

FOR MY HAITIAN DAUGHTER'S BIRTH MOTHER.

Sometimes I imagine your tear-filled eyes as you carried your frail and emaciated baby girl to the public hospital in Port-au-Prince. I imagine you kissing her precious face for the last time before you had to turn and walk away into the dusty Haitian heat, knowing you would never see your baby again.

My spirit aches knowing that because of extreme poverty, you had to choose between watching your baby starve and abandoning her. No mother should ever have to make that choice.

Your sacrifice was not in vain. It drives me forward daily to be a voice for you and for others like you living in extreme poverty, suffering in silence.

As long as there is breath within me, I will be your voice.

CONTENTS

INTRODUCTION

ONE.

This little word could possibly be the most neglected word in all of Scripture. So many Christians overlook it. I've heard several Bible study teachers and even pastors forget to quote it as they teach lessons and preach sermons. I certainly can't point fingers. I've read Matthew 25:40 dozens of times, but I misquoted it like everyone else by leaving out that crucial little word: "The King will tell them, 'I assure you, when you did it to the least of these my brothers and sisters, you were doing it to me!'"

The verse actually reads, "I assure you, when you did it to *one* of the least of these my brothers and sisters, you were doing it to me!" I had never noticed the word *one* until a crisp fall morning when I sat on the screened-in porch of my mountain home reading my Bible. The word *one* glared at me like a neon light.

One. Such a simple word. How could I have missed it so many times before?

I was all alone as I read that morning, but it was as if God himself were sitting beside me on the porch whispering that neglected word over and over again until it sank deep into the depths of my soul—*One. Just one.*

But, could that little word really make a difference? I thought of the suffering I had witnessed in Africa and Haiti. The smell of death at the AIDS hospital, the orphaned girl who cried uncontrollably and wouldn't let me come near her, the teenage girl who sold her body to feed herself and her siblings because their parents were dead, the boy with a high fever who reached up for me to hold him, the women gathering water from a dirty stream, the man dressed in

CUP OF COLD WATER

filthy rags begging on the street corner, the children stepping in raw sewage. All of these images came flooding back to me. I teared up as I remembered their faces. Still God continued to whisper, *One. Whatever you did to just one.*

I sat quietly weeping as I read that verse again and again as if I'd never read it before. I began to question God in my spirit, "But, God, does *one* really matter in a broken world where there are 145 million orphans? Where a child dies every five seconds of hunger-related causes and 925 million people are chronically undernourished? Where 40 million people are living with HIV/AIDS, and 1.1 billion do not have access to potable water? Where 3 billion people live on less than $2.50 a day, and 800,000 women and children are sold into human trafficking and brought across international borders each year? Where famine and disease seem to engulf masses of humanity? Does helping just *one* person really matter, God?"

As I continued to read with opened, spiritual eyes, I found the answer to my questions in the rest of Matthew 25, where Jesus speaks about the end of the age when He will separate the righteous from the unrighteous:

But when the Son of Man comes in his glory, and all the angels with him, then he will sit upon his glorious throne. All the nations will be gathered in his presence, and he will separate them as a shepherd separates the sheep from the goats. He will place the sheep at his right hand and the goats at his left. Then the King will say to those on the right, "Come, you who are blessed by my Father, inherit the Kingdom prepared for you from the foundation of the world. For I was hungry, and you fed me. I was thirsty, and you gave me a drink. I was a stranger, and you invited me into your home. I was naked, and you gave me clothing. I was sick, and you cared for me. I was in prison, and you visited me."

Then these righteous ones will reply, "Lord, when did we ever see you hungry and feed you? Or thirsty and give you something to drink? Or a stranger and show you hospitality? Or naked and give you clothing? When did we ever see you sick or in prison, and visit you?"

And the King will tell them, "I assure you, when you did it to one of the least of these my brothers and sisters, you were doing it to me!" (vv. 31–40)

"When you did it to *one* . . ." Those words sank to the deepest part of my being. That morning, God completely broke me and showed me the power in helping just one needy person.

In this world of so much suffering and economic disparity, so much pain and heartbreak, many of us feel overwhelmed by the magnitude of the need. Where do we even begin? As I've ministered to orphans, good Christian people have asked me what difference it makes to help one fatherless child when millions of other orphans suffer around the world. But the truth is that Jesus rarely calls one person to minister to masses of suffering people. Instead, He teaches us in Matthew 25:40 the importance of helping one needy person. Our Savior put so much emphasis on helping just one person that He tells us that when we help a needy person, we have done it to Jesus himself.

> And if you give even a cup of cold water to one of the least of my followers, you will surely be rewarded.
>
> **MATTHEW 10:42**

So, does *one* really matter? Oh yes. *One* definitely matters.

Wherever you are in life, whether you are a busy college student, a homemaker with little ones, a business person with a demanding career, a single parent working two jobs, or a retired person looking to volunteer, Christ will meet you right where you are in your desire to care for the hurting. You can accept Jesus' invitation to care for the needy no matter your schedule, financial situation, education level, or past failures. When you pray and ask the Lord to reveal ways that you can help the needy in your everyday life, you will begin to see those around you through His eyes.

Our God views people differently than we do. Daily we are bombarded with the latest gossip on Hollywood stars as if they were privileged royalty, but the poor of this world suffer and die every day in needless silence. God's system is the complete opposite. He calls us to treat the "least of these" as if they were royal daughters and sons. And they are. The poor, the orphan, the widow, the stranger, the suffering, the needy, and the oppressed are the King's children, and they are the ones who will be first in God's kingdom (Matthew 20:16). Helping them is how we are the hands and feet of Christ here on earth.

This book is uniquely arranged to help you accept Jesus' invitation to care for the needy on any level. Many of you are ready to begin. You are looking for everyday ways to help the needy around you in Jesus' name—you are ready to go *deep*. For others, you may have the time and the resources to go even *deeper* in your acceptance of Jesus' invitation to care for the needy. And for some of you, your heart beats with the realization that it is time to go *deeper still* in your life's race to help the needy. No matter your level of commitment, this book will give you creative ideas that you can use to accept Jesus' invitation to care for the least of these.

As you read and bookmark ideas that you can implement in your life, remember that whatever you do in Jesus' name to just *one* person in need, even if it's just to give a cup of cold water, you have done it to Christ himself.

One really does matter.

FEEDING THE HUNGRY AND THE THIRSTY

"For I was hungry, and you fed me. I was thirsty, and you gave me a drink."

1. BUY EXTRA NONPERISHABLE FOOD ITEMS EACH TIME YOU VISIT THE GROCERY STORE AND DONATE THEM TO A FOOD PANTRY.

It was a typical Thursday evening in our country home. My older brother and I sat at the kitchen table working on homework. My mother was at the stove preparing dinner. My father, an insurance salesman, was still at work.

Through the window, we could see the setting sun across the cow pasture in front of our house. Our little brick home was secluded. We lived so far off the beaten path that we rarely had visitors. I wasn't even sure we had a doorbell until that Thursday evening when its piercing ring jolted me out of my seat at the kitchen table.

Now I realize that in many families the doorbell rings frequently and it's not a big deal to open the door to a stranger when you live in a nice, quiet neighborhood. But when you live in the country, with no one within shouting distance, and your dad is not home, and it's nearly dark outside, and you're eleven years old, the ring of the doorbell is not a comfortable sound.

The three of us looked at each other. Instantly I knew the unease rising up in me was in them as well—I could see it in their eyes. We crept to the front window and slowly pulled back the curtain. What I saw sent a wave of fear through my eleven-year-old mind. There on the other side of our door stood a man dressed like one of the hobos from my storybooks.

The man had greasy blond hair that poked out like porcupine quills from underneath a filthy, dark, knitted cap. He wore black cut-finger gloves. His skin was dirty, and he looked like he hadn't shaved or changed his clothes for more than a week.

As I stood studying this stranger and becoming more terrified of his appearance by the second, my mother did the unthinkable. She opened the door. She said with fear under control, "May I help you?"

> To me, a faith in Jesus Christ that is not aligned with the poor . . . it's nothing.
>
> BONO, LEAD SINGER OF U2

The words that man uttered in reply will be etched forever in my mind. With eyes full of desperation, he said, "Ma'am, I am so hungry. Would you allow me to beg you for food?" And with that, he fell to his knees. I saw my mother's fear melt into deep compassion. Without hesitation, she brought him a full plate of the food she had been preparing for dinner.

My mother, wanting to protect us, gave the man the plate of food to eat on our front porch, and then shut the door. Full of curiosity for this strange man, I peered at him through the front window. As I watched, he ate that plate of food in about five seconds. I had never before seen anyone eat food the way he did. He ate it like he hadn't eaten in a week.

As he nearly inhaled the food, tears welled up in my eyes. For the first time in my life, my heart broke for a poor person. My heart broke for someone who was hungry. It didn't matter to me where he had come from or what his situation was. It didn't matter to me that it may have been his own foolish choices that had brought him to such a low place. I didn't care about his history or the road that had brought him to my front porch. And when that man left our porch, I watched him walk down our long dirt driveway until his silhouette disappeared from view. But his silhouette has never left my heart. It appears every time I see someone in need, every time I see a lonely orphan, a grieving widow, or a person lacking food.

IN HIS NAME

Food. Such a simple word, yet our bodies must have it to survive. For so many people, food is scarce. According to UNICEF, every 3.6 seconds a person dies of starvation—usually a child under the age of five. In the time it took you to read the first three pages of this book, twelve children died from starvation.

When our Savior walked this earth, He knew the importance of meeting the physical needs of the people around Him. In John 6:1–14, we read the familiar story of Jesus feeding the multitudes with a little boy's lunch of five loaves of bread and two small fish. Five thousand men were fed that day, along with women and children, with that one small lunch.

I've often thought of that little boy and what he had to give for that incredible miracle to take place. He could have kept his lunch for himself. It was late in the day and he was likely very hungry. He could have kept half of his lunch and given half to Jesus to make certain his own needs were met. But he didn't.

I've heard many sermons where pastors emphasize that the little boy "shared" his lunch. But really, he didn't share any of it.

THE STATS

The US is the world's wealthiest nation, yet 1 in 4 children live in households that struggle to put food on the table.

Each day more than 135,000,000 pounds of food are wasted in the United States.

CUP OF COLD WATER

He gave it *all* away! And only then did Jesus bless it, break it, and multiply it. Isn't it amazing how God's math works? When we give what we have, our Father blesses it, breaks it, and then multiplies it as only He can!

I don't think it's any coincidence that one of the most profound miracles of Jesus' earthly ministry centered on feeding the hungry.

A CUP OF COLD WATER

Overseas in third world countries where extreme poverty abounds, food is not a daily guarantee. Even in the Western world, food can be difficult to afford. For those of us who have been given the monetary resources to simply go to the grocery store or supermarket and purchase food for our families, why not buy a little extra each time you shop to donate to a local food pantry?

> *For $25, you can provide a family of four with two hundred meals.*
> *Visit FeedingAmerica.org.*

To find a local food pantry, visit FeedingAmerica.org and select your home state or click "Find My Food Bank" and type in your zip code. The Feeding America site will bring up a page with phone numbers, e-mail addresses, and maps to your local food banks. The site will also show you local statistics such as how many people are served and how many pounds of food are distributed.

It takes only a few dollars and a little effort to buy nonperishable items to support your local food pantry. The most needed items include canned meats and soups, rice, dry pasta, peanut butter, crackers, and dry or canned fruits.

Like the little boy with the fishes and loaves, God will use what you give. He will bless it, break it, and multiply it as only He can.

Abba, I often take for granted how much you have blessed me. If I am hungry, I can walk into any number of grocery stores in my community and buy something to eat. May I never browse the aisles of a supermarket again without a thankful heart and an open hand ready to bless others in my community from the overflow of what you have given me.

2. TAKE A MEAL TO THE RONALD MCDONALD HOUSE CHARITIES.

Baby Grace was born in Liberia, Africa, on a balmy Sunday afternoon in November while her daddy, Pastor David, preached in his cinder block church. Cecelia, Grace's mother, knew as soon as her baby was born that something was terribly wrong. The midwives had cheered at the birth of each of her five children. This time they gasped when they saw Grace. Baby Grace's abdominal organs were on the outside of her body.

Quickly the news spread to the nearby village where Pastor David and Cecelia lived. Many of the villagers ascribed the condition to black magic, and they urged Cecelia to let the "throwaway" baby die. But Cecelia and David knew better. They knew that God had knit their baby together in Cecelia's womb. They loved their baby and kept her away from the villagers who insisted she was a "devil child." But they also knew Grace needed medical care desperately. They prayed for a miracle.

Cecelia and David took her to the local government hospital where a Chinese doctor, who just happened to be in the country, closed up Grace's abdomen. But he warned that Grace would die before her first birthday if she didn't have a second, more involved surgery. Once again, Pastor David and his wife prayed for a miracle.

This time, their miracle took them all the way to Nashville, Tennessee. When a group of Christian speakers came to Liberia on a mission trip and met Grace, who was

> It is one of the most beautiful compensations of life that no man can sincerely try to help another without helping himself.
>
> **RALPH WALDO EMERSON**

now eight months old, they returned to the United States determined to help this precious baby get the lifesaving surgery she needed. Through a series of incredible circumstances that only God himself could have orchestrated, Grace's surgery and her hospitalization costs were donated by Vanderbilt Children's Hospital in Tennessee. Delta even donated airline tickets for Grace, David, and Cecelia. The only obstacle that remained was housing for the family while they were in the States for three months.

That's where a Ronald McDonald House came in. The Ronald McDonald House Charities have homes all over the United States where families of hospitalized individuals can stay free of charge. David and Cecelia were granted a stay at the Ronald McDonald House (RMH) of Nashville, where they remained during Grace's surgery and recovery. The RMH Charities are funded by donations from private individuals and corporate companies.

IN HIS NAME

Love. Such a simple word, yet the Bible teaches us it is greater than faith and greater than hope. Paul tells us in 1 Corinthians that even if we can speak with eloquence like an angel, but we lack love in doing so, we are nothing but a noisy gong or a clanging cymbal. He goes on to say that we can even have the faith to move a mountain, but if we don't have love, we are nothing (13:1–2).

Following Christ's example in caring for the needy is more than just performing acts of kindness for others to see. Those acts of kindness must be deeply rooted in love. The outpouring of God's love toward us is what leads us to care for others' needs. Letting His love flow through us as we live our everyday lives will enable us to help the needy out of an overflow of how much we are loved by God himself.

Focusing on how much we love God will always leave us legalistically striving to love others. We can never measure up when we focus on our love for God! But focusing on how much God loves us will lead to a natural outpouring of love onto the needy around us. Even a simple act of kindness, like a meal for a family at the RMH, when wrapped in true Christian love can impact others in ways we may not be able to know on this side of heaven.

Pastor David and Cecelia could not have afforded a hotel stay or meals during Grace's surgery and long recovery time in the US without the kindness of others wrapped in the love of Christ. And during her recovery, Grace even celebrated her first birthday—the one she was told she wouldn't live to see without the lifesaving surgery. Grace's surgery and recovery were a success and she returned with her parents to her homeland in Africa, healthy and whole! Praise God for His love that leads us to love others in His name!

> **THE STATS**
>
> The first Ronald McDonald House was founded in 1974 in Philadelphia.
>
> Today, there are more than 300 Ronald McDonald houses worldwide.

A CUP OF COLD WATER

Grace and her parents are one of thousands of families who have been impacted by the Ronald McDonald Charities. On any given day, in any of the three hundred Ronald McDonald Houses worldwide, families are being given a place to stay free of charge while their loved one is hospitalized.

Taking a meal to the RMH in your area is a small gesture of love that goes a long way for a displaced family in a strange city while their loved one is ill. The RMH depends on the kindness of people in the community to bring meals to the houses for families living there.

> *If every customer in the US donated a penny every time he or she visited a McDonald's restaurant, more than $62 million dollars would be collected to support children and families.*

You do not have to know anyone who is living at an RMH to take a meal. You just have to be ready to love and give to a family who is dealing with the illness of a loved one at an RMH. To contact the Ronald McDonald House Charities and find a house near you, visit rmhc.org/who-we-are/chapter-search/. On the organization's home page (rmhc.org), you can also get information about other volunteer opportunities with the Ronald McDonald House Charities.

Abba, in a gesture as simple as cooking a meal for a family at the Ronald McDonald House, let me shine your light and your love as I minister in my community. Remind me that it's your immeasurable love that leads me to love others.

3. PARTICIPATE IN A LOCAL PRODUCE CO-OP OR BUY IN BULK.

Margaret and her husband, Herald, had been married more than sixty years when Herald lost his battle with Alzheimer's disease. Margaret had always been a homemaker and now, widowed and without the financial support of her husband, she lives on a limited income.

Margaret's daughter helps take care of her. Last summer, she drove Margaret to the social services office and helped her fill out the application for government food assistance. They assumed that because Margaret lived on such a limited income and was widowed, she would get the help she

> It is a tragic mix-up when the United States spends $500,000 for every enemy soldier killed, and only $53 annually on the victims of poverty.
>
> **MARTIN LUTHER KING JR.**

needed to purchase food. But they were wrong. Although Margaret was approved, she was allotted only fourteen dollars of food stamps per month. Fourteen dollars per month. That was it. When Margaret gasped at the low amount, the social worker said there was nothing she could do to help her further.

IN HIS NAME

Often we assume that people who are hungry can get food stamps through the government. While this is true in some cases, food stamps alone don't provide the sustenance families need. And frankly, is it really the government's job to care for the poor?

Jesus' answer for taking care of the poor was simple—His people. For ages God's people have been caring for the needs of the poor around the world. In the Old Testament, God frequently told His people to care for the impoverished and the needy. Deuteronomy 24:19 says, "When you are harvesting your crops and forget to bring in a bundle of grain from your field, don't go back to get it. Leave it for the foreigners, orphans, and *widows*. Then the Lord your God will bless you in all you do" (emphasis added). Proverbs 29:7 teaches, "The godly care about the rights of the poor; the wicked don't care at all."

I once heard Rick Warren of Saddleback Church say that the church, the body of Christ, is the only organization big enough to care for the poor, the widowed, and the orphaned. He went on to say that we, as Christians, are in nearly every nation and speak nearly every language on this planet. We have a call from our Savior to care for the less fortunate.

While I am so thankful to live in a country where we have programs in place to help the needy, as Christians, it's imperative that we understand that caring for the needy is our responsibility. We can't assume that a government program will take care of the needs around us.

THE STATS

In the US more than 6 million adults over the age of sixty face daily hunger and are forced to skip meals or purchase poor-quality foods.

Nearly 9% of the elderly live below the poverty line.

A CUP OF COLD WATER

A neighborhood produce co-op is one creative way to meet needs in your community. Utilizing a co-op will provide families with healthy produce at a deeply discounted rate that almost anyone can afford.

Most produce co-ops originate by contacting produce distributors like the ones who deliver to local restaurants. The distributor can sell the food to the co-op participants at a discounted price because it comes by the case. Through a produce co-op based in Charlotte, North Carolina, each family pays just $17.50 for a large basket of fresh produce. Smaller baskets are $11.50 and a fruit basket is $8.50. This is a fraction of the supermarket cost for the same items.

When the cases are delivered each week, volunteers split up the produce evenly among participating families. This is an ingenious way for families of any size to eat healthy fruits and vegetables at a low price. You can encourage needy families to participate or better yet, purchase two baskets—one for your family and one for a needy family. For an example of a successful produce co-op and information on how it functions, visit yourneighborhoodproduce.net.

> *When you give to Angel Food Ministries, you are taking care of more than just the physical needs of the hungry. Angel Food places a salvation tract in every box of food they package for needy families.*

Much like a co-op, Angel Food Ministries packages food together and sells it at a deep discount. Bundles of food vary in quantity and some bundles are packaged specifically for children. Meats, vegetables, produce, and pastas are all available through Angel Foods. Prices are given on their website for each bundle of food and preorders are needed. Orders can be placed online, but must be picked up at a participating location. To find a location near you, visit www.angelfoodministries.com. At the website, you can find information on ordering, donating, and even on how to begin a host site for Angel Food.

Produce co-ops and ministries like Angel Food give alternatives to retail pricing at traditional grocery stores for those with limited incomes who need to purchase food at a discounted rate. It also gives us the ability to purchase food at a low cost to give to those around us who may be in need.

Abba, in this world where children die of starvation every day, I have been given so much. I can say, with great thanksgiving to you, that I don't know what it means to be truly hungry. Show me what I can do to reduce the suffering of hungry people right here in my own community.

4. ANONYMOUSLY GIVE GROCERIES TO A SINGLE PARENT OR A WIDOW OR WIDOWER.

When Leah and her older brother were in elementary school, her mom and dad divorced, leaving Leah's mother with few resources to care for her two children. As a young girl, Leah didn't completely understand what her mother had to face during that difficult time, but she remembers vividly a day when a stranger's gift brought her mother to tears.

It was already dark when Leah, her brother, and her mom arrived at home from church one Wednesday night. Immediately they noticed a brown cardboard box on their front porch. They weren't expecting a package in the mail, and the box had no address or note attached. Leah's mother brought the package inside and put it on the kitchen counter.

Leah's brother looked at Leah with eyes as big as saucers as their mother opened the box and began to unpack the items inside one by one. There was a box of rice, a frozen turkey, a bag of potatoes, and a jar of peanut butter—but it was the remaining items that brought their mother to tears. At the bottom of the box was a kid's treasure trove of goodies. Ravioli, Pop-Tarts, Captain Crunch cereal, and Eggo waffles made Leah and her brother gasp and cheer with glee. They began to jump up and down in the kitchen as their mother unpacked each item. It was like Christmas!

When Leah looked at her mother, she had tears streaming down her face. It

> Is what you're living for worth Christ dying for?
>
> **LEONARD RAVENHILL**

wasn't just the kind gesture of giving the box of food that brought her mother to tears. It was that someone had taken the time to think of her children. Whoever had brought the groceries to them had shopped with her children in mind. It was a small act of kindness that meant the world to a struggling single mom who couldn't afford to buy those "fun foods" for her kids on her limited income.

Leah is now thirty-nine years old, but she can still remember the excitement of seeing the groceries that someone had bought for her and her brother. And seeing the tears on her mother's face is a memory that is still ingrained in her mind after all these years. To this day, Leah has no idea who left that box of food on her family's doorstep, but the impact it made in her life is as real today as it was nearly thirty years ago.

IN HIS NAME

The early church was familiar with sharing what they had with those in need. We read in Acts 4:32 that the believers shared their possessions so that no one among them had need for anything: "All the believers were united in heart and mind. And they felt that what they owned was not their own, so they shared everything they had."

As the church, we are good at seeing the needs outside our church walls, but what about the needs within our own congregations? In nearly every church are single mothers who are struggling, husbands who have been laid off from their jobs, and families who have mounting medical bills. As the body of Christ, we have a responsibility to do what we can to take care of the needs that are within our own church families. Sometimes the needy are not just the people holding cardboard signs on street corners. They may also be right beside us in the pew on Sunday morning.

A CUP OF COLD WATER

Being aware of the Holy Spirit's leading is key to accepting Jesus' invitation to care for the needy. Within the church body, financial needs are not always announced. Some are obvious, such as a husband who has suddenly lost his job or a wife who has just lost her husband to cancer. Others are not as obvious, such as a family paying for expensive medical treatments for a loved one. Members of the church may or may not voice their needs, but you can be sure that the single mothers in your congregation are likely struggling financially. Many single mothers and widows or widowers live paycheck to paycheck as they try to make ends meet on a limited income.

> *For a single parent, or a widow/widower, receiving a bag of groceries given anonymously is about more than help—it's about hope.*

If you know a single mother or a widow or widower, don't wait for them to voice their needs. Go ahead and bless them by periodically leaving groceries on their porch. And don't be a "back of the pantry" giver. Donating chicken broth that's been in the back of the cupboard for six months or a can of tuna that you'll never use is not what we should be giving to meet the needs of others. Where is the sacrifice in that kind of giving? Instead, shop for groceries that you would like to have while keeping in mind the needs and even some of the wants of the children involved. Buying a few age-appropriate "fun foods" for a single mom's children will mean more than you know! You can bet that it will be like Christmas in their kitchen when they open the box of goodies that you took the time to buy just for them.

Abba, I can't always know who around me needs extra help with groceries, but you know exactly who they are and what they need. Bring to my mind the families around me who may need help and use me to meet their needs.

5. KEEP FIVE-DOLLAR GIFT CARDS IN YOUR PURSE OR WALLET FOR THE NEEDY.

A recent poll found that half of all American pet owners consider their pets a part of the family. Our family of nine is no exception. We have a tiny terrier that we affectionately named Belle when we rescued her from a dog pound six years ago. Although she has become a part of our family and my kids love her dearly, she isn't the most attractive little dog. In fact, her wiry hair and long tail make her look like a cat. We have her groomed about four times a year so she has some semblance of looking like a dog. We always laugh when we pick her up after being groomed and see the big bows in her hair and the tiny doggie bandana around her neck. The groomers try their best to make her look cute, but the poor thing is just not a cute dog!

One day when we picked her up from the groomers we laughed particularly hard at her as we put her in the car. She seemed irritated with her new look and tried to scratch the bows out of her hair. When she found it to be of no use, she gave in to our laughter, climbed in the front seat, and stretched her neck to see out the passenger side window. That's about the time we came to a stop sign where a young couple stood holding a sign that I couldn't quite make out. Belle's little head kept bobbing up and down, keeping me from reading the sign. All I could see through her freshly groomed ears and big pink bows was the word *HUNGRY* written with a faint marker.

> I can't talk religion to a man with bodily hunger in his eyes.
>
> GEORGE BERNARD SHAW

I knew there was no money in my wallet because I had given the last of my cash to Belle's groomers as a tip. When it was my turn to go through the four-way stop, I drove my van through the intersection. But I didn't make it far before the Holy Spirit whispered clearly in my spirit. How could I spend thirty-five dollars, plus a tip, on my dog—*my DOG*—and then immediately pass by a couple who may truly be in need and give them nothing? I was so ashamed.

That day, because I was close to a Wal-Mart store with a McDonald's restaurant, I parked the van, went inside, and purchased a few five-dollar gift cards for the couple. I knew they could easily walk to the store and purchase anything they might need, including food. If I could pay thirty-five dollars for dog grooming, then surely I could spend twenty dollars on a few gift cards to help someone in need. Belle's big pink bows not only got in the way of me reading the cardboard sign that day, they almost got in the way of my Savior using me to help someone in need.

THE STATS

Most people think that urban areas of the US have the highest poverty rates. Not so. In rural areas it is more difficult for food banks and food emergency assistance programs to support poverty-stricken families effectively.

More than 19 million people in the US are considered "the working poor."

IN HIS NAME

Did you know that Americans spent $47.7 billion dollars on pet products in 2010? While I understand that pets bring joy to our lives, it also is mind-boggling that we spend that much money on our animals while many charities struggle to find resources to help the less fortunate in our communities. Every community in America has people who are needy and hungry.

Just as people beg for food on street corners today, when Jesus walked the earth beggars asked for handouts from people passing by. One such man was Lazarus (see Luke 16:19–23). He begged outside the gates of a rich man. Certainly the rich man had to pass Lazarus each day, as did his rich friends when they came to the elegant parties that the rich man gave. Lazarus was always passed by as if he were invisible. But when Lazarus died, the Bible says he was carried by angels to heaven.

No one is invisible to our God. No one. He is close to the broken, the hungry, and the destitute. And He uses His people to see and minister to the needy. We, as Christians, must be willing to let God open our spiritual eyes to see the needs around us.

A CUP OF COLD WATER

Many of us are leery of helping someone who is on the street begging for food or money. I admit that it is sometimes hard to know just what to do when we are encountered by these people. I always wonder, *Are they genuinely needy or are they just trying to get money? If I give them money, will they use it for drugs or cigarettes instead of food?* It's hard to know. That's why it's so important to pray and ask the Holy Spirit to guide you each time you encounter a person begging on the street.

> *For the money it takes to purchase one large bag of pet food, you could purchase four $5 gift cards to keep on hand for an encounter with a needy person.*

I have in the past given people on the street money; I now try to keep gift cards to Wal-Mart and McDonald's in my car or in my purse for such times. Buying gift cards of five dollars each is not a huge financial burden and with a McDonald's on nearly every corner and a Wal-Mart store in nearly every town, purchasing these cards ahead of time takes the stress out of seeing a needy person and wondering what they may do with cash that's given to them.

So, if you are able, purchase a few five-dollar gift cards, put them in your wallet or in your car, and the next time you come in contact with someone on the street who is in need, you'll be ready to help.

Abba, it is so easy for me to turn away when I see someone begging on the street. I assume they will use the money they are given to buy drugs or alcohol. Remind me that you see every gift given in love, and let me give out of the love you have lavished on me.

6. START A FOOD PANTRY AT YOUR CHURCH.

Driving through the poor side of town to get to the ball field where her husband played Major League Baseball was something Kathy did several times a week. It didn't take many trips for her to see the stark contrast between her nice suburban neighborhood and the poverty-stricken streets lined with project housing. Abandoned cars. Trash-lined sidewalks. Noisy apartments. Driving through this type of neighborhood sends most people into a learned routine—lock the doors and drive through as quickly as possible. But Kathy is not like most people. She saw the needs of the people she passed as an invitation to be the hands and feet of Jesus.

Instead of putting her leftovers from dinner into the refrigerator, each night Kathy packed them up and took them with her on her drive to the ball field. As she passed people in the housing projects, she would stop to give them her extra food. Soon, she had developed relationships with many of the families, and she was able to share Christ in a tangible way as she met their needs. The families were always genuinely appreciative. Helping these people brought a greater question to Kathy's mind—*How many more families struggle with hunger in my city?*

> I am only one; but still I am one. I cannot do everything, but still I can do something. I will not refuse to do the something I can do.
>
> **HELEN KELLER**

As Kathy prayed about how to help the hungry of her area, she had an idea. She decided to start a food pantry at her church where families and individuals could come regularly to get nourishing food. With the faces of the children and parents she had helped at the forefront of her mind, Kathy wasted no time. She contacted her church and asked if her pastor would pray about having a food pantry at their church. Kathy offered to head up the entire effort if she could have the church's approval and support. With the pastor's blessing, Kathy and her husband contacted a large local food bank distribution center. The center listed their church as an official food distribution ministry. That status gave Kathy the ability to purchase food at a reduced rate each week at the food bank.

With the help of church volunteers and faithful people who give monetary gifts, Kathy travels once a week to the food bank to purchase canned meats, canned soups, boxed nonperishable items, produce, and dry milk. She then divides the food into boxes that she distributes from her church every Wednesday to families in her city who need food. Some are homeless. Some are unemployed. Some just have more month than they do money.

Her idea that began with taking leftover food to a few families in the inner-city housing projects has grown to an ongoing ministry that feeds hundreds of needy families throughout her city. When Kathy talks about this ministry that God birthed in her heart, she smiles from ear to ear and says,

It's just something that burned in my heart. The thought of people going hungry while I have plenty to eat gave me the desire to do something for them. It's time consuming. I have a full-time job and I'm the mother of four active children, but it's a deep joy for me to serve the Lord by giving food to the hungry. One of my greatest joys comes in meeting and loving on the people who come to our church for food. I try to make sure they leave with much more than a box of food. I want them to leave knowing their needs were taken care of by Jesus himself. I'm just a vessel to meet those needs.

IN HIS NAME

Many times it is within our means to help the less fortunate, but we fail to see their needs. It is so important for us to pray each day to have eyes that can see the hurts and needs that surround us. Jesus didn't die so we would live blinded to the needs of others. He saved us to be a blessing to those around us, to be a light in this dark world for Him. Being a blessing to others involves rising out of our comfortable lives, seeing the needs around us through God's eyes, and asking Him to show us how to meet those needs in creative and compassionate ways.

God likes to meets us where we are. When we are ready to accept His invitation to help the needy, we don't have to go searching for opportunities. Instead, when we are following hard after Jesus through prayer and Bible study, God will put opportunities to serve Him in our path.

THE STATS

There is a misconception that only uneducated people are hungry. Of those interviewed in a hunger study by Feeding America, 26% indicated some college education.

More than 10 million US households serviced regularly by Feeding America experience food insecurity, meaning they don't have dependable access to enough food to sustain a healthy life.

Kathy didn't search for ways to help the needy. She, in following Christ each day, was led to a place of service for Him. Passing needy families on the way to the ball field was God's invitation to Kathy to help the needy that He placed in her everyday life. Ephesians 2:10 says, "For we are God's masterpiece. He has created us anew in Christ Jesus, so we can do the good things he planned for us long ago." I love that each of us has works uniquely designed by God himself and that He planned them in advance. For Kathy, one of those works is feeding the hungry. Feeding the hungry through a food pantry is a tangible way for us to touch the lives of the poor and the needy in our very own communities.

A CUP OF COLD WATER

Starting a food pantry at your church involves a few steps. First, contact your local food ministry distributor. You can find a distributor in your state by searching FeedingAmerica.org for local distributors. On the site they list their names, addresses, and contact information. In the yellow pages, many food distributors are listed under "food banks."

Many cities have a food bank distribution center where donations are brought. Not only do these food banks store and organize food in warehouses, they also allow different ministries to purchase the stocked food at a reduced rate. Some food banks even sell their food by the pound, and many times produce is given free of charge. Therefore, apply with them for your church to become a ministry food pantry. If you live in a rural area or an area that is not served by one of these food distribution banks, you can contact grocery stores in your area and ask for donations to start your church's food pantry. They may even be willing to help with a food drive by putting a donation bin for your food pantry in their store.

> *Food drives at schools, day care centers, and local businesses can help you get your new pantry stocked with needed food.*

Second, once you are listed as an official ministry food pantry, set up a time to purchase food each week at the food distribution center. Depending on the size of your purchase, you may want to organize a small team of volunteers to help pick up the food and later pack the food into "family boxes." Kathy makes boxes with fewer items for individuals and smaller families and boxes with more food for larger families. Even children and teens can help fill the boxes.

Next, set up a regular day and time for needy families in your area to come to get the boxes of food, and then advertise the time through flyers and word of mouth. Also, because you will be listed as a food ministry with your city's food bank distribution center, when needy families call the center, they can let those families know the day and time that your church gives out food.

Finally, once the boxes are ready and your pantry is open, make sure that each family or individual fills out a form asking for contact information, where they are employed, and how many people are in their family. Having good records will allow you to determine how much food to purchase in the future.

When I asked Kathy what advice she would give to those starting a food pantry, her answer was heartfelt: "Tell them to touch the people who come to get the food boxes. So many times these people just need a physical touch. Hug them. Give them a pat on the back. Laugh with them. Call them by name. Smile and let them know they are loved—just like Jesus would do."

Abba, give me favor as I contact people about beginning a food pantry in my church. Show me how to be organized and deliberate as I take this step of faith to feed hungry people in my city. Bring alongside me those in my church who also have a heart to help the poor, so that we can work together to serve others in your name.

7. SPONSOR AN ORPHAN IN AN IMPOVERISHED NATION.

It was blazing hot under the African sun as child after child approached the whiteboard. I asked each one, "Can you spell your name for me?" Most of them could spell their name. The little ones who couldn't spell had an older sibling or friend to speak for them. After I wrote their name on the whiteboard, they stood beside the board for their photo. Kriek, a missionary in Swaziland, Africa, took a picture for each child's sponsorship card. Each card had the child's name, age, grade, and what care point they came to each day. (At one of the many care points in Africa, children can play together and receive a nurturing smile or hug from a grandmother figure, who they affectionately call "Go-Go." In ideal situations, when food is available, the Go-Go will cook "pop" for the children—a porridge-type meal made from ground corn maize.)

Some children smiled easily for the photo, but others seemed afraid of the camera and no amount of coaxing and tickling would force smiles on their faces. Every child wore old and tattered clothes, even if they were wearing their school uniforms. Most of them had no shoes.

For the children, sponsorship would mean a meal each day at the care point, help with education, basic health care, and most importantly spiritual discipleship. If enough sponsorship monies came in, they would be pooled for clothing and shoe giveaways or to make improvements to the care point such as adding a small kitchen, playground equipment, an education center, a multipurpose building, and possibly even a well with clean water to drink. I was thrilled to be a small part of the excitement of taking photos and gathering information for the sponsorship packets.

When I returned from that trip to Africa, I organized an "Orphan Sunday" at my church where the entire morning service centered on orphan awareness. Tom Davis, author of *Fields of the Fatherless* and *Red Letters,* flew in from Colorado Springs to preach the sermon. Special music and videos were played and adoptive and foster parents were recognized. In the gymnasium we set up tables for church members to browse through child sponsorship packets.

I was overjoyed to see the pictures of the children I had encountered while in Swaziland. As hundreds of church members thumbed through the packets and chose children to sponsor, I was overcome with emotion. Child after child that I had seen, touched, hugged, and held got sponsored that day! They were not just names and photos on pieces of paper—they were children in desperate poverty who would now get the help they needed.

Orphan Sunday was a few years ago and I have been privileged to see what the sponsorship monies have now done. New kitchens have been built. New multipurpose buildings for worship and play have been erected. New playground equipment has been installed. New wells have been dug. But most of all, children have accepted Christ through discipleship programs. And all because of a little miracle called child sponsorship.

> Every child you encounter is a divine appointment.
>
> **WESS STAFFORD,
> PRESIDENT, COMPASSION
> INTERNATIONAL**

IN HIS NAME

Did you know that more than two thousand verses in the Bible pertain to the poor? Psalm 12:5–6 is one of my favorite passages about God's love for the poor because it speaks of God rising up to help them:

The Lord replies, "I have seen violence done to the helpless, and I have heard the groans of the poor. Now I will rise up to rescue them, as they have longed for me to do." The Lord's promises are pure, like silver refined in a furnace, purified seven times over.

God hears the moaning of the needy and the poor and rises up to protect and defend them. But the way He rises up is through us, His people. What a wonderful picture—God arises in us to defend and protect the poor! When I read these verses, I can't help but cry out to the Lord, "Here I am! Use me, use my life! Arise in me! Arise in me!"

Whenever I get a letter from Abush, my family's sponsored child in Ethiopia, and I see the progress he has made since we began to sponsor him, I realize that sponsorship is a simple way to let God rise in me to care for the poor.

THE STATS

Sub-Saharan Africa has more orphans than the combined population of children in Denmark, Ireland, Norway, Canada, and Sweden.

Every day 5,760 children become orphans.

A CUP OF COLD WATER

Many wonderful humanitarian ministries and organizations do a good job for the Lord with sponsorship of children in impoverished nations. My family has sponsored Abush in Ethiopia for several years. We sponsor him through Compassion International, but Compassion is just one of many solid sponsorship ministries from which to choose. Some are listed below with their websites.

CUP OF COLD WATER

- Child Fund International: *www.childfund.org*
- Childcare Worldwide: *www.childcareworldwide.org*
- Children's HopeChest: *www.hopechest.org*
- Compassion International: *www.compassion.com*
- Save the Children: *www.savethechildren.org*
- World Vision: *www.worldvision.org*

> *For $25 a month through Compassion International's Child Survival Program, you can provide lifesaving aid to mothers and babies living in areas where the top causes of infant death are malaria, diarrhea, measles, AIDS, and malnutrition.*

The cost to sponsor a child is around thirty-eight dollars per month. In most cases you can correspond with your sponsored child through letters. Many of the sponsorship organizations also have programs where you can send gifts and even visit your sponsored child. Some also have catalogs where you can help an impoverished family by purchasing for them livestock, a brood of chickens, or a dairy cow.

An impoverished child will be helped in so many ways for a little over a dollar a day through child sponsorship. You can know that as you send your sponsorship check each month, God is *arising* in you to help a needy child.

Abba, what a joy to know that programs like Compassion International and Children's HopeChest care for children living in extreme poverty. Lead me to the child you would have me sponsor, and use my sponsorship to better that child's life and pierce the darkness of poverty with the light and hope of Christ.

8. ORGANIZE A FEED THE CHILDREN FUND-RAISING CAMPAIGN.

When I was in college taking classes toward a degree in elementary education, I remember thinking a professor's suggestion was ridiculous. She told us to make sure that as teachers we kept a jar of peanut butter, saltine crackers, and napkins in our desk drawer. She said that no matter where we taught school, whether in an affluent area or a poor area, we would always encounter children who came to school hungry because they didn't have enough food at home.

I knew that the United States had pockets where children didn't have enough to eat, but was it so extreme in my area that I needed to keep food in my desk drawer for hungry little students? I tucked her advice away thinking I wouldn't ever need it.

Two years later, I received my first teaching position at a local elementary school. I taught third grade in an affluent suburban area near a fairly large city. I had twenty-eight eager and active students, and each morning we hit the ground running with lessons in reducing fractions, spelling sight words, reading classic children's literature, and discovering earth science.

I had a classroom full of children with different learning styles, but one student stood out to me. His name was C. J. He was an adorable African-American boy with a dimple on one cheek. He always had his homework done and seemed very smart. But each morning when he came to school, he was quiet and reserved, sluggish in his morning work. Yet he perked up after lunchtime. I couldn't figure out why he did so well in his work after lunch but seemed to struggle with morning assignments.

After six weeks of school, I saw something in C. J. I hadn't noticed before. A parent had sent cupcakes that morning for her daughter's birthday, and I let each child have a cupcake during morning recess. I watched C. J. devour his cupcake like he hadn't eaten in days. I called him aside and asked if he had eaten breakfast. He hadn't. I asked him why, and he said there wasn't food in his house. After some prodding, I found out that there was never much food in C. J.'s house and he always left for school without breakfast. I didn't even want to ask about whether or not he ate dinner. I was afraid to hear the answer. I knew C. J.'s mom was a single parent, but I had no idea how much C. J. and his mother were struggling.

That's when I remembered my college professor's suggestion and decided to purchase peanut butter and crackers for my desk drawer. The next day, when the children went out for morning recess, I asked C. J. to stay back. I opened my desk drawer and showed him the crackers and peanut butter. His eyes lit up at the sight of his teacher having such yummy treats in her desk! I made him some peanut butter crackers and told him that each morning he could come to my desk during recess and get himself a snack. I told him that he didn't even have to ask; it was his special drawer. This little secret of ours went on for the rest of the school year. C. J. went on to make the honor roll three times in a row while he was my student! I can't claim it was because of his "morning power snack" of crackers and peanut butter, but I have to think it at least helped!

> Lord, to those who hunger, give bread. And to those who have bread, give the hunger for justice.
>
> **LATIN AMERICAN PRAYER**

IN HIS NAME

We all have seen pictures of starving children in third world countries who desperately need food, but some families right here in the United States are hungry as well. Knowing terms used to describe hunger will help you to better understand the levels of need right here in our own country.

Food security means having access at all times to enough food for an active, healthy lifestyle for every member in the household. *Food insecurity* is the uncertainty of having or getting enough food to meet the needs of every person in the household. People experience food insecurity because they don't have enough money to buy food, or don't have access to the needed resources to get food. The number of households with food insecurity is calculated by adding together the number of households with low food security and very low food security.

People in *low food security* households may use various strategies to avoid having to reduce their food intake or dramatically change their eating patterns. The strategies might include eating less-varied diets, participating in federal food assistance programs (such as WIC or food stamps), or even getting emergency food from local food pantries.

People in *very low food security* households reduce their food intake or change their eating patterns because they simply don't have enough money for food. For example, sometimes a parent in a very low food security household will skip a meal so that a child in the household can eat.

Here are some surprising facts about hunger in the United States:

- *In 2009, 5.6 million households accessed emergency food from a food pantry one or more times.*
- *In 2009, 50.2 million Americans lived in food insecure households—17.2 million were children.*
- *Nearly 1 in 4 children lives in households that struggle to put food on the table.*
- *One in every 2 babies born is enrolled in the WIC program.*
- *One in 8 people lives below the poverty line.*

Poverty and hunger are found in nearly every city in our nation. This means that all of us can have an opportunity to minister to people in our communities who are suffering from a lack of food. The power of one life to touch another life is at the core of Christ's teaching about ministering to others.

A CUP OF COLD WATER

You may not know of someone who is directly affected by hunger, but you can certainly help those who are affected by food insecurity. A great place to start is with Feed the Children. Their website, www.feedthechildren.org, gives a variety of ways that average people can give of their time, talents, and resources to help hungry families all over the United States.

> *For $50, Feeding America can provide 350 meals for families suffering from food insecurity. Visit FeedingAmerica.org.*

One such way is to submit a special project that you, your church, your business, or your ministry have created to support hungry children. Some creative suggestions are corporate pledges, benefit dinners, auctions, bake sales, and workplace campaigns (like casual dress days). Creating a campaign like a casual dress day is as easy as obtaining permission from a supervisor. Coworkers simply donate five dollars in exchange for permission to wear jeans instead of the usual professional attire. This results in a fun atmosphere for employees while they raise money to feed the hungry. (To add another touch to your casual dress day, create stickers or buttons that participants can wear that say, "I'm dressed down to fight hunger in [your town's name]. Ask me how you can fight hunger too.")

If you submit a project proposal and get it approved by Feed the Children, then they can give you resources that will help make your project successful. The more successful your project, the greater the impact on needy children and families. On the website you will also find other ways to give, such as donating a vehicle, sponsoring a child, participating in a mission trip, and planned giving.

Abba, create in me a heart that cares deeply about hungry children and families in my country and around the globe. Open my spiritual eyes to the needs around me and keep my hands open to give from the abundance you have given to me.

9. COOK AND HOST BREAKFAST FOR THE HOMELESS.

When David Blackwell was a freshman in college, God rocked his world, and now through this young college graduate God is changing the face of homelessness in Orlando, Florida. Here is David's story in his own words:

I grew up in middle-class suburban America. My only experiences with the poor were a few mission trips to Brazil that I took in high school. Even then, after we told the poor about Jesus, we went back to a five-star hotel to sleep. My friend Ben was in the same boat. His only experience with the poor was driving around with his youth pastor in a minivan passing out plates of spaghetti. He said it was more like a drive-by than stopping to minister to the poor. We felt God was calling us to change that.

We went downtown after a University of Central Florida football game and passed out peanut butter and jelly sandwiches. We sat down and talked to the homeless and asked them for their stories and what their biggest needs were. I can remember so perfectly the first homeless man I ever met. He called himself Whiskers; he had a bushy red beard and glasses. When I asked him what his biggest needs were, he answered, "Clean socks." Then he thought about the question and added, "And someone to talk to."

> The hunger for love is much more difficult to remove than the hunger for bread.
>
> **MOTHER TERESA**

In those first few months, I felt like God was saying that I could do more than give someone a sandwich. In January of 2007, I went to the

Passion Conference in Atlanta. At that time, I had a ten-year plan: finish school in four years, my master's degree in two, and my doctorate in three. I wanted to be a seminary professor. I felt God asking me, "That's great that you have plans, but what are you doing now?" All I could come up with is that I had passed out a few sandwiches with my friends, Ben and Brian. I heard God clearly tell me to start a nonprofit to work with homeless people in Orlando.

We didn't have any money, but we had plenty of friends. We decided that we could ask all of our friends to bring a dish to the park and we would have enough to feed forty to fifty people. We started having potluck-style picnics at the park. By December we had a few hundred people coming to the park.

Relationship has always been a driving force behind what God has called me to do. Ultimately if I helped a hundred homeless people off the streets and into homes and jobs where they were self-sustained but they didn't receive love from me, then it was worthless. If they don't know Christ, then they are missing out on the best of what life has to offer.

Jesus was very relational. To take out that aspect from ministry would be to undercut the very foundation of Jesus' own ministry. He was focused on a relationship with God first and foremost, and then a relationship with humanity.

IN HIS NAME

It's so important for us to remember that when we minister to the "least of these" we are ministering to Jesus himself. I don't know how it works, but God's

Word is clear: when we help someone who is destitute, downtrodden, afflicted, sick, or needy, we are doing it for Jesus Christ.

I once heard my friend Jason tell a story about a time when he and his wife were on staff at an inner-city ministry. They took students to a ministry that prepared a meal for 250 homeless people every Sunday night. Jason said,

> One of the staff members there was named Ray. Ray had been homeless at one time himself, but after getting help and coming to Jesus, he was now serving others full-time. As we were milling around the long plain tables that were to be set for dinner, Ray called all of the day's volunteers together. I'll never forget what he said next: "Guys, you can see that we don't have fancy stuff. The silverware is plastic and the tablecloths are paper. But, when you set the table, you need to do it as though you were using fine china. The tablecloths need to be straight. The napkins and flatware need to be arranged just right. Jesus is coming to dinner tonight, and it needs to be perfect."

Oh, how often we forget the truth of Matthew 25:40: "The King will reply, 'Truly I tell you, whatever you did for one of the least of these brothers and sisters of mine, you did for me.'"

A CUP OF COLD WATER

Although David's ministry, Home Sweet Homeless, is fairly new, already it is reaching hundreds of homeless men and women in Orlando. His ministry website, hshomeless.com, has information on two outreaches that David has spearheaded.

One outreach ministry is monthly potlucks. The potlucks involve Christians bringing a dish to an area park that homeless people frequent. A huge picnic potluck dinner ensues with families and individuals not only bringing a meal to the homeless, but also engaging in their lives. In David's own words, "The idea behind the potluck is to get outside the thought of a 'homeless feeding.' Instead we want to join with the homeless population and share a meal with them." David asks participants to "come prepared to serve, to make friends, and to have a great time." In addition to food, David encourages people to bring a blanket, game, or musical instrument to the potluck picnics.

> *Not ready to begin a large ministry to the homeless? Then start small. Bring an extra sandwich to your workplace to share with a homeless person near your place of business.*

Another outreach ministry of Home Sweet Homeless is breakfast for the homeless on Fridays at two labor agencies that the homeless frequent in hopes of being hired for day labor. This is a project that any church or ministry group can do for the homeless in their area. At the Orlando ministry, volunteers stay up all night on Thursdays baking homemade bread, boiling dozens of eggs, and preparing fresh fruit. Much of the food is donated by local farmers.

The food is then delivered by the volunteers to the labor agencies at 4:30 AM on Friday. Homeless shelters are also ideal places to deliver breakfast for the homeless. This is an incredible way for Christians to show their love for the needy in a simple gesture of serving them breakfast.

Abba, remind me when I forget, that you love the poor, that you are close to the broken, and that your heart breaks for the needy. Remind me that you were once homeless and poor. Remind me that you have not forgotten the homeless, and that I can provide love to help them renew their dignity.

10. START A "COOK & PLAY" MINISTRY.

Many moms will tell you that making a menu and shopping for healthy foods can be very stressful. While convenience foods can seem like a good choice, they are usually very expensive and typically loaded with preservatives. Cooking with whole foods and making a menu prior to grocery shopping can be time consuming, but very beneficial for saving money and making healthy choices for our families. I have seven children, ages nineteen years old down to an infant, and for me, finding healthy meals that are easy to prepare, affordable, and something all of us will like is always a challenge. That was also the challenge for Jackie.

Jackie is a busy mom of four small children, yet she has found a way to combine her love of cooking, her knowledge of nutrition, her knack for bargain grocery shopping, and her compassion for the needy into one ministry. She calls it "Cook and Play."

When I first met Jackie, she was teaching a nutrition class at my church. Her class was different from any I had taken before. In her class, she not only stressed healthy eating with whole foods, she also taught cost-saving techniques to cut down on grocery bills. Her knowledge of how to make one chicken last for several meals fascinated me. I felt confident that I could make the meals again because her recipes were easy to prepare.

> Jesus will judge us not only for what we did, but also for what we could have done and didn't.
>
> GEORGE OTIS

Jackie took this class a step further with Cook and Play. Through this unique ministry, she buys healthy foods in bulk and has a group of women over to her home once a month to teach them how to cook a healthy meal. The women cook the meals in Jackie's kitchen while their children play in another room. What makes this ministry even more unique is that each woman makes two meals—one for their family and one to give away as a blessing to someone else. Jackie encourages the moms to pray about who should receive their extra meal. Her ministry has grown over the past several years because it serves others while encouraging them to pass the blessing on.

IN HIS NAME

Serving others is a part of the Christian walk. But so many times we don't feel like we have interests or gifts that will make a difference in the lives of others. Every born-again believer has gifts and talents that can and should be used to serve others. Paul writes, "There are different kinds of spiritual gifts, but the same Spirit is the source of them all. There are different kinds of service, but we serve the same Lord. God works in different ways, but it is the same God who does the work in all of us" (1 Corinthians 12:4–6). For Jackie, her enjoyment comes through cooking, and she turned it into a ministry. God met her in her everyday life and showed her how her love of cooking could be used to serve others.

What do you love to do? Cook? Play music? Paint or draw? Sew or make crafts? Fish or hunt? Play golf or tennis? Fix up old cars? Sail? Garden? Our interests were given to us by the Lord. Pray about a creative way to use the activities you enjoy to serve others. Even if in just a small way, let the activities that bring you joy be an offering to the Lord through service to other people.

A CUP OF COLD WATER

Starting a Cook and Play ministry will involve organization and patience but the benefits will be worth the effort. First, look for recipes that are easy to make and use healthy, affordable ingredients. Next, invite other mothers to join you. Be sure the women know to set aside two to three hours for the class. Women should sign up and pay ahead of time so you can purchase the right amount of food. Jackie sends out an e-mail invitation/newsletter every month and women sign up for each month's class on a first-come, first-served basis. Don't be discouraged if only a few women sign up at first. Starting small with a few close friends may be wise.

> *To learn more about how Cook and Play donates to women's shelters, visit Jackie's website at momonamission.me.*

During the class, encourage a rotation of moms to watch the children in another room. Older children may be able to help by playing with the younger children, or by measuring and stirring in the kitchen with their mothers. Jackie's ministry is directed toward women with young children, but your cooking ministry can certainly be geared toward any group—young moms, couples, newlyweds, retirees, teenagers, etc. Men can start cooking ministries geared toward couples or just men. My husband loves to cook and he especially enjoys teaching our sons to grill!

If your classes outgrow your kitchen or you don't want to host the ministry at your home, ask for permission to use your church's kitchen. Rotating the class from one participant's home to another may also be an option. Finally, when you invite people to your cooking ministry class, make sure they understand that you will be making two dishes of food—one to keep and one to give. That way, your ministry will be a double blessing!

Whether it's cooking or another interest or hobby you may have, using it as a ministry will bless others in your church and community.

Abba, you have gifted me and all of your children with talents and interests that help us enjoy this life. Show me how to creatively channel the leisure activities that I enjoy into a ministry that will give back to others.

11. RAISE FUNDS TO DIG A WELL IN AFRICA.

Drinking clean water is vital to life. Because every cell in our bodies contains mostly water, our organs begin to shut down within seventy-two hours if no water is consumed. Water protects our joints and organs, regulates body temperature, transports oxygen to our cells, and removes waste. Put simply, our bodies die without clean, potable drinking water. But did you know that an estimated 50 percent of people living in Africa do not have access to clean drinking water? Fifty percent. I can hardly wrap my mind around that number.

Many humanitarian organizations are working hard to change that statistic. They are drilling wells in remote areas of Africa and Asia, but many more are needed. When I visited Africa, I was surprised to see a hand pump in the middle of the bush. It had been drilled by a humanitarian organization, and as a result countless lives have been saved through the gift of clean water. Prior to the well, people had to walk for miles to get to a water source, and even then the water wasn't clean.

Other parts of Africa I visited had no wells in sight. The weather was so hot when we helped with an "Orphan Camp" for over three hundred impoverished children. The day consisted of face painting, foot races, soccer, and other outdoor games. Some of the children were pouring with sweat but kept right on playing. I was so thirsty that I felt almost faint when the afternoon was over. When I got back to the hotel, I turned up a full water bottle and drank every drop. I couldn't help but think about the children who had no source of water at their homes. The water they drank, if they got any that day, was probably dirty and contaminated. Thankfully, since my visit, churches have partnered with villages in that area and clean, potable water from newly drilled wells helps keep those children alive.

IN HIS NAME

Helping an impoverished village by building a community well physically saves lives, and it also provides an opportunity to tell the nations about the source of living water. John 4:1–26 tells the story of when Jesus met a desperate woman at a well. As she drew water to drink, He told her, "Anyone who drinks this water will soon become thirsty again. But those who drink the water I give will never be thirsty again. It becomes a fresh, bubbling spring within them, giving them eternal life" (vv. 13–14). Jesus knew she needed more than water. He knew she needed the grace and forgiveness that could come only from the free gift of salvation in Him alone. Jesus was aware of her sinful past, yet He loved her unconditionally. She, for the first time, felt a love that transcended her sin and penetrated to the deepest part of her soul. She sat face-to-face with pure, amazing grace when she encountered the Savior at that well.

> God uses people to perform His work. He does not send angels . . . He uses burdened, broken-hearted, weeping men and women.
>
> **DAVID WILKERSON**

Being able to share with an impoverished community that the clean water pouring from their new well can bring health and wellness pales in comparison to sharing with them the good news of the living water. The water from the well will leave them thirsty again, but Jesus Christ gives living water that will cleanse, forgive, and bring eternal life.

Drilling a well will certainly meet the physical needs of an entire community. Clean water brings life, health, and wellness. But giving an entire community the hope of Christ will bring eternal life, peace, and forgiveness.

A CUP OF COLD WATER

Half the people in Africa do not have access to a clean, potable water source. This is a statistic that the church simply cannot ignore. The average cost to drill a well in Africa ranges from $4,500 to $10,000, depending on the country (countries have different prices for the use of drilling equipment). This is a relatively small price to pay for the lives that will be saved by the potable water.

There are many ways that individuals, churches, ministry groups, and humanitarian organizations can raise money for drilling. One way is to purchase bottles of water to resell at church events or community-wide festivals. Replace the labels with your own adhesive-backed, computer-made labels that share how the money from the sale of the water bottles will go toward drilling a well in Africa. Don't forget to also display a sign letting buyers know that you accept donations.

> *For every $10 you donate at thewaterproject.org, one person can be provided with clean water for 10 years.*

Another idea is to collect used water bottles, remove the labels, cut a slit in the side of each bottle, and ask people in your church to take a bottle and fill it with money. Children will especially enjoy filling a water bottle with spare change.

Of course, benefit dinners, silent auctions, and special offerings are also great ways to raise money to purchase a well.

How do you decide where to send the money you've raised? The following humanitarian organizations and ministries build wells in Africa and Asia. Most are faith based, although some are secular. I advise working with a Christian ministry that uses well drilling as a means of sharing the gospel with the communities it services. When you visit the websites below, look for a mission statement on the front page or on the "About Us" page. If they are a Christian ministry, they will typically state it in one of those two sections of their site.

- Africa 6000 International: *www.africa6000intl.com*
- Charity Water: *www.charitywater.org*
- Edge Outreach: *www.edgeoutreach.com*
- Gospel for Asia: *www.gfa.org/ministries/jesuswells*
- Hydromissions International: *www.hydromissions.com*
- Life Today: *www.lifetoday.org*
- Lifewater: *www.lifewater.ca*
- Lifewater International: *www.lifewater.org*
- Sanma: *www.sanma.org/waterwell.htm*
- Water Missions International: *www.watermissions.org*
- The Water Project: *thewaterproject.org*
- Water Wells for Africa: *waterwellsforafrica.org*

- World Concern: *www.worldconcern.org/water*
- World Serve: *www.worldserveintl.org/water-sanitation*

When you research a ministry, make sure to find out how long the organization has been drilling wells and how they maintain and service the wells after they are drilled. Maintenance and service of wells is just as important as the initial drilling.

Water is so basic to our human existence. Bringing clean, potable water to thirsty people, as well as bringing the gospel to their thirsty souls, is an eternal investment.

Abba, it is a true blessing to have clear, clean, refreshing water that flows from the faucet in my home. Millions of people will walk many miles today for water that is filled with parasites and bacteria. Remind me as clean, clear water passes across my lips that I have been blessed so that I can be a blessing to others.

12. TAKE A MISSION TRIP TO AN IMPOVERISHED AREA.

Most of us have never been truly hungry or thirsty. We've experienced hunger pangs or deep thirst for short periods of time, but we have had the resources to eventually fill our stomachs and quench our thirst. We live in places where grocery stores and supermarkets contain more food than we could eat in a year. We have clean, potable water flowing into our homes. But not everyone lives with such luxuries. They are truly hungry. They are truly thirsty.

This realization has never been so real and so raw to me as it was on my first trip to Africa. On the third day of our trip, when we visited our second care point, my mission team was horrified to learn that the care point had no food. The wind had blown off the roof of the shack where they housed the maize, and when the bags got wet, they attracted insects. All their bags of maize were now infested. The children literally had nothing to eat—nothing. They had not eaten in days. And they were truly hungry.

I thought of how I feel when I am very hungry—the sick feeling, the faintness. I was brought to tears realizing that these children live with that feeling every day! Many of them get only one meal a day. Now that meal was not even available for them because of the ruined maize.

> When a poor person dies of hunger, it has not happened because God did not take care of him or her. It has happened because neither you nor I wanted to give that person what he or she needed.
>
> **MOTHER TERESA**

I knew there were snacks in my bag—snacks I had brought along just for myself in case I got hungry. I went to the van and got them. I gave them to the woman who ran the care point. I had to wipe away tears as I watched her take each snack and break it into pieces for the entire group of children. She tore my granola bar into ten pieces and gave each child a tiny bit. They gobbled it up in seconds and held out their tiny hands for more. The beef jerky was next. The woman put a tiny piece of meat into each little hand. Then the raisins: one to this child, two to that one . . .

I had to turn around so that no one would see me crying. Even now, as I type this story, I am in tears remembering that experience. True hunger was so real to me that day. It was like a spear that pierced to the depths of my spirit. With every bite those children took, the spear went deeper and deeper. I was broken. Later the team was able to go into town to get the children a proper meal, but I'll never forget those little hands reaching out for the tiny morsels of food. Hunger took on an entirely new meaning for me that day.

IN HIS NAME

A foreign mission trip can change your life. It will minister to those whom Jesus loves so dearly—the broken, the poor, the marginalized, the orphaned, the widowed, the downtrodden, the destitute, and the forgotten. It will profoundly change your heart into a heart like Jesus'. Until I saw extreme poverty for myself, and stepped outside my comfy world into the world of the suffering, hunger statistics were just numbers on a page. Now I've seen suffering and I can never go back to the way I was. Never. Nor do I want to.

The faces of the people I met are forever etched in my mind. They have hopes, fears, dreams, desires, and feelings—just like I do. They want the best for their children—just like I do. They long for friendship, acceptance, love, and wellness—just like I do. But, for reasons that I can't understand, I was born in a place of abundance and they were born in a place of extreme poverty.

As our lives and paths crossed during that foreign mission trip, my heart was forever changed. I carry their memory with me each day as a reminder of the words in the last half of Luke 12:48, "When someone has been given much, much will be required in return; and when someone has been entrusted with much, even more will be required."

A CUP OF COLD WATER

Traveling to an impoverished nation changes everything. Everything. It's now difficult for me to throw food away after a meal. Even a spoonful! I think about the hungry people I've encountered around the world, and I just can't bring myself to throw even a small amount of food in the trash.

Being more aware of the food we throw away seems to be a universal reaction for those who have traveled on a mission trip to an impoverished nation. You assume you will go to a nation like Haiti, Swaziland, or India and help the people with your "American blessings," but what ends up happening is that *you* get the blessing of seeing life differently and having a new appreciation for the abundance in your everyday life. I've never met anyone who went on a mission trip who wasn't forever changed by what he or she encountered.

> *When you take a mission trip to Africa with Children's HopeChest or Adventures in Missions, you can help serve a meal of ground corn maize to a group of hungry orphans.*

Because there is no more profound way to grasp poverty and true hunger than to actually see it, touch it, smell it, and experience it firsthand, a mission trip is a must for those Christians who are physically able to do so.

Many wonderful mission organizations help with food distribution around the globe, and they allow people to join them on mission trips. Explore the following list and find a ministry that fits your needs. All of them feed the hungry and they welcome and encourage Christians to join them in their efforts.

- Adventures in Missions: *www.Adventures.org*
- Children's HopeChest: *www.hopechest.org/travel*
- Compassion International: *www.compassion.com/get-involved/trips-visits.htm*
- Samaritan's Purse: *www.samaritanspurse.org*
- Serving in Mission: *www.sim.org*

In appendixes A and B you will find resources to help you prepare to serve on a short-term mission trip.

Jesus loved the poor and He made it a point to go to them while He was here on this earth. As you prepare to step out of your world into the world of poverty, prepare your spirit by praying to have a heart like Jesus.

Abba, are you calling me to a mission trip? I have fears about going. Take away my fears because I know they are not from you. Where you lead, Abba, I will follow. I want to be fully obedient to everything you have planned for me so I can be fully alive in you.

INVITING IN THE STRANGER

"I was a stranger, and you invited me in."

13. BRING NEIGHBORHOOD CHILDREN TO VACATION BIBLE SCHOOL AT YOUR CHURCH.

When I first met Grace, she was a single mother of three teenage children. She worked hard at her full-time job and lived on a meager income. She wanted to set a good example for her children in caring for the poor and she wanted to accept Jesus' invitation to care for the needy, but taking a mission trip, starting a food pantry, or volunteering at a soup kitchen was not in her budget, nor did she have the time for such commitments. But there was one thing she knew she could do to impact the needy for God's kingdom.

> The only thing necessary for the triumph of evil is for good people to do nothing.
>
> EDMUND BURKE

Every summer she would load up her minivan with neighborhood children and bring them to vacation Bible school (VBS) at our church. The children were always a loud and rambunctious bunch, far from the calm and "disciplined" children our church typically saw. These children ran in the hallways, pushed and shoved their way through the snack lines, clobbered the other children at recreation time, and even smashed a decoration or two before the week was over. But each year those needy children, who may not have ever heard about Jesus if it weren't for Grace's commitment, learned the truth of God's Word. Some of them even gave their lives to Christ before the week was over.

One year during VBS week, on a bright and warm June morning, I watched Grace once again pull up her van to the church door. Her noisy little passengers raced each other into the church building and she parked her minivan. As she tried to catch up with her rowdy bunch that was shoving its way through the hallways, I smiled and said, "Grace, I don't know how you do it! I admire you!" To which she gave a quick smile and a heartfelt reply, "Lorie, sometimes God's will is not our own." In other words, she was letting me know that it wasn't easy to bring these kids to VBS—in fact, it was hard! But it was her way of doing what she could to help the needy. Bringing needy children to VBS became Grace's personal ministry. Her sacrifice was her part in accepting Jesus' invitation to care for needy children.

IN HIS NAME

In Matthew 19:13–15, some people of Judea brought little children to Jesus so He could bless them, but the disciples rebuked the people for doing this. In turn, Jesus rebuked the disciples and insisted that the children not be hindered. Jesus wanted to bless them! He wanted to touch them and pray for them!

When I think of this passage, I imagine that the disciples pushed the children away because the little children were loud and giggly and all trying to climb into the Savior's lap at one time. Perhaps the disciples thought Jesus would be bothered by such wiggly and active children, but Jesus loved it! He wanted the children to come near to Him! He fully understood how active and rambunctious children are at times—especially when they are excited! And He fully understood how precious children are.

Are there children in your life—in your neighborhood, your extended family, or your workplace—who need to be brought to Jesus? If the Lord is prompting your heart and you're thinking of a particular child or a certain group of children as you read this, then pray about how you can bring them to Jesus like Grace did.

A CUP OF COLD WATER

No matter your profession, no matter your income, no matter your marital status, there is always something you can do for the needy. Grace had a busy life. She had no time in her day to volunteer and no money in her budget to give away. But she still found a way to help the needy by something as simple, yet as profound, as bringing needy children to church to hear the good news of Christ.

If you have a car, you too can care for the needy in this simple way. During the summer, many mothers would love for someone to care enough to take their children to a church's vacation Bible school. So many school-age kids are "latchkey children" during the summer months, meaning they are home alone while their parents are at work. Why not bring them to your church's VBS or church camp? Be sure to get a parent's permission before taking the children to church.

> *Is there an empty seat in your car on Sunday mornings?*
> *Consider bringing a neighborhood child or teen to church.*

Many churches provide summer VBS at no charge and certainly welcome any children who want to come and learn about Jesus. If your church charges a fee for summer programs, ask the pastor or children's ministry leader well ahead of time if scholarships could be made available. It also would be a good idea to let the VBS coordinator know about the number of children you will be bringing as well as any children who may have behavioral issues.

Like many things God asks of us, bringing needy children to church can be challenging and rewarding at the same time. The children you bring may never thank you. They may never have good behavior in the church hallways. They may never sit still and listen like you want them to. They may even use a bad word or two. But, friend, their lives will be forever impacted by what you did for them. Bringing Jesus into their lives will be well worth your sacrifice.

As I think about the children in my neighborhood, give me favor, Abba, with their parents as I ask to take their children to VBS. Give me patience, understanding, and joy as I serve you by bringing these little ones to church. Help me to remember that the seeds planted when children are young will grow and bloom in your time.

14. CREATE BAGS OF HOPE.

I couldn't believe I had forgotten the batteries, but I had walked right out the door without them. Back then, the little camera I owned took AA rechargeable batteries, and I had left them in the charger on my kitchen counter. I didn't realize it until I got all the way to the church and tried to take a picture of our group. The group was getting ready to load the church vans for a workday in the inner city. We were dressed in matching T-shirts that had a picture of the outstretched hand of Christ on the front and verses from Isaiah on the back.

I was so frustrated when I realized I couldn't take even one picture with my camera! I checked my watch and made a decision—if I hurried, really hurried, I could make it to the corner store to buy batteries and get back before we loaded up the vans. I decided to chance it and took off in my car.

When I got to the store, I zipped into a parking place, slammed the car door, and sprinted through the parking lot. That's when I saw him. He was a young guy, maybe thirty years old, in a wheelchair. He was holding a small bucket of sunglasses, trying to sell them to each customer who passed by him in the parking lot. As soon as I saw him, I thought, *Here we go . . . someone trying to sell something to make a buck.*

I avoided eye contact, hoping the man wouldn't stop me. I checked my watch—I had ten minutes to get in the store, buy the batteries, and get back to the church before they started loading the vans. But the man *did* see me. And he *did* ask me to buy a pair of his sunglasses. He said he was trying to make money to take home to his family.

He seemed genuine enough, but I just didn't have time right then. I said, "No, thank you," and kept sprinting to the store. I made it to the threshold and caught a reflection of myself in the automatic door. My heart sank as I saw the picture of the hand of Christ on the front of my shirt. And as I turned, I saw the verses from Isaiah 58 printed on my back—"This is the kind of fasting I want: Free those who are wrongly imprisoned; lighten the burden of those who work for you. Let the oppressed go free, and remove the chains that bind people. Share your food with the hungry, and give shelter to the homeless. Give clothes to those who need them, and do not hide from relatives who need your help" (vv. 6–7).

I could hardly concentrate as I purchased the batteries because the still, small voice of my Savior was ringing in my spirit. I was so ashamed. Here I was passing by a man who may have truly been in need because I was in a hurry to go and help the poor downtown with my friends from church. I walked right by a needy person so I wouldn't be inconvenienced. And all the while I had Scripture on my T-shirt about helping the poor. I even had a picture of the outstretched hand of Christ on the front of my shirt.

As I left the store, I made a conscious effort to find that man in the parking lot and give him some money. I made it back to the church with two minutes to spare. I'm thankful that God reminded me that day that I "wear" His name everywhere I go—whether I'm at church, at a downtown mission, or at the corner store.

> The world is a dangerous place, not because of those who do evil, but because of those who look on and do nothing.
>
> ALBERT EINSTEIN

IN HIS NAME

"Wearing" the name of Christ goes much deeper than having a verse and religious picture on your T-shirt. As Christians, we wear the name of Christ wherever we go. His picture is stamped on our hearts and we are to be His hands to everyone we encounter.

A day doesn't go by that I don't pray for God to help me "add to" and not "subtract from" the people I come in contact with each day. From the waitress who brings me my salad, to the exterminator who sprays my house, to the woman in line in front of me at the dry cleaner's, to the man begging on the street corner, I want to "give" to their lives and not "take away" from their lives. Even if it's just a common courtesy like a smile to say "hello," we should be Jesus to those we come in contact with every day.

We especially need to be aware of the needs around us and not let opportunities to do a good deed in Jesus' name slip by. Jesus calls us as His followers to be lights in this dark world because He is the light of the world and He shines through us, His children. In John 8:12, Jesus said, "I am the light of the world. If you follow me, you won't have to walk in darkness, because you will have the light that leads to life." Then in Matthew 5:14–15 Jesus tells us, "You are the light of the world—like a city on a hilltop that cannot be hidden. No one lights a lamp and then puts it under a basket. Instead, a lamp is placed on a stand, where it gives light to everyone in the house." We are called to be lights for Christ in our everyday lives.

I have a pastor friend who prays each morning for an opportunity to help a needy person before the day is over. Most days he doesn't encounter someone with a cardboard sign or someone asking for a handout. Instead, he meets ordinary people as he goes about his days. But those are just the people who may be in need of a warm smile or a friendly "hello" or even a "How are you?" as you hold the door for them.

We are called to be the hands of Christ every day and in every situation. As Paul reminds us in 2 Thessalonians 3:13, "Brothers and sisters, never tire of doing what is good."

A CUP OF COLD WATER

Making sure we are always ready to do good to those we encounter takes prayer and an attitude of selflessness. It's not always easy to "add to" those we come in contact with. But the Holy Spirit can prompt us to let the love inside of us ooze onto everyone we encounter—especially those who have blatant needs like the man I encountered in the store parking lot.

> *Imagine the impact you could make if you gave a smile and a "hello" to everyone you encounter.*

A great way to make sure you're always ready when you encounter someone in need is to have a few "Bags of Hope" on hand. These are simply plastic bags filled with items that a person in need could use. Bags of Hope include but are not limited to trial-size toiletries, snacks, water bottles, small Bibles, and religious tracks. Making these bags and putting them in your car will ensure that you are always ready to help someone in need.

You can also have your Sunday school class, Bible study group, or other ministry organization donate items and gather together to make the bags.

When you've finished putting the bags together, distribute them among group members. Make this a fun night for your group by having everyone bring a snack to share or maybe host a cookout at your house. After eating, as you fellowship together with friends, you can fill your bags of hope.

Remember as you fill and ultimately give away your bags of hope, you wear the name of Christ everywhere you go.

Today, Abba, keep me ever mindful that I wear your name. I represent Jesus Christ—the Savior who is the light of the world and who calls me to shine in this dark world. For every personal encounter I will have today, let me "add" to the lives of others.

15. HOST A WORLD CRAFT PARTY.

For just a moment, try to imagine a life of extreme poverty where you are forced to leave your village to find a servant job in the city. Even though you are a talented weaver, due to unrest in your country, you must leave your village to find work. Becoming a servant in the city is the only way to provide for your family. Unfortunately the life of a servant includes beatings, verbal abuse, and even sexual abuse.

This is the plight of so many women in India. But the Priscilla Center is working to change that. The Priscilla Center partners with these women, allowing them to stay in their own villages and weave items on a handloom that are then sold. This provides the women a source of income so that they can sustain themselves and their children. The items they weave can be purchased through a ministry called World Crafts, which ensures that the women of the Priscilla Center get a fair price for their items.

World Crafts (a division of Women Mission Union) partners with missionaries and ministries, like the Priscilla Center, to help impoverished men and women sell their goods at a fair price in order to have sustainable income. All of these men and women live in impoverished areas of the world such as Bangladesh, Laos, Tanzania, Cambodia, Vietnam, Zimbabwe, Uganda, Kosovo, and North Africa. Their handmade goods include bracelets, woven skirts, purses, necklaces, satchels, notepads, ornaments, boxes, beaded jewelry sets, aprons, Bible covers, picture frames, and bookmarks.

One of the most meaningful Christmas presents I ever received was a handmade wooden nativity ornament. When my

> Every believer from every nation brings out the color and diversity of the tapestry of heaven.
>
> **MAX LUCADO**

husband's cousin told me she had ordered it from World Crafts, and that the sale of that ornament had helped an impoverished man in the West Bank, I decided to keep the ornament displayed all year. It was just too beautiful to be put away with the Christmas decorations!

IN HIS NAME

Showing God's love to the world begins with relationships. Relationships teach others to trust us as we tell them about a Savior who died for their sins. Missionaries seek to establish relationships with the people they live among in order to tell them about Christ. They selflessly immerse themselves in another culture to gain the trust of the people they serve. Many times, showing them the love of Christ through practical means allows them to talk about the Lord.

Through World Crafts, artisans in various countries are shown the love of Christ when the missionaries help them sell their goods. By helping people sustain themselves, the missionaries establish important relationships and open the doors to share the gospel. Purchasing a handmade item through World Crafts is about much more than buying a woven purse or a beaded necklace. It's about sharing Christ with the nations in a unique and powerful way.

THE STATS

Thirty-three countries are represented through World Crafts.

Nearly 60 worldwide Christian ministries have contributing artisans to World Crafts.

A CUP OF COLD WATER

With World Crafts, you can not only order individual items through a secure website (www.worldcraftsvillage.com), but you can also host a World Craft party any time of the year. Unlike a Tupperware party or a jewelry party, you can know that when you order from World Crafts, you are saving lives. You are empowering artisans in impoverished areas to sustain themselves and their families through the fair market price of their handmade goods.

World Craft parties can be done with friends, family, coworkers, or Sunday school or Bible study groups. Ministry organizations and churches can host parties for international missions events or women's retreats. The website walks you through how to host a World Craft party, step-by-step. The site is user-friendly, with detailed information. When you click on "Parties," you will find everything from a guide to making invitations, to a script for what to say at your party. There is even a link to recipes from around the world for you to make!

The site recommends that you allow thirty to ninety minutes for your party. Be sure to order enough catalogs well in advance of your party date. At parties, take orders from the World Crafts catalogs and collect money for the orders. The host simply sends off the order forms and payment, and the ordered items are mailed a few weeks later.

> *When you purchase a handmade item from Word Crafts,*
> *you are giving hope and financial security to a man or woman*
> *on the other side of the world.*

The ministry of World Crafts is threefold. First, they help provide an income for impoverished men and women in other countries. Second, they help local missionaries and contact persons establish vital relationships with local artisans. And finally, they provide ways for people to purchase unique gifts from artisans around the world.

World Crafts is fulfilling the Great Commission of Acts 1:8 while empowering impoverished artisans around the world.

Abba, I can't always go on every mission trip that sparks my interest, but hosting a party in my home is something I can do for foreign missions. As I plan a World Craft party, help me to know just who to invite so that all of us can have fun together while meaningfully and tangibly impacting those in foreign lands who are being ministered to by missionaries.

16. ANONYMOUSLY SEND FLOWERS TO A SINGLE MOM.

I stood staring at the picture from the Christmas card. I could hardly believe it. The card was from a friend in Georgia. It had been three years since I had talked with her—three years since my husband took a job in another state and we moved our family away from the small community in Georgia where we had lived for most of our married life.

While we loved our new home and new friends, we also loved to hear from our friends back in Georgia. Christmas cards were especially nice because many of them included pictures. But this Christmas when I received a card and family photo from my friend, my heart dropped. Her husband was not in the picture. My eyes darted to the signature at the bottom of the card. It was signed by my friend and her children.

I closed my eyes in disbelief and thought about the fun our families had had when our children were little. The trips to the amusement parks, the summer cookouts, the hot summer days when our children would splash around in their wading pools while we talked about how blessed we were to have such great kids. My husband and I had attended Bible studies many times in their home. Right in their living room, we had prayed together with other Christian couples for our children and our marriages.

> The greatest feats of love are performed by those who have had much practice in performing daily acts of kindness.
>
> ANONYMOUS

For several days, I couldn't get my friends out of my mind. This precious Christian couple's split seemed impossible. I had known them for years. I found out later that their divorce had been nasty, a hard separation for both sides. Because I dearly loved both parties involved, I didn't want to know details. The details didn't matter: a home was now broken, children were caught in a battle, and two hearts were forever torn. It's no wonder God hates divorce.

It was heartbreaking to imagine my friend as a single mother. I wanted to do something for her, but what? I decided to ask someone who had been in my friend's shoes a few years before. Linda was now happily remarried, but she had been a single mom for many years, and she had a heart for single moms. I asked her what the hardest part of being a single mom had been for her. Her answer surprised me. Aside from the financial struggles, the custody battles, and the loneliness, she told me one of the hardest things was to see other women get flowers from their husbands.

I was taken aback by her answer. Flowers. For single mothers who had gone through the pain of separation and divorce, seeing other women get flowers from their husbands would make for a depressing day. With Linda's single days still fresh in her mind, she suggested I send my newly divorced friend a big bouquet of flowers to let her know that I was thinking of her. Who knew a simple gesture could mean so much to someone who is hurting?

IN HIS NAME

Divorce tears families apart. It causes terrible pain and suffering. And it's true that God hates divorce (Malachi 2:16). But it's also true that God loves His precious children, and He uses us to touch the lives of the needy and the hurting. I've heard so many single mothers say that having a divorce in their past can be like a scarlet letter. Criticism and judgment are not what they need. No matter the circumstances surrounding a marital separation, the hurt is deep and the pain is lasting.

The Bible says in Psalm 56:8, "You keep track of all my sorrows. You have collected all my tears in your bottle. You have recorded each one in your book." Our God sees every tear we cry as we struggle with the inevitable hurts and pain that this life brings. Divorce tears apart what God joined together, and it is painful, full of misery and tears. It leaves individuals with deep hurts that only God can heal. Since we, as Christians, are called to be the hands and feet of Jesus to the hurting and the needy, we can certainly be used to reach out to single mothers who need encouragement.

A CUP OF COLD WATER

Being a single mother has to be one of the hardest jobs in the world. Juggling child care, a career or multiple jobs, financial pressures, custody issues, holidays, housework, and schedules can be exhausting. Why not ease the stress of a single mother by sending her a bouquet of flowers? You can even send them anonymously if you want to enjoy the smile on her face without her knowing they were from you.

> *When you anonymously send flowers to a single mother, include a Scripture verse in the card to encourage her.*

Begin looking around at work, at church, or in your neighborhood for a single mother who may need encouragement. It won't take long for the Holy Spirit to reveal a sweet single mother to you. And don't think that because a mother has been divorced or separated for many years, she doesn't need encouragement. All single moms need encouragement! You'll be amazed at how merry you will feel after you've brightened the day of a hardworking single mom.

I plan to send flowers to a single mother, but I don't know what types of flowers are special to her. Abba, you know. So whisper to my spirit creative ideas for the flowers that will bring her special joy and brighten her day. It's my great honor and privilege to serve you in this way by bringing a little joy into the life of a single mother.

17. INVITE THOSE WHO ARE SURE TO BE ALONE DURING THE HOLIDAYS TO YOUR HOME.

Too serious. Too mushy. Too silly. It seemed every Mother's Day card I read in the store that day would not work for my mother or my mother-in-law. As I picked up card after card to try to find the right one, my eye caught a small lavender card with pink and yellow wildflowers in the corners and a heading that read, "For Someone Special." Curious, I opened to the card's message: "Although you're not my mother, you're someone very special to me."

Immediately, there in the card store, God brought someone to my mind—Mrs. Rebecca. My family had known Mrs. Rebecca and her husband, Mr. George, for many years. They were in their mid-seventies and attended our church. Mr. George had been my son Jacob's Sunday school teacher for years. Jacob adored Mrs. Rebecca and Mr. George. They always had big smiles and hugs for Jacob and the other little ones in the class. They enjoyed having the entire class of preschoolers over to their house regularly for cookouts and ice cream.

I noticed when I went to Mr. George and Mrs. Rebecca's house for these parties that they didn't display pictures of children, grandchildren, or great grandchildren. I found out later that Mr. George and Mrs. Rebecca, as much as they adored little children, had never been able to have any children of their own.

As I stood there in the store reading that card and thinking of Mrs. Rebecca and Mr. George and their love for children, I realized that Mrs. Rebecca has never, in all her years, had a Mother's Day of her own. In that moment, the Holy Spirit told me, *Give Mrs. Rebecca a Mother's Day this year.* So I bought that card and a bouquet of flowers, and the next morning, Mother's Day morning, I stood with my husband and my four small children outside her ladies' Bible study class. Another friend went inside to tell her that someone was waiting for her outside the door.

> Sympathy is no substitute for action.
>
> DAVID LIVINGSTONE

Mrs. Rebecca has back problems and it took her a few minutes to make her way to the door. When she opened it, the six of us were standing there with flowers in hand. We all said, "Happy Mother's Day, Mrs. Rebecca!" Mrs. Rebecca closed her eyes, buried her face in her hands, and began to weep quietly. My little children wrapped their arms around her waist and told her she was our special "Grand-friend." Through her tears, she told us how much she loved us, and then she wrapped her loving arms around us all. She was deeply moved by our gesture of kindness and said she'd never forget what we had done for her that day.

Afterward, my husband went ahead to the church service to help with ushering and I took our children to their Sunday school classes. When I finally entered the church sanctuary, the service was in full swing and the congregation was standing and singing a familiar praise song. As I got settled, I saw the words to the song scrolling on the screen in front and I tried so hard to sing, but I just couldn't concentrate on the words. I was so full from what had just happened with Mrs. Rebecca! My soul was overflowing with joy!

Finally, I apologized to the Lord in my spirit: *Lord, forgive me! I'm so full of joy right now, I can't even concentrate on worshiping you!* And in that very moment, the Holy Spirit whispered to my heart, *Sweet Daughter, you already worshiped me through what you did for Mrs. Rebecca.* And what incredible worship it was to know that our family had brought such joy to a precious friend.

IN HIS NAME

Many times we think of helping the needy outside our sanctuary doors only. While this is desperately needed and profoundly necessary because usually the poor *are* found outside our churches, sometimes the needy are also in our very own congregations. And sometimes their needs are so much more than physical needs. Especially among the elderly, loneliness can be overwhelming. We were created for fellowship and relationship with each other, and the bonds of friendship help us stand during times of trouble. The Bible speaks to the strong bond created within friendships in Ecclesiastes 4:12: "A person standing alone can be attacked and defeated, but two can stand back-to-back and conquer. Three are even better, for a triple-braided cord is not easily broken."

Like Mrs. Rebecca, many elderly persons, single parents, widows or widowers, and those going through profound losses can benefit from a special touch from another Christian. For these hurting brothers and sisters in Christ, holidays such as Christmas, Thanksgiving, Mother's Day, and Father's Day can be especially difficult. Because people sometimes hurt in silence, it's important that we are sensitive to the Holy Spirit's prompting in caring for the emotional needs of these hurting dear ones.

> **THE STATS**
>
> Loneliness and isolation have been linked to health problems. Isolated men are 1 to 4 times more likely to die of all causes at any age versus non-isolated men. Isolated women are 1 to 3 times more likely.

A CUP OF COLD WATER

Well in advance of this Thanksgiving and Christmas season, ask the Lord to bring to your mind those in your church, your workplace, or your neighborhood who may be spending the holidays alone. Perhaps you know a single parent, an elderly couple, a widow or widower, a college student, or a family who has just moved to the area and cannot travel "home" to be with extended family. Make an effort to invite those who the Lord brings to your mind into your home to join your family during the holiday season. Be persistent with your invitation. Some people may be hesitant to say yes the first time you invite them. If they see that you are sincere and you really do want them to join your family, they will feel more comfortable accepting your invitation the next time you ask.

> *Do you know someone who has recently lost a parent?*
> *This Father's Day or Mother's Day, send him or her a "thinking of you"*
> *card. This simple gesture can encourage a grieving heart.*

What a blessing it will be to you and your family to open your home to someone who is lonely during the next holiday season. Be willing to use your home, no matter its size, for God's glory. I've heard it said, "Be ready to *bless* and not *impress* through hospitality with the home God has given you." Some people are uncomfortable welcoming others into their home because they think their furniture is not "the best" like their neighbor's home, or they think their kitchen is too small. When others come to your home, focus on blessing them with hospitality and don't fret about the little things that may bother you about your home. Bringing friends into your house and enjoying each other's company will bring joy into each of your lives.

And don't forget those who may be hurting near other holidays such as Mother's Day and Father's Day. A "thinking of you" card in the mail or a bouquet of flowers sent to someone who has lost a child or parent (or those who have never had children of their own) can speak volumes to a hurting heart on Mother's Day or Father's Day.

Bring to my mind, Abba, those in my church, workplace, and neighborhood who are hurting and need a special invitation to join my family this year during the holidays. Help me to make their visit a special time for them to enjoy friendship and traditions that make the holidays so special.

18. ORGANIZE A COMMUNITY WORKDAY.

The rural Southern community where I grew up had a country church on nearly every corner. When I was a teenager, I passed by several of them each afternoon on my way to my part-time job. I can still remember one church clearly. It was small and painted white with beautiful stained glass windows and a cross at the top of the steeple. It looked like a picture on a postcard with its manicured green lawn and gravel driveway. Someone obviously took great care each week to take care of the grounds, including trimming the hedges around the small parking lot and sweeping the porch steps that led up to the whitewashed double doors.

I remember the church vividly, now more than twenty years later, not so much because it stood out from the other country churches in my town, but because of what was right beside the church. Not fifty yards away, in the lot next door, stood an old shack. It was made of weathered, dark brown wood and had a rust-stained tin roof. The weathered wood exterior made it look uninhabitable, but it was lived in. The front yard had no grass—just dirt where chickens roamed free. The family who lived there would sometimes sit on the crooked porch in the evenings, and they always waved to me when I drove by after work.

What made this such a strange sight was the fence that had been erected between the church and the old shack. It was a wooden privacy fence about twelve feet tall. It ran down only one side of the church property—the side where the shack was. On one side of the fence was the nice, whitewashed church. On the other side of the fence was a shack suggesting extreme poverty. What a contrast. I couldn't help but suspect that the church had put up the fence to block out the view of the poor people living right next door.

I cringe to think that the fence the country church erected is indicative of

> It's amazing what can be accomplished if you don't worry about who gets the credit.
>
> CLARENCE W. JONES

what churches sometimes do within many communities. No, we may not erect twelve-foot-high fences around our churches, but the reality is that we, as God's hands and feet, can get so busy with our "holy huddles" that we forget there are suffering and needy people right outside our doors in our very own communities.

IN HIS NAME

When churches reach out to their communities as representatives of Christ, they send a message that Christians care about the needs of the people around them. Christians can be good at merely talking about Christ. But when we get out of the pews and really begin to show love to our communities, our "talk" turns into our "walk." When unsaved people see that Christians care by our actions *outside* the church, they are far more likely to want to be a part of what's going on *inside* the church.

It's time to tear down the "wooden fences" that separate our churches from our communities. We should never forget that as Christians, we are ambassadors. Second Corinthians 5:20 reminds us that we are to be about the Father's business wherever we go: "So we are Christ's ambassadors; God is making his appeal through us." The communities where we live, work, play, and attend school are fertile mission fields where we can and should be attentive ambassadors for our Savior.

A CUP OF COLD WATER

Finding ways to intentionally show love to our communities is imperative for the health of a church. One such way is to create periodic workdays where church members are encouraged to do acts of kindness for their communities. No matter the size of your church, set aside time to care for those who work and live in your community. Your efforts will speak volumes to your neighbors about the love of Christ.

My church family sets aside two days a year for what we call "Love Loud" days—one day in early fall and one day in the spring. If you decide to initiate a workday for your church, talk with your pastor and explain your ideas of branching out into the community to serve. Your pastor knows of specific needs that can be addressed, such as visiting shut-ins or doing yard work for widows. After speaking with your pastor, enlist a team to help you coordinate each area of need. Church members can then begin signing up for teams or they can work with their Sunday school classes or Bible study groups. For your church's first workday, it may be necessary to give each team a list of community projects from which to choose. Eventually, groups can create their own projects and implement them on their own.

> *More than 9 out of 10 unchurched people say they would come to church if they were invited. But only 2% of church members have invited an unchurched person to church. What are we waiting for?*

To create a list of projects your teams could do, contact local school principals, police officers, fire departments, mission organizations, hospitals, food banks, clinics, and social workers to ask what specific needs they may have or know about. Before my pastor, Bruce Frank, initiated the Love Loud day at my church, he contacted our city's mayor to see how our church could be involved with the community. He pledged our church's prayer support for our mayor and our local government officials. This established a relationship with local officials and let them know that our church was serious about being the hands and feet of Jesus in our city.

Some local project suggestions are:

- *Painting rooms in elementary schools.*
- *Taking dinner to fire or police departments.*
- *Taking care baskets to nurses' stations at hospitals.*
- *Doing yard work for nursing homes.*
- *Cleaning or painting at the Department of Children's Services.*
- *Providing breakfast for social workers.*
- *Picking up trash along city streets.*

Of course, projects will vary greatly in different communities. That's why it is important to check with your local contacts to ask what needs they may have.

Whatever projects you do for the community, remember to do them with a smile and a servant's heart, expecting nothing in return. Remember, working in the community and showing love to those outside our church doors is what *being* the church is truly about.

It seems like such a simple thing, Abba, to reach into my community and show love to people through acts of kindness. As I ponder and plan a community workday, give me your creativity. Give me and my fellow workers servants' hearts as we venture outside the church walls to reach the community with your love.

19. PROVIDE RESPITE CARE FOR FOSTER FAMILIES.

Each year I attend the Christian Orphan Alliance Summit. The Alliance is a group of ministries, agencies, and churches that support efforts to defend orphaned and destitute children. Every year I am inspired by ordinary Christians who give their resources, talents, and time to help needy children in the United States and around the world. Some advocate for children through adoption. Others specialize in caring for orphans in crisis on foreign soil. Still others focus on helping children in the foster care system.

One agency that helps foster children is 4Kids. Located in Ft. Lauderdale, Florida, 4Kids is a ministry of Christ Chapel Church. Before the ministry was started, members of Christ Chapel went to their local Department of Children's Services and met with the social workers to apologize. Yeah, apologize. The church members explained to the social workers that for far too long the church had not met the needs of children in crisis, and they aimed to change that. They asked for the forgiveness of the social workers, and then asked them what their church could do to help children in foster care. The social workers actually wept. The conversation that followed sparked a vision for safe places where children in crisis could be placed. Christian families within their church opened their homes to these children in crisis. Since that heartfelt meeting, church members have successfully provided temporary and permanent homes to thousands of children in South Florida over the past

> From my many years' experience I can unhesitatingly say that the cross bears those who bear the cross.
>
> SADHU SUNDAR SINGH

eleven years. Their vision for the 4Kids ministry is simple—"A Home for Every Child in Crisis."

When I visited Christ Chapel during the Orphan Summit in 2008, I was able to tour many of the foster and group homes that are part of the 4Kids network. I was amazed at how many children had been helped and adopted by Christians affiliated with the ministry. What Christ Chapel had accomplished for children in crisis situations in just a few short years was mind-boggling. Thousands of children's lives had been touched and changed.

As I toured the group homes, the guide pointed out the pictures on the walls of the children who lived there at that time and told us stories about the children overcoming immense odds during their stay in that foster home. Some of the children had been in foster care for a short time while others had been there for many years. The homes were so warm and inviting. I was told that the children divided up the household chores and ate together as a "family" as often as possible. The group home "parents" worked very hard to make sure the children experienced the love of a family—some for the first time in their lives.

Foster parents work on the front lines caring for at-risk children and teens. They work tirelessly to create a home atmosphere for the most vulnerable—children in state care. When I asked the tour guide how foster parents are able to provide such attentive care to at-risk children day in and day out without becoming overly fatigued, he explained that they are able to take breaks often when "substitute" parents provide what is called *respite care*. Respite care is occasional foster care, an arrangement where respite care providers house children for a few days at a time so foster parents can rest. Foster parents depend on respite care to keep them inspired to continue their work for the Lord in caring for troubled children and teenagers.

CUP OF COLD WATER

IN HIS NAME

When I think about Christians helping other Christians, such as when foster parents are given a break through respite care, Aaron and Hur come to my mind. Once during an important battle, they gave help in a unique way to Moses, who was the leader of God's people, the Israelites, and the advocate and intercessor for them before the Lord. On many occasions Moses found himself pleading the cause of the Israelites before God. One such time was when the Amalekites attacked them at a place called Rephidim. As the Israelite men fought valiantly, Moses, Aaron, and Hur went to the top of a hill to watch the battle. As long as Moses held up his hands, God's people were winning. But if he lowered his hands, the enemy would overpower them. That's when Aaron and Hur came beside Moses, put a rock under him as a seat, and held up his hands so that Moses wouldn't grow faint (Exodus 17:8–16).

THE STATS

24% of foster children live in relatives' homes.

48% live in nonrelative foster family homes.

The remaining percentage live in group homes, emergency shelters, residential facilities, and preadoptive homes.

What a picture of how we are to help each other as brothers and sisters in Christ! We can and should hold each other up in the battles of life. When a brother or sister is tired, we can hold them up through prayer and through practical help. For foster parents, giving them a respite from parenting is one way to help those on the front lines of caring for impoverished and at-risk children. We can "hold up their arms" and let the parents rest just like Aaron and Hur did for Moses during the battle.

LORIE NEWMAN

A CUP OF COLD WATER

Providing respite care for foster children gives foster parents a much-needed break while also giving children a time away from their normal routines. Training for foster parents and respite care workers is often the same, because respite care workers may experience the same issues that arise with foster parents, just within a concentrated time. Most respite work is done on the weekends, providing foster parents a break once a month. But respite care can also be arranged during the summer months, or anytime foster parents need a vacation.

If you have considered foster care but are not quite ready to foster full-time, respite care may be the ministry for you. If you are a nurse or have other medical skills, there is a need for specialized respite care for children with special needs.

> *Respite care can also be a needed service for birth or adoptive parents with a special needs child.*

To find out what you need to do to become a respite care provider, contact your local Department of Children's Services. The National Foster Care Directory website has a search engine that will allow you to enter your state and find foster care resources in your local area. Visit www.childwelfare.gov/nfcad to reach the search engine. You can also read articles and learn more about respite care in general by visiting www.childwelfare.gov/adoption/adopt_parenting/services/respite.cfm.

By providing respite care for full-time foster parents, you become like Aaron and Hur as they held up the arms of Moses in battle. As long as they held up Moses' arms, God's people were victorious in battle.

Abba, there are so many children in foster care. The numbers are staggering, but you know each child by name and you have a plan for each of their lives. Show me how to be a part of the solution to the growing number of children in the foster care system and keep reminding me that to touch just one child's life is of immeasurable eternal importance.

20. SET UP A PRAYER TABLE AND GIVE OUT COLD WATER AT A COMMUNITY EVENT.

Three years ago when Julie married Allen, her prince charming, in a tiny country church in the rolling hills of Virginia, she never imagined their fairy tale would end this way.

On a seemingly normal Tuesday afternoon in May, with absolutely no warning, Julie's prince charming took his own life beside a quiet stream in the woods not far from their home. In one dreadful day, Julie's life fell apart. All her hopes and dreams for her marriage slipped through her hands like soft, dusty sand. Her prince charming was gone and she was forced to carry a label no young woman ever wants to bear—*widow*.

In the weeks and months following Allen's death, Julie began the painful task of sorting through his belongings. In the process, she organized her entire home, determined to simplify and sell any nonessential household items. Julie was resolved to live her new life as a widow in a place of financial security, free from the attachment to material possessions, while giving much of her income to mission work.

One Saturday morning before dawn, after weeks of organizing, Julie loaded furniture, trinkets, clothes, and linens onto a truck and headed to a flea market, praying for a of good sales. With mixed emotions, Julie filled several flea market tables with her various items. It was shaping up to be a difficult and emotional day as she unpacked and placed many of her and Allen's belongings on the tables.

As the sun began coming up over the flea market tents, Julie noticed two women setting up at a table across from hers. The strange thing was that these ladies didn't have anything to sell. Instead, they had several coolers full of bottled water. They also put out pencils and paper on their table. It didn't take long for the two ladies to walk over to Julie's table and introduce themselves. They explained that they set up a table each week at the flea market as a part of their church's prayer ministry. They offered Julie a bottle of cold water, and then asked how they could pray for her.

Julie was amazed at these two ladies. Here they were at a flea market early on a warm Saturday morning with nothing to sell, just giving out bottles of cold water and offering to pray for strangers as they passed by. And how was it that on this difficult day for Julie, God placed these two prayer warriors directly across from her table? God knew Julie would need them at that very time.

Julie told the women about the path she was now walking in life, and the three women held hands, right there in the flea market, and prayed together. Julie felt a sense of peace wash over her aching spirit as the women lifted their prayers to God's throne.

That day as Julie sold many of her items, she kept a curious and watchful eye on the prayer table across from her. Several people passed by the ministry's table. Some took the cold water offered to them, some didn't. Some gave their prayer requests, some didn't. But the ladies offered love to each stranger that passed by their table, whether the free gifts of water and prayer were accepted or not. The love and prayer support they gave to Julie that day, at just the right time in her life, was a gift that Julie will not soon forget.

> The more you train yourself to be dependent on the Spirit of God, the more He bears His fruit in your life.
>
> ANGELA THOMAS

IN HIS NAME

It was our Savior himself who said in Matthew 10:42, "And if you give even a cup of cold water to one of the least of my followers, you will surely be rewarded." Matthew 10 begins with Jesus calling His twelve disciples together and giving them instructions before He sends them out to cities in Israel. While they are together, He gives them the authority to cast out evil spirits and to heal every disease and illness (v. 1), and tells them to go to the lost sheep of Israel and preach that the kingdom of heaven is near (vv. 5–7). "Heal the sick, raise the dead, cure those with leprosy, and cast out demons. Give as freely as you have received!" Jesus says (v. 8).

He goes on to inform them that He is sending them out among wolves (v. 16), but they are to remember that God will give them the words to say when they are needed most: "When you are arrested, don't worry about what to say in your defense, because you will be given the right words at the right time. For it won't be you doing the talking—it will be the Spirit of your Father speaking through you" (vv. 19–20). Finally He tells them that they will be rewarded for obeying Him: "And if you give even a cup of cold water to one of the least of my followers, you will surely be rewarded" (v. 42).

Those instructions were given more than two thousand years ago to Jesus' disciples, but today, we are also called His disciples (Matthew 28:19–20). The setting is different, the culture is different, but God's Word never changes. Our instructions are the same today. Jesus still tells us, His followers, to warn people that His kingdom is near. He still tells us, His followers, that He will give us the words to say at the right time if we meet resistance due to our faith in Him. And He still tells us, His followers, that we will surely be rewarded if we give even a cup of cold water in His name (Matthew 10:42).

A CUP OF COLD WATER

The flea market prayer ministry had two parts. First, the women offered cold water to everyone who passed by. If strangers accepted their free water, then the ladies would simply ask them if they could pray for them. If they gave a request, the ladies would either pray with them right then, or write the request on a piece of paper to pray over at a later time. If a stranger didn't offer a prayer request, the person could simply take the cold water bottle—no strings attached.

> *Provide a prayer request box on your table. Some people may be more comfortable giving a request if they can write it down and put it in a box rather than in your hand.*

Setting up a table at a flea market, farmers' market, craft show, or other community event requires a small amount of preparation. Some events insist on registration beforehand and payment of a fee to reserve a table. Be sure to call ahead to see what the fee will be and pay in advance if necessary. You may be able to reserve several weeks' worth of tables at a time. Other events do not require advanced registration at all. Their table assignments are first-come, first-served. If this is the case, be sure to arrive early to find a good table. Fees vary depending on the size and location of the event or market. Read your local newspaper, check with your chamber of commerce, or go to radio or TV station websites for lists of upcoming community events. You can also visit www.greatfleamarket.com for a list of flea markets in each state.

Bottled water should be purchased and chilled ahead of time. If you are able, you can even print your own sticky labels for each bottle. Take off the original labels and replace them with ones you have made displaying a Bible verse about prayer. Be sure your labels are printed on waterproof paper with ink that won't run when condensation forms on the cold bottles. At your table, also have plenty of paper and pencils for people to write their prayer requests.

Resist the temptation to give out gospel tracts or brochures for your church or ministry. Your focus should be on serving without making people feel an obligation to take something in return for the water or prayers. They should understand that they can give a request or take a bottle of water with no strings attached. If they ask about your church, certainly give the information, but otherwise use your table simply as a prayer ministry to strangers.

If they want a bottle of water and don't want to give a prayer request, honor their decision with a smile, knowing that you have done what Jesus asked— you have given a cup of cold water in His name.

Abba, a community event seems like such an unlikely place for a prayer ministry. Yet you always meet people where they are. Help me to do the same as I plan and begin a prayer ministry. As I pray over strangers' requests, give me a boldness to pray with passion for them. Give me your love for each stranger so that they can sense and feel how much you deeply care about every detail and every aspect of their lives.

21. VOLUNTEER AT AN INTERFAITH HOSPITALITY NETWORK CHAPTER.

For years, when I heard the word "homeless," I envisioned a dirty bum stumbling on a downtown street with a bottle of booze in his hand. That image of homelessness was blown from my mind when I met the Halley family. They were a family of five—Mom, Dad, two school-aged children, and a toddler. They looked just like any other average American family. But without warning, the dad had been laid off from his job through no fault of his own. After being unable to pay their rent for four months, the Halleys were evicted from their home. With nowhere to go, the unthinkable became a reality for this family: They were homeless.

That's when they got help from the Interfaith Hospitality Network. Because most homeless shelters are either for men only or for women and children, the Interfaith Hospitality Network (IHN) keeps homeless families together by utilizing local places of worship as temporary shelters for families during the week. That's how I met the Halleys. They were staying at my church through the IHN when my family came to volunteer one night. My husband and I, along with all of our children, arrived around 6:00 PM to spend the night with the families who were staying at our church. Each family is carefully screened for emotional and psychological problems prior to admission to the program and cannot be serviced through IHN if issues are found, so we felt safe in volunteering with our children for the night.

We helped clean up the dinner tables, and then played a board game with the children. As bedtime approached, the Halley family went to their "bedroom" in a Sunday school classroom and our family went to the host room. My husband

and I slept on twin cots and our children slept in their sleeping bags on the floor. As I lay there on my cot in the dark, I could hear the dad in the room next to us playing with his children—just like my husband did each night at our home. Then I heard the mother singing and praying with her little children as she put them to bed—just like I did each night at our home. At that moment I realized that the Halley family was not that different from my own family.

> He is no fool who gives what he cannot keep to gain what he cannot lose.
>
> **JIM ELLIOT**

The next morning when the IHN van arrived to take the Halley family to the IHN Day Center, we told them goodbye, and then made our cots and went home. My kids had truly enjoyed "camping out" on the floor of the church as well as playing with the Halley children. Volunteering that night was one of the easiest yet most memorable ways that our family has ever been able to volunteer together.

Until we moved to another state, our family regularly volunteered to stay the night with the IHN families when they stayed at our church. Each time we volunteered, there were new families to meet, and we counted it a real joy to get to know each one of them. The Interfaith Hospitality Network completely changed the way I view homelessness.

IN HIS NAME

When we think of homelessness, many times we envision a disheveled man who is addicted to drugs and abuses alcohol. But did you know that 40 percent of the homeless are actually intact family units? In fact, one of every four homeless persons is a child.

Being homeless is about more than losing a place to live. In the process, dignity is lost. To help a homeless family get back on its feet is to help restore that dignity. Men find much of their identity in their work. It is simply the way God created them. In Genesis 2:15, God gave the garden of Eden to Adam and the job "to tend and watch over it." Adam was to watch over and guard the garden, to work and care for the ground. Adam's work assignment was given before Eve was created.

The first man, Adam, had a God-given mission to work and produce something he could take pride in: something of value. During a time of unemployment and homelessness, the husbands of homeless families feel the weight of being unable to provide for their families. This sense of burden can make for a stressful situation within these homeless families. According to an article on the causes and effects of poverty, homeless families experience even greater life stress than other families, including increased disruption in work, school, family relationships, and friendships.

THE STATS

Approximately half of all homeless children are under the age of five.

Homeless children experience more mental health problems, such as anxiety, depression, and withdrawal. They are twice as likely to experience hunger, and four times as likely to have delayed development.

Utilizing local church buildings and the Christians within those churches (as volunteers through the Interfaith Hospitality Network) is a way to not only restore dignity to the families by providing them shelter, but also a chance to offer the much-needed spiritual restoration that only Christ can bring.

A CUP OF COLD WATER

Interfaith Hospitality Network is a nationwide organization that links homeless families with local churches willing to house them at night. During the day, the families go to a Day Center where they can get help with job training, job placement, and social services, as well as receive child care for their children. On Sundays, the families are taken to a different place of worship where they stay for the week. An IHN van transports the families each day either to their place of work or the IHN Day Center.

IHN partners with any church denomination to help homeless families get back on their feet again. Once a family has a sustainable income, they are moved to transitional housing. Eighty percent of the families serviced through the IHN go on to long-term housing that they are able to pay for themselves. Helping families achieve lasting independence is a primary goal.

> *In 2010, more than 135,000 volunteers in 5,000 congregations helped with Interfaith Hospitality.*

The IHN is currently working in forty-one states and the District of Columbia, and they allow volunteers of all faiths to help families overcome homelessness. Ways you can volunteer include:

- *Cooking and serving meals.*
- *Helping with résumés and other special services.*
- *Helping children with homework.*
- *Helping at an IHN child care center.*

- *Staying overnight at churches with guest families.*
- *Mentoring.*

If you are interested in starting a chapter of the Interfaith Hospitality Network within your community, you can find contact information at their website: www.familypromise.org/program/interfaith-hospitality-network. At the site, you can also search to find IHN chapters in your state, as well as learn more about how the Interfaith Hospitality Network began and how it operates.

By volunteering with IHN, you can be a part of the solution for homeless families and encourage them as they regain independence and dignity with your simple acts of kindness done in Jesus' name.

I admit, Abba, that my view of homelessness hasn't involved the plight of homeless families and children. Now that I know, show me how to respond to the need in my own community through programs that already help homeless families, like Interfaith Hospitality Network. Give me eyes to see the homeless as real people that you love and deeply care for. Help me not to judge them as my human nature so often leads me to do.

22. ORGANIZE A BLOCK PARTY IN A NEEDY AREA.

The members of my former church in Georgia look forward to it every year—the annual block party downtown. Hours and hours of work from individuals representing multiple churches and ministries go into the creation of the block party near an inner-city housing project. The block party is one day of free fun, free medical care, free school supplies, free haircuts, free concerts, and most importantly the message of the gospel of Christ.

Before we moved to another state, I volunteered at different stations every year. The year I remember most was when I volunteered at the haircutting station. I didn't know much about cutting hair, and I certainly had no real training. My "training" had come by trial and error, as I had been cutting my children's hair for many years. On the day of the block party, at the early morning volunteer meeting, only one lady raised her hand to work the haircutting station, and the volunteer coordinator begged for anyone who had any knowledge of haircutting to help her. With reluctance, I raised my hand.

> Never doubt that a small group of concerned citizens can change the world, indeed it's the only thing that has.
>
> MARGARET MEAD

So there I was, cutting hair at the annual block party. That's how I met Clarence. He was an older man, about sixty years of age, and he sat in my chair on the lawn outside the large housing project where he lived. Music from the praise band thumped in the background and little kids ran to line up at the inflatables as I began to trim Clarence's dark, curly hair. Slowly, as if with great care, he told me part of his life story. Recently he had been released from prison, and he was desperate to start his life anew. He fought back tears and his voice cracked as he told me that he had lost everything—his family, his career, and his dignity. He felt as though he had wasted so many years of his life.

As I trimmed the curls around his forehead and ears, he and I talked about how God can make all things new and how God can take a broken life and make something beautiful from it. Clarence already knew Jesus. He had given his life to Jesus in prison, and now that Clarence was out of jail, he felt like God had given him a second chance at life—a second chance to make something of himself. I took my time cutting Clarence's hair because I wanted to make sure we had plenty of time to talk about Jesus' power to restore and renew.

When I finally finished Clarence's hair, I let him hold a small hand mirror so he could see whether his new haircut was suitable. I watched him give his reflection a long, hard look. But I don't think it was his hair that Clarence was really looking at. After a long look into that little mirror, Clarence handed it back to me with a smile and said, "It's good." Somehow I knew he was talking about more than just his new haircut. His new life was going to be good, because Clarence was now confident in the truth that Jesus Christ makes all things new.

IN HIS NAME

Having a servant's heart is not always easy. Our desires rise up and demand to be fulfilled first. Putting ourselves in the place of a servant and helping the needy can be taxing. It can be messy. And it can be a thankless job. But it's just what our Savior did. In fact, it was the last thing He did for His closest friends just before His death. John 13 recounts the story of when Jesus rose up from where He was reclining, removed His outer robe, tied a towel around His waist, and began to wash the dusty feet of those around Him.

His example for us is clear. We too are to be servants while here on earth. Jesus says to His disciples,

> You call me "Teacher" and "Lord," and you are right, because that's what I am. And since I, your Lord and Teacher, have washed your feet, you ought to wash each other's feet. I have given you an example to follow. Do as I have done to you. I tell you the truth, slaves are not greater than their master. Nor is the messenger more important than the one who sends the message. Now that you know these things, God will bless you for doing them. (John 13:13–17)

Ministering to the poor and the needy through a block party is a lot of work. And not one of the people you help may ever thank you. They may not ever realize the depth of your sacrifice to meet their needs and tell them about a Savior who died for them. But God sees. He sees every act of obedience and humility done in His name. So rise up, friend, from where you may be reclining in your spiritual walk. Wrap a towel around your waist like Jesus did and be ready to become a servant to those around you.

THE STATS

Top reasons many Americans are unable to receive basic health care: lack of medical insurance, lack of transportation services, need and expense of child care, limited hours and days of operation at medical facilities, and failure to practice preventive medicine.

A CUP OF COLD WATER

Organizing a block party in a needy area takes many months of planning. Late summer is a great time to host one so that children can get necessary school supplies, medical checkups, and clothes that they may need for school. But, of course, the block party is for those of any age. Its purpose is to bring the good news of Christ to the people of needy areas through meeting some of their basic needs.

> **The most vulnerable of the urban poor are women and children.**

You will need to begin your planning in early spring. Depending on the scope of your planned block party, you may want to involve other churches in the planning and implementation. Create a list of "stations" that you want to make available at the party. The following list will get you started. Choose ones that will work for your particular area and add or delete where needed.

- *Clothing giveaway station*
- *School supply giveaway station*
- *Haircutting station*
- *Diabetes screening station*
- *Blood pressure station*
- *Eye exam station*
- *Dental exam station (with toothbrush giveaway)*
- *Picnic tables and free lunch station, serving hot dogs, chips, soda, bottled water, etc.*

- *Kids' stations with inflatables, carnival-type games with candy giveaways, face painting, etc.*
- *Child identification and fingerprinting station. (Local police can provide this free of charge. Also gives a needed police presence.)*
- *Stage for periodic live music, the gospel message preached several times throughout the day, and kids' shows (puppets, story time, etc.)*

Also, be sure to ask for donations for your stations. For example, ask church members to donate money or grocery or department store gift cards. Local grocery stores may even be willing to donate candy or bottled water.

Four to eight weeks before the event, announce to your church that volunteers are needed and place a sign-up sheet in a highly visible location in your church. Volunteers will be needed in each station area, or rotations of volunteers, if you have enough manpower. For each station, assign one person to oversee the setup and supplies needed. For example, in the inflatables area for children, assign an overseer to make sure the inflatables will be delivered and inflated on time, that small tables are available for face painting and other carnival games, that enough volunteers are assigned to monitor each game, that candy donations are adequate, and that cleanup of that area is taken care of. You'll also need a crew of volunteers to clean up trash from all stations after the party is over. This is very important as you want to leave the grounds in good shape after the event.

If you don't have nurses, dentists, and doctors in your congregation who can help with the medical clinics, consider asking hospitals if they will provide such services for the event. And don't forget to encourage your church's students to volunteer. Teenagers can help with any area of the party.

Most importantly, pray with your volunteers. Give each volunteer a list of prayer requests well in advance of the party so that every area of your event can be covered in prayer. Remember, the gospel message should be shared at least once from the stage, if not multiple times. With advanced planning and organization, your block party can become an annual or biannual event for your church to use to reach the needy of your community with the love of Christ.

Abba, as I consider leading the charge to begin planning a block party, show me which needy area of my community would be a good place to host the party. Give me favor as I seek help and volunteers who will come alongside me to make this block party a reality. Give me a desire to lead and organize, as well as a heart full of compassion and love for the needy in my area.

23. CREATE A PARTNERSHIP WITH YOUR CHURCH AND AN AFRICAN VILLAGE.

Pastor Walter is one of the most humble men I've ever had the privilege to meet. His congregation meets in a small cinder block church in the bush of Africa. Most of the people attending his church are orphaned children and widowed women. Their lives have been radically altered by the AIDS pandemic. When I met Pastor Walter, his wife, and their four small children several years ago, he was financially supporting several of the orphans and widows in his church even though he is a poor African man himself.

As several of us from our mission team knelt down on the dusty cement floor of Pastor Walter's church and prayed over his ministry, I prayed that God would make a way for the people of my church back in America to support and uplift this man's efforts to help the poor of his African community. My answer came a few weeks later when a partnership between Pastor Walter's church and my home church was born. The members of my church embraced the idea of financially supporting the orphans of Pastor's Walter's congregation, and thus began a partnership enabling Pastor Walter to care for more people in his impoverished community.

The following is an excerpt from my personal journal on the day our church began this partnership:

I saw Jesus yesterday! It's true! But He didn't look at all the way I expected. He wasn't wearing a regal robe on His shoulders. He didn't have a royal crown on His head. No legion of angels announced His arrival. *But I saw Him! He was there!* He had dark skin and deep brown eyes. He wore tattered clothes and no shoes. He had dirt on His face and His eyes were weak and sad. Through His eyes I could see abandonment and a hunger for affection. I might have missed seeing Jesus altogether if it hadn't been for God's reminder through Tom Davis.

Tom Davis, president of Children's HopeChest, was the guest pastor at our church yesterday. As God spoke His message through Tom, I was reminded in Matthew 25 of what Jesus looks like:

"'I was hungry, and you fed me. I was thirsty, and you gave me a drink. I was a stranger, and you invited me into your home. I was naked, and you gave me clothing. I was sick, and you cared for me. I was in prison, and you visited me.'

"Then these righteous ones will reply, 'Lord, when did we ever see you hungry and feed you? Or thirsty and give you something to drink? Or a stranger and show you hospitality? Or naked and give you clothing? When did we ever see you sick or in prison and visit you?'

> How little chance the Holy Ghost has nowadays. The churches and missionary societies have so bound him in red tape that they practically ask Him to sit in a corner while they do the work themselves.
>
> C. T. STUDD

"And the King will say, 'I tell you the truth, when you did it to one of the least of these my brothers and sisters, you were doing it to me!'" (Matthew 25:35–40).

After the worship service, as individuals and families chose children for sponsorships, I looked into the eyes of the sweet children in the sponsorship packet photos. I remembered many of them from my trip to Africa last month. I remembered playing ball with them, hugging them and kissing them, holding them in my arms, looking into their eyes. But yesterday, as I looked into one boy's eyes once again—this time in a photo that was being taken home by a church member—I saw Jesus.

You see, when we care for the orphan, the widow, the imprisoned, and the sick, we are caring for Jesus himself.

That day the church congregation was moved by God's compassion and sponsored more than 270 orphaned and impoverished African children.

THE STATS

About 40% of Africans live in slums.

More than 50% of Africans suffer from diseases spread by water such as cholera, infant diarrhea, dysentery, and river blindness.

Nearly one third of children in sub-Saharan Africa are underweight.

IN HIS NAME

The Great Commission in Acts 1:8 is clear: "But you will receive power when the Holy Spirit comes upon you. And you will be my witnesses, telling people about me everywhere—in Jerusalem, throughout Judea, in Samaria, and to the ends of the earth." People everywhere need to hear the gospel of Jesus Christ, and churches around the world struggle to bring that message. The pastors and laypersons in those churches are our brothers and sisters in Christ. Helping them to reach their villages and communities with the love of Christ through financial partnerships can give them the empowerment they need to fulfill our commission as Christians to "go and make disciples of all the nations" (Matthew 28:19).

CUP OF COLD WATER

A CUP OF COLD WATER

It's not necessary to have traveled to an impoverished African country to create a partnership with a village in Africa. You just have to be a part of a mission-minded church congregation that is ready to embrace a church on the other side of the world. These partnerships begin with Children's HopeChest in Colorado Springs, Colorado. The organization's website, www.hopechest.org, has contact information and the details you will need to get started. (Click the Transform tab for information on community partnerships.) These partnerships are usually made with churches, although businesses are also welcome to become involved. Many partnerships are with African villages, but villages in Russia and Ukraine also need partnerships.

> *Children's HopeChest can send a representative from their ministry to your church to help increase involvement for your church's partnership with an African village.*

Children's HopeChest sends sponsorship packets to a contact person within your church who presents the packets to the congregation. Many churches set aside a Launch Sunday where these packets are explained during the service, and then put on a display table outside the sanctuary for church members to view. Each packet contains all the necessary information to sponsor a child for thirty-eight dollars a month, including a photo and contact information so members can write to their sponsored child. If a church chooses, a member of the HopeChest staff can even come and speak or preach at your sponsorship kickoff event.

Once the children are sponsored, the monthly pledge money is pooled together and sent to the HopeChest missionaries in your partner village. The money is used for various humanitarian efforts such as feeding, clothing, and evangelizing orphans, and supporting the pastor and local church. Churches and businesses are asked to commit to their partnership for at least three years. During those three years, individuals are encouraged to take mission trips to their sponsored village.

The partnership is designed to change the lives of the impoverished villagers, both spiritually and physically, but the sponsoring churches quickly find that the partnerships change lives within their own congregation. When a church congregation can care for the needs of another church in an impoverished area, a beautiful weaving of lives takes place. Partnering with a church overseas gives the receiving church the financial resources they need to help those who are suffering in their villages and communities. And it gives the donating church the opportunity to help with needs that they might not otherwise even be aware of.

It takes only one person to ignite a fire of interest and involvement and motivate an entire congregation to move with compassion to partner with a village church in Africa. As I look back at the partnership that has developed in my former church with a church in Swaziland, Africa, and the lives that have been touched and changed, I stand amazed that God used me to ignite such a fire of compassion for the impoverished people of Swaziland. I am just one person. But what I've learned is that when even one person has God on their side, it makes them the majority.

To read the blog of two missionaries in Africa involved in such partnerships with Children's HopeChest, visit jumbogerber.myadventures.org.

Oh Abba! Keep reminding me through your Word that when you call me to help the poor and the needy, I am not to wait until it's convenient or when I have mustered up an army of helpers. I can start now! As I walk in obedience to show love to the hurting, I have you there with me, and Abba, that makes me the majority!

24. BECOME A FOSTER PARENT.

Seven-year-old Alaina is a typical little girl who likes to play dress up in her mom's high-heeled shoes. Barbies, pink hair bows, and sparkly crayons are some of her favorite things. Her bedroom is decorated with pink and purple frills and lifelike baby dolls. Her days consist of running from the cootie-filled boys during recess and finger painting pictures for her daddy in Mrs. Jenkin's art class. She can count to ten in Spanish and she can sing the books of the New Testament. She's learning how to share, how to pray, and how to be a little girl who walks with Jesus.

In every way imaginable, Alaina is a beautiful, healthy, well-adjusted little girl. But her life certainly didn't start out that way. By the time Alaina was eight months old, she had suffered abuse and severe neglect at the hand of her mother. Alaina was taken into state custody by a social worker, became a ward of her state, and was placed into a foster home. That's where John and Caryn met her. Alaina was already in her first foster home when John and Caryn got the call asking if they would take her into their home. They didn't hesitate, even though they were already foster parenting a newborn baby boy, in addition to their two biological children. They had been approved to be foster parents only two months before, and they finished their foster care training only a few weeks before they got the call. They agreed to take little Alaina.

> There can be no keener revelation of a society's soul than the way in which it treats its children.
>
> **NELSON MANDELA**

Within the year, the birthmother's rights were terminated and Alaina was released for adoption. Immediately, John and Caryn started the process to adopt Alaina, as well as the baby boy they had been fostering. Alaina and her little brother just celebrated another "Gotcha Day," or adoption anniversary, last month with their forever family.

Although Alaina's story has a happy ending and she was adopted by a loving, Christian family, there are still 115,000 children in the United States who are legally free and clear for adoption. They are just waiting for a forever family—waiting for someone to make room in their home and in their heart for them. According to the Adoption and Foster Care Analysis and Reporting System Report released in 2010, there were 423,773 children in the US foster care system. That is a staggering number. And these children have been taken from their parents through no fault of their own.

There is an incredible need for foster families who will give these children temporary homes. Some children need foster care for a short time while others need care for an extended period. No matter the length of time a child is in state foster care, a Christian foster parent can give a child security, acceptance, safety, and unconditional love.

IN HIS NAME

I once met a social worker who advocated with her state for children in foster care. She told me that when she is called to the hospital to take a newborn into state foster care, she prays over the baby. She prays that every one of the tiny babies will never have to know that they were unwanted, and she asks God to provide forever families to adopt each child and love him or her as their very own.

There are over 423,000 children in state foster care. How can the church ignore that number? These children are not in a far-off, impoverished third world nation. They are right here in the United States—within our own communities. So many of the children have experienced horrific abuse that we can hardly fathom. And only God can heal their deep hurts from abuse and neglect.

In 2 Samuel 9, King David asks his servant if there is anyone left in the household of the former king, Saul, that he can show kindness to. His servant finds one man, Mephibosheth, who had crippled feet. As the former king's grandson, Mephibosheth had lost everything that had rightfully been his. To show kindness to him, King David invited Mephibosheth to his home, restored everything that had been taken from him, and then set a place for him at the royal dinner table not just for that night, but for all of his days.

THE STATS

In the US, there are over 423,000 children living in foster care.

Of those children, 115,000 are available for adoption.

What a picture for us! So many children in foster care have had everything taken from them—their homes, their security, their innocence. In the same way that King David showed kindness to Mephibosheth by restoring everything that had been taken from him and giving him a place of honor at the royal table, when a Christian couple fosters a needy child and gives that child a place of honor in their home, they too are restoring what the world has taken from these precious children.

A CUP OF COLD WATER

Many times I've heard couples say that they would like to help children in crisis, but they don't think they could handle growing attached to foster children just to have them leave. While it is certainly true that foster children can come and go in foster homes, what a privilege it could be to have the children in your home for even a short time to show them the love of Christ!

The first step in the journey to become a foster parent is gathering information. A few websites will help you learn about foster parenting. The Administration for Children and Families web page, www.acf.hhs.gov/index.html, provides answers to frequently asked questions about foster parenting. Click on "Questions," and then choose "Child Welfare" from the Search by Category drop-down menu. At the US Department of Health and Human Services website, www.childwelfare.gov, you can read articles and find current information on foster care. You can also visit www.adoptus.org to find information on the children in your state who are free and clear for adoption through the state foster care system.

Being as informed as possible will allow you to make an educated decision on whether to go through your Department of Children's Services or use a private agency for foster training. Many private agencies contract with the government to provide foster care and adoption services. Although the amount of time spent in foster parent training is set by each state, the training times can sometimes be more flexible with a private agency. For example, many states require training for foster parenting that lasts eight to ten weeks (typically one night per week for a one- or two-hour class), but with a private agency, their training may take place on three Saturdays or over a weekend to accommodate potential foster parents' schedules. Some churches also offer classes along with free child care.

> *When adopting a child from the US foster care system, adoptive parents pay no fees. In many cases, adoptive parents are paid a monthly subsidy until the child is eighteen years old.*

For foster care, you do not have to own your home and you can foster as a single adult. You also can get a stipend each month from your state to cover expenses such as food, clothing, and child care for each foster child. Even those who work full-time can foster because the state will pay for day care. In some cases, if you adopt a child that you have been fostering, your stipend can continue until the child reaches the age of eighteen.

Clearly the government is willing to accommodate potential foster parents, as many options exist for couples and individuals who want to light a needy child's dark world by providing short-term or long-term foster care. For a child who has experienced tremendous loss through no fault of their own, making room at your table, room in your home, and room in your heart for them can speak volumes about God's unconditional love to a little heart that bleeds for acceptance, love, and affection.

Abba, it seems I do have room in my home and certainly in my heart for a foster child. But it's hard to imagine getting attached to a child just to have the child leave. Yet even if I foster a child only for a brief time, I could have a real, eternal impact on a child. I may be the only Jesus they ever see by being their foster parent. Help me, Abba, to rise above my fear.

25. ADOPT AN ORPHAN.

Forgotten. Dirty. Cast aside. Unwanted. Abandoned. All of these words described the orphaned girl in the picture. I wanted to look away from the photograph . . . but I couldn't. I wanted to walk away and pretend she wasn't there . . . but I couldn't. I wanted to go back to ironing, cleaning, cooking—anything to take my mind off the image that was glaring at me from my computer screen . . . but I couldn't. I kept hearing God whispering in my spirit, *Look. You must look at her.* He was telling me, *Look closely into her eyes until you see a reflection of me.*

The little two-year-old girl in the picture was one of twenty-four adoptable children at an orphanage in Africa. Some were brought to the orphanage by their father after their mother died in childbirth. Others

> God's part is to put forth power; our part is to put forth faith.
>
> ANDREW A. BONAR

were brought by a desperate and impoverished mother clinging to the hope that through adoption, her children may have a better life. Still others were brought by neighbors or extended family members after the child's parents both died of AIDS.

Whatever the reasons surrounding how and why children arrive at an orphanage, they no longer matter once the children are there. In an orphanage, the labels "forgotten," "alone," "unwanted," and "cast out" are the world's banners over them. They have nothing. They have no home. They have no parents. And they have no voice.

Adoption is the one word that can remove all the banners over an orphaned child. But the adoption process can bring so many questions. Big questions. I've been there. When God called my husband and me to adoption, serious questions were at the forefront of our minds: *Can we take another child? Do we have the room? Do we have the resources? How will we send them all to college? Will we need a bigger vehicle? Can we really do this?*

Even with so many questions in my mind, somehow all of them melted away as I looked into the little girl's desperate eyes. As I stared at her picture, fighting my desire to turn away and forget her, something rose up in my spirit. It rose up and overpowered my fear. It rose up and overpowered my questioning. It rose up and overpowered my desire to turn away. Nothing mattered but saving her. Nothing mattered but replacing "forgotten" with "remembered," "alone" with "together," "unwanted" with "wanted," "abandoned" with "chosen."

IN HIS NAME

One of the greatest kings in the Old Testament is Josiah. After Josiah's father was killed, the people made eight-year-old Josiah their king. He turned out to be one of the godliest of all of Judah's leaders. We read part of his story in 2 Kings 23. At the young age of sixteen, Josiah renewed Judah's covenant with the Lord, and then he ordered the removal of the tools of Baal worship from the temple of the Lord and did away with the idolatrous priests. He desecrated and burned altars where the people had sacrificed their children to false gods. He essentially "cleaned up" and turned God's people back to the one true, living God. He was a mighty man who knew and followed God alone.

And to think that Josiah started out as a fatherless child. Yet this once fatherless child was used by God to lead and turn the hearts of an entire nation back to himself! God specializes in using the most unlikely of candidates to do His work—even fatherless children!

A CUP OF COLD WATER

Many reputable Christian adoption agencies have helped adoptive parents navigate the system to bring orphaned children into families. There are three types of adoptions that are available to potential adoptive families. While most agencies specialize in just one type of adoption, some agencies can help parents with any of the three types. See appendix C for the websites and contact information of various agencies.

Private domestic adoption. In a private domestic adoption, potential parents first choose an agency to conduct a home study. In a home study, a social worker looks at the potential parents' home, interviews them extensively, assesses their finances, and determines whether or not they will give approval for the parents to adopt. In most cases the agency doing the home study is the same agency that will handle the adoption, but if the chosen agency is out of state, a separate agency in the parents' home state is used to perform the home study, which must be done by an in-state social worker. Home studies can be invasive, but they are a necessary step required for any adoption.

After the home study is completed, usually the parents are put on a waiting list to be chosen by a birth mother who will be surrendering her baby for adoption. The adoptive parents can normally indicate what gender and ethnicity they prefer, as well as any special needs they may or may not be comfortable with. Waiting times for a healthy baby can range from a few weeks to many years. If an adoptive couple is willing to adopt a baby of any ethnicity, or a baby with special health needs, the wait can sometimes be significantly reduced.

While some agencies work with birth mothers who are surrendering an older child or toddler for adoption, most agencies work exclusively with pregnant birth mothers. Private adoption attorneys can also, in some states, match potential adoptive parents with birth mothers.

Fees for a private domestic adoption can vary widely depending on the agency or attorney the parents choose. Most private adoptions cost between $8,000 and $35,000.

Adoption through the state foster care system. A child adopted through the state foster care system at some point has been taken from his or her home due to abuse or neglect, and the parents' rights have been terminated. Potential adoptive parents must have a home study done by a social worker in their state of residence. (State adoption laws can vary from state to state, but home studies are a requirement in every state.) Adopting a child from the state foster care system is free. There may even be a monthly subsidy for adoptive parents until the adopted child is eighteen years of age. Every state has children in the state foster care system waiting for an adoptive home. Many of them are in sibling groups, and most are over seven years of age.

International adoption. An international adoption involves a child who meets the US immigration criteria of an orphaned child. Children are adopted from an overseas orphanage, children's home, or foster home. As with any other adoption, adopting internationally requires a home study by a social worker in the adoptive parents' state of residence, although the study differs from the domestic home study due to immigration requirements. Once an international home study is completed, the social worker will send it to the in-state immigration office where the adoptive parents must also file immigration papers to bring an orphaned child into the United States as their own child. Adoption laws in the child's nation of birth must also be satisfied before the child can leave his or her country.

Many agencies specialize in one or more countries where US citizens can adopt orphans, and they can handle all aspects of international adoptions. Fees as well as "wait times" can vary greatly depending on the child's birth country. Typically fees range from $8,000 to $25,000 plus travel expenses.

> *Many ministries, such as Life Song for Orphans and Shaohannah's Hope, offer grants to offset the cost of private and international adoption.*

For more information on foster care adoption and agencies in your state, use the search engine at www.childwelfare.gov/nfcad and check the "Public Foster Care and Adoption Agencies" box. Just like fatherless King Josiah, one of Judah's most God-fearing kings, God has a perfect plan for every orphaned child. Being an adoptive parent, you will have a front-row seat to God's marvelous, perfect plan as it unfolds in your adopted child's life. What a privilege to partner with God in such a life-changing way!

Abba, the thought of giving an orphaned child a home has been stirring in my mind and heart for a while now. But as I look at the requirements, the red tape, and the paperwork, it seems like a mountain I can't climb! Help me to understand the process and help me to remember that at the end of the long process is a child—a child that desperately needs a home.

CLOTHING THE NAKED

"I needed clothes and you clothed me."

26. DONATE TOYS OR CLOTHES TO A WOMEN'S SHELTER.

When I met Charise she was busy with her ten-month-old little girl, Alicia. We had all just finished dinner, and Alicia had lasagna noodles all over her bib and in her hair. She was adorable! Her mother smiled at her baby, who was wearing more noodles than she had eaten. But as Charise unstrapped her daughter from the high chair and tried to clean the baby's face and hair, I couldn't help but notice that she was very tired from a long day at work.

Knowing Charise was tired, I volunteered to bathe Alicia in the sink while her mom took a shower. As we walked the long hallway to the bathroom area where the showers were, Alicia giggled out loud as her mother tickled her chin. They seemed to be a typical mother and daughter winding down their day with dinner and bath time. Except for the fact that Charise and her daughter were living in a women's shelter. I didn't know the circumstances that brought Charise to the shelter—I certainly didn't ask. But for many women, domestic violence is what causes them to flee to the safety of a shelter like the one where Charise was living.

> You don't give for God's sake. You give for your sake.
>
> MAX LUCADO

Whenever I volunteered at the shelter, I brought dinner and ate with whoever happened to be staying there at the time. The women I met while volunteering always amazed me. They were strong women who worked hard and loved their children. Most of them had left an abusive situation and were trying desperately to get on their feet financially to sustain themselves.

CUP OF COLD WATER

Because many of them had left their homes abruptly, the shelter always needed clothing. The women especially needed nice business clothes that they could wear for job interviews. I also took toys to the shelter on occasion for the children. I knew the clothes and toys I brought would be put to good use. Cleaning out my closet and my children's toy boxes and bringing the clothes and toys we didn't need anymore to the shelter was a simple way to help displaced mothers and children like Charise and Alicia, who were looking for a new start.

> **THE STATS**
>
> An estimated 1.3 million women are victims of physical assault each year by an intimate partner.
>
> Reasons for being in a shelter can include domestic violence, interpersonal conflict, and eviction.

IN HIS NAME

Jesus specializes in making "everything new" (Revelation 21:5). He can take any situation, any sin, any challenge, any failure, any dilemma, and any messes that life throws our way, and make something beautiful from them. Second Corinthians 5:17 reminds us that God is in the transforming business: "This means that anyone who belongs to Christ has become a new person. The old life is gone; a new life has begun!"

If we are willing to give Him our messes, He can take them, break them, and make them into something new for us. I'm sure Charise and others like her who find themselves in a women's shelter never imagined their lives would take such a turn. But God is there. And He's there through us, His children. We are His hands and feet to the hurting.

A CUP OF COLD WATER

Nearly all of us have clothes in our closets that we don't wear for a number of reasons. Some we can't fit into, some are outdated, and some we never wore—they're hanging in the closet with the tags still on them! Why not donate these items to a local women's shelter? Make sure the clothes are free from stains, tears, and missing buttons and have them laundered or dry cleaned before donating. Shoes, belts, and handbags are also needed at the shelters.

> *If you haven't worn an article of clothing for a year, you likely will never wear it again. Why not donate it to a women's shelter?*

Visit www.womenshelters.org and click on your state to find a women's shelter in your area. If the shelter does not have an address listed, you will have to contact someone at the shelter to learn the best way to drop off donations. Some shelters keep their locations secret to keep the women safe. Another resource, the National Coalition Against Domestic Violence website (www.ncadv.org), has a wealth of information on programs and issues related to battered women and children. The Coalition gives even more ways for you to volunteer, donate, and help at battered women's shelters.

As you volunteer and donate items, you can be a part of real restoration as God makes "everything new" in the life of a woman living in a shelter.

Abba, you alone are the Restorer of broken lives. In my city are women living in shelters due to abuse. As they seek safety and restoration, show me how I can be a part of their healing. Thank you that you are the Living God who heals, restores, and makes everything new.

27. DONATE TOILETRIES TO A HOMELESS SHELTER.

I was only ten, but I remember it well. I was on a trip with my best friend, Heather, and her family. Her father frequently went out of town on business, but this time Heather and her mom were able to travel with him. At the last minute, they invited me to tag along to keep Heather company. When we arrived in the big city of Atlanta, it was already nighttime. My senses were on overload with all the lights, sights, and sounds of one of the busiest cities in the world. Our hotel was situated downtown in the heart of the city and because we were close to restaurants and attractions, we walked nearly everywhere we went.

One morning, as we made our way up a bustling downtown sidewalk to get breakfast, we passed people lying alongside the street. They were homeless. But I had never seen a homeless person—ever. I had no idea why these people were sleeping on the sidewalk. In my naïveté I was frightened. I actually thought the people were hurt, and my mind was racing with what had happened to hurt all of those people at once.

I suppose Heather's mother could see the concern on my face. When we got to the restaurant, she explained that the people we had seen had no place to live, so they slept on the streets. I was shocked.

> You can't comfort the afflicted without afflicting the comfortable.
>
> **DIANA, PRINCESS OF WALES**

I couldn't understand how anyone could sleep on the cold, hard sidewalk. Why didn't anyone help them? Why didn't someone let them stay at a hotel? Couldn't they sleep at a church? Surely the churches should help them. The entire time we were at that restaurant, I was quiet.

When we left the restaurant, I noticed that many of the homeless people we had passed before were gone. Now that the sun was up and shining, they had left the places they had slept for the night—all except for one man. The black man in a brown dirty overcoat was lying propped up but eyes closed against a brick building with his legs across the sidewalk. As we got closer, I could see that people were just stepping over him—literally stepping over this human being as if he were a heap of rotting garbage on the street. I was dumbfounded. It just didn't seem right to me. Even though I was only ten years old, in my mind something seemed terribly wrong with what I was witnessing. A human being was in need and all the adults ignored him and stepped over him like he was yesterday's trash. Life just kept going all around this homeless man. He seemed forgotten. Invisible.

IN HIS NAME

Now that I'm an adult, I know why the grown-ups chose to step over this homeless man instead of helping him. They were busy. They had places to go. They had families and homes to tend to. They had important jobs. The office was waiting. The taxi was coming. The appointment was soon. Besides, homeless people are just a part of every city, right? Our fast-paced world doesn't offer much time to help other people. Stepping over a sleeping homeless person is so much easier than helping him, isn't it?

THE STATS

Nineteen percent of homeless people are employed.

Oh, friends, what have we accomplished as a society if we are so busy with our appointments and staring at our smartphones that we treat a homeless

CUP OF COLD WATER

person in need as if he's invisible? It must truly grieve the heart of God for us as His body to ignore a person in need. Proverbs 3:27 says, "Do not withhold good from those who deserve it when it's in your power to help them." Most of us do have the power to help, even in small ways, but will we take the time?

I don't know what happened to that man on the street in Atlanta, but God has used that experience to impart a clear message to me about the homeless—their lives and needs are not invisible to God and they should never be invisible to us.

A CUP OF COLD WATER

So many wonderful missions help the homeless on a daily basis. Homeless shelters can minister to the homeless in varied ways, from offering a bed on a cold night to helping with job placement. One way to help the homeless is to help those who help them. By this I mean supporting one of the many homeless shelters that already has programs in place to help the homeless.

> *The next time you travel to a hotel, save the trial-size shampoos, soaps, and lotions to donate to a homeless shelter.*

An immediate need of homeless shelters and ministries is personal hygiene items. Because items such as soap, toothbrushes, toothpaste, deodorant, shaving cream, and shampoo are given away each day, these shelters need donations regularly to keep their shelves stocked.

How many of us have those tiny soaps and shampoos from hotels just sitting in a drawer somewhere? Why not take them to a homeless shelter?

Or the next time you visit the pharmacy, pick up a few extra bars of soap and shaving cream. These small items can help shelters take care of the personal hygiene needs of the homeless that come to them each day. It's an easy way to show the love of Christ.

The following list of websites will help you find a homeless shelter or organization near your town. Some of them are Christian ministry sites and some are secular sites.

- Homeless Shelter Directory: *www.homelessshelterdirectory.org*
- Mama's Health:
  www.mamashealth.com/help/communityhelp/homelessshelters.asp
- National Coalition for the Homeless:
  www.nationalhomeless.org/directories/index.html
- National Housing Database for the Homeless:
  www.shelterlistings.org/find_shelter.html
- National Soup Kitchen Directory:
  http://www.homelessshelterdirectory.org/foodbanks/index.html

Although it's easy for us to overlook a homeless person, they are never overlooked by our God. And although providing something as small as a bar of soap may be overlooked by many people as an act too small to take notice of, even a small act of kindness is never overlooked by our God.

Taking toiletries to a homeless shelter is something I can do, Abba. It seems like such a small gesture, but continue to remind me as I learn to care for the needs of others that anything done in your name, even giving a cup of cold water, is seen by you.

28. BUY PERSONAL CARE PRODUCTS FOR A SCHOOL'S GUIDANCE COUNSELOR TO GIVE TO NEEDY TEENS.

I was twelve years old and in middle school. In my class was a bully named Steven whom everyone avoided. Everyone. He was mean and nasty. I don't think he had even one friend and I personally didn't care. He had a mean and degrading comment for anyone who so much as looked at him the wrong way. And frankly, everyone made fun of Steven. He dressed funny, smelled like he hadn't bathed in days, and always wore clothes that were either too small or too big. But one spring day my attitude changed toward Steven.

It was the last day of school, and I was sitting in the school office waiting for my mother to pick me up. Through the window, I saw that someone had spread the lost and found items from the entire school year on the sidewalk, in hopes that the owners would claim them before summer vacation. I thought I saw one of my sweaters in the mix, but being so timid and shy, I was too embarrassed to go and pick it up off the ground. Instead I hoped that no one would know it was mine.

As I waited, the minutes turned into nearly an hour. I was getting concerned that the custodians would lock me in the school for the summer! Then I noticed something

> I choose kindness . . . I will be kind to the poor, for they are alone. Kind to the rich, for they are afraid. And kind to the unkind, for such is how God has treated me.
>
> **MAX LUCADO**

LORIE NEWMAN

out the window that made me do a double take. It was Steven. He was looking in all directions, as if he was making sure no one was around. I thought he was going to do something terrible like start the school on fire.

Just as I was about to tattle on him, he bent down to the ground and picked up a pair of gym pants from the lost and found items. He held them up to his waist. He then picked up a jacket and tried it on for size. My heart broke as I watched him rummage through the clothes in search of clothes that might fit. He had no idea I was watching, and I'm sure he would have been mortified if he had known I could see him.

I slowly began to put the puzzle together in my twelve-year-old mind. Steven wore old, tattered clothes because that's all he had. Other kids made fun of him because of the funny way he dressed and the way he smelled, which made him feel inferior. His inferiority manifested itself as bullying. Tears swelled in my eyes as I watched the school bully rummage through leftover clothes because his family was so poor. Although I was still young, I knew that under Steven's cold, hardened exterior was a boy just longing to be accepted.

THE STATS

Inner-city schools are often under-funded. As a result, students tend to receive poorer instruction, have fewer high-caliber teachers, and have access to fewer resources.

Children who both live in poverty and read below grade level by third grade are three times as likely to not graduate from high school as students who have never been poor.

IN HIS NAME

How wonderful that God allowed me to be a momentary, silent witness to Steven's life. I believe it was just another way God was shaping my spirit. Even at a young age, my heart was being molded and shaped into a heart like God's—a heart of mercy and compassion for the oppressed and the needy.

The example of Steven is a good one for us to consider when we accept Jesus' invitation to care for the needy. Many times, those who may need help are not the nicest people to be around. Let's face it, there are many mean "Stevens" in this world. They have needs, but they walk around with a scowl on their face and a mean word for everyone on their lips.

Does this disqualify them from the help Jesus invites us to give in Matthew 25? Of course not. Many people are angry and bitter because of their unmet needs, and if we take the time to touch their lives and meet those needs, we may see, like I saw in Steven, that under a hardened exterior is a heart that is tender and soft.

A CUP OF COLD WATER

There are countless "Stevens" and other needy children in public schools today. Some are found in inner-city schools, others are found in rural schools. Poverty is real to these kids. Many of them do not practice basic hygiene, not because they choose this for themselves, but because they are not taught at home how to care for themselves properly. These kids are often referred to the school nurse or the school guidance counselor in an effort to educate them about personal hygiene and grooming. But schools do not normally have the funds to provide personal care products for these students.

> *When you call a local school, ask for the school nurse who can tell you exactly what items need to be donated.*

My mother worked as a school nurse for over twenty-five years and made many home visits. After these visits, she oftentimes spent her own money to purchase personal care supplies for the children. By donating these personal items to a local school, you can give a poverty-stricken child in your community ways to care for themselves. Here is a list of commonly needed items you can donate:

- *Men's and women's deodorant*
- *Feminine pads*
- *Body/hand lotion*
- *Hairbrushes, combs, headbands, and hair clips*
- *Antibacterial soap*
- *Shower gel*
- *Lice shampoo*

Also, you can contact your community's middle school or high school guidance counselor or school nurse to ask what specific items are most needed at that particular school.

Each year, at the end of summer, many back-to-school drives collect school supplies for needy children. While these are wonderful and needed drives, some children may also need personal care items throughout the school year. Collecting these personal care items to give to the school nurse or guidance counselor can meet the needs of poor children throughout the academic year.

Abba, by donating personal care products to a school, I can touch the lives of many needy children I will never meet. Take the items I donate and use them to build the self-esteem of every needy child that uses them.

29. BUY BACK-TO-SCHOOL SUPPLIES FOR A FOSTER FAMILY.

When I first saw Cyndi, she was pushing the wheelchair of a teenage boy who was paraplegic. With great care, she helped him get comfortable at the dinner table in our church's fellowship hall. While my family and I had already visited the church in our new town three times on a Sunday morning, we were visiting on a Wednesday night for the midweek fellowship meal for the first time. As we made our way through the dinner crowd, I couldn't help but watch Cyndi. I knew the child in the wheelchair had to be adopted or perhaps a foster child since the boy was African-American and Cyndi was Caucasian.

Cyndi was definitely someone I wanted to meet. Being an adoptive mom myself, I felt an instant connection with her, even though we had never met. By the time the night was over, I had introduced myself and my family. Cyndi confirmed my curiosity—the teen in the wheelchair was her foster child. I learned that she and her husband had fostered over eighty children, in addition to raising their own three biological children and six adopted children.

Over the next year as I got to know Cyndi better, her heart for foster children inspired me. I watched her family grow when they added another child to their already large family—a special needs African-American baby. God had given Cyndi a soft heart for the hard-to-place children in the foster care system who desperately needed families. Put quite simply, Cyndi

> I have come to realize more and more that the greatest disease and the greatest suffering is to be unwanted, unloved, uncared for, to be shunned by everybody, to be just nobody.
>
> **MOTHER TERESA**

loved the children that no one else wanted. She was, and still is, a real missionary in the foster care system of our city.

But having a large family takes lots of resources, and every one of Cyndi's adopted children has special needs. Those needs range from psychological needs induced by sexual abuse, to physical needs due to birth defects. Regularly Cyndi takes the children to doctor appointments and therapy visits.

Cyndi never complained, but I knew that the fall months were an expensive time of year for her family because back-to-school items needed to be purchased. For families who have just one or two children in school, it's a great expense to buy new notebooks, backpacks, calculators, lunch boxes, clothes, shoes, and other necessities for a new school year. For nine, it was a huge bill. Cyndi once told me that it was common for her to spend over five hundred dollars for basic school supplies.

That's why she was so excited one August when a businessman contacted her to say that he was going to provide her entire family with the school supplies they needed. Cyndi was beyond thrilled! In fact, she teared up while telling me about the generosity of this man. When Cyndi received this incredible gift, I realized there must be other adoptive and foster families who also struggle to purchase needed school supplies each year. It is so simple to purchase a few school supplies for an adoptive or foster family, yet the gesture will have a tremendous impact on a family who ministers every day to needy children.

IN HIS NAME

Not all of us are called to adoption or foster care. But all Christians are called to care for the fatherless. Isaiah 1:17 says, "Learn to do good. Seek justice. Help the oppressed. Defend the cause of orphans. Fight for the rights of widows." For those who have answered yes to the call to foster or adopt, the church can make sure that the family is not financially burdened with the additional care needs of the children. Wrapping our arms around adoptive and foster families within our churches and communities with emotional and financial support is a way to care for the needy tangibly.

A CUP OF COLD WATER

Each year, at the end of summer, look for families in your church or your community who have adopted children or who are foster parents. You can help them by purchasing school supplies for their families. This can be done by either directly giving the families the supplies, or by purchasing gift cards to an office supply store or superstore like Wal-Mart. Because different schools and grades usually require different supplies, you may want to ask the foster or adoptive parents for a list of needed supplies before purchasing your items. If you want to help several adoptive or foster families, consider leading the charge to involve your Sunday school class or Bible study group in the project.

> *Consider a school supply drive for the children of adoptive and foster families within your church or community.*

If you want to take this idea a step further, you can organize a school supply drive at your church or workplace. The collected school supplies can be given to the Department of Children's Services for them to distribute to foster children in your area. This will also help you make a connection between your church and the social workers at the Department of Children's Services who work tirelessly in our communities to care for children in crisis situations. Showing the love of Christ to children through these organizations will let social workers know the church is serious about caring for fatherless and needy children.

Abba, bring to mind families in my church or community that have adopted children or foster children in their home. Show me how I can bless them with school supplies this upcoming academic year. It's my great privilege to link arms in your name with adoptive and foster families to "defend the cause of orphans" in my community.

30. DECORATE A CHRISTMAS TREE WITH ITEMS FOR A HOMELESS SHELTER.

Christmas is my absolute favorite time of year. To celebrate Immanuel, God with us (see Matthew 1:23), is such a precious and sacred privilege. My most memorable Christmas was when I was eight years old. My family decided to spend Christmas Eve at my grandparents' house in the country, thirty minutes from our home. I was afraid that Santa would not know where to leave the presents, so I asked my daddy to climb up a ladder to nail a letter to Santa on the chimney. The letter explained that I was at Grandma and Grandpa's house for the night. My dad said he would put the letter on the chimney, but I wasn't satisfied. I stood outside and watched my dad climb the ladder, walk on the slanted roof, and nail the letter to the chimney. My dad must have really loved his little girl to climb up that tall, rickety ladder in the cold December weather!

Although my children have never celebrated with Santa bringing them gifts, at Christmas our home is filled with laughter, wonderful food, gifts under the tree, decorations, prayer, and sincere thankfulness for the gift of grace that was wrapped in a manger two thousand years ago in Bethlehem. The combination of being with friends and family, eating homemade food, enjoying sparkling decorations and the smells of cinnamon, and knowing that God in flesh came to earth as a humble little baby gives Christmas a specialness that no one can ignore.

> No matter how little you have, you can always give some of it away.
>
> CATHERINE MARSHALL

Each year millions of people give to charities during Christmastime. In fact, in a recent poll, 52 percent of respondents said a recession would likely not have an effect on their giving to charity. People just seem to be more generous at Christmastime when the needs of the poor are highlighted. While it is wonderful that most Americans donate to charities during the holidays, the needs of the poor do not cease after December when the decorations are packed away.

IN HIS NAME

When I consider the Old Testament sacrifices where an animal's blood had to be shed for the sins of God's people, it is almost unimaginable that God made himself flesh and came to earth to die on a cross as a sacrifice to atone for the sins of humankind. The Old Testament sacrifices required a spotless, perfect animal to die for the sins of God's people. When Jesus Christ died, He had lived a spotless, perfect life on earth. Then He shed His blood on a cross and died in our place. God loved us so much He would rather die than live without us.

But the grave had no power over Jesus! He's the Son of almighty God! When He rose to life on the third day, He overcame the grave for us. Because of His shed blood, we can know that when we die, we will live forever in the presence of God in heaven! This message is as simple today as it was then—whoever will believe that Jesus Christ really is the Son of God and accept His sacrifice for their sins can have eternal life with God.

The message of Christmas is pure love and pure hope. It's no wonder that people around the world love Christmastime! The Bible says in 1 John 4:12,

CUP OF COLD WATER

"No one has ever seen God. But if we love each other, God lives in us, and his love is brought to full expression in us." Making Christmastime one of the many times each year when we share hope and love with the hurting and the needy lets us show the world that God is alive in us.

A CUP OF COLD WATER

To keep the spirit of giving going even after the decorations are taken down, why not use that bare green Christmas tree? After the ornaments and decorations have been taken off the Christmas trees at work, church, or school, leave the bare green trees up in prominent areas. Artificial trees work best for this, but if there is still some life left in your real Christmas trees, they can be used as well. Have coworkers, church members, or fellow students put items on the bare trees to donate to a homeless shelter.

> *Put the Christmas cards you receive in a basket on your kitchen table. Each night at dinner, pull out one card and pray for that family during your blessing for the meal.*

The end of December is a perfect time to collect small winter items, and they can be pinned or placed on tree branches for this clothing drive. Items that shelters almost always need in winter are:

- Scarves
- Gloves
- Winter hats

- *Mittens*
- *Wool socks*
- *Undershirts*
- *Long johns*

Most dollar stores sell winter gear. For less than five dollars, you can purchase a set of winter items for a person at a homeless shelter. Collecting warm clothing for shelters is a great way to continue the spirit of giving after Christmas.

In the summer months, you can use this same idea for a "Christmas in July" project for a church group or place of business. If winter gear is hard to find in the summer, collect toiletries instead.

The message of Christmas, God's perfect love for us manifested in the birth of Christ, sometimes can be understood best by others through our actions. Giving to the homeless is a perfect way for God's love to be brought to full expression through us.

Your love for us, Abba, is perfect. Sending your love to us in the form of a humble baby in a manger was certainly not what the world was expecting. Show me how to humbly serve others with your perfect love. As I collect winter items for the homeless, use me to be a spark that ignites love among others for the least of these.

31. MAKE A "NEEDY BOX" FOR YOUR CAR.

It was freezing outside. In fact, as Margie strapped her children in their car seats after church one frigid Wednesday evening, she heard the weather reporter over the radio give the record-breaking temperature—nineteen degrees. As she pulled away from the parking lot and approached a traffic light, she noticed a dark figure under an overpass. It was dusk, so she strained her eyes to see. There was an elderly man sitting by the road. The homeless man was begging from the cars that passed through the traffic light.

Margie's heart broke when she realized the man had no gloves, no scarf—not even a hat to keep him warm. The light turned red and Margie stopped to speak to the man. She slowly let down her car window as the man approached her car. Normally Margie would have been too afraid to make herself so vulnerable, but on this blustery evening, her heart broke for this homeless man.

When he came to the window, Margie looked around her car and gave him the only thing she had with her—a bottle of water. As she gave it to him, she took hold of his hands. They were ice cold. She knew the light was to turn green at any moment, so she asked him if she could pray for him.

> The first joint priority of the churches of any city should be that of making it hard for people to go to hell from that city.
>
> **DAVID SHIBLEY**

She held his freezing hands and prayed over him through her car window. When she looked up, the light was green. It had obviously been green for several seconds, but no one behind her had honked their horns in irritation. They seemed to understand her efforts to help this homeless man.

Margie said goodbye to the man and drove home, but she couldn't get him out of her mind. The thought of a human being enduring such extreme cold was heartbreaking—especially an elderly man. So she decided to go back to the overpass. Margie packed a pair of warm gloves, a scarf, and a knit hat in her car. But when she got to the overpass, the homeless man was gone. Disappointed at a missed opportunity, she drove back home. She started to put the gloves, hat, and scarf away but instead decided to keep them in her car for the next time she saw a homeless person. In fact, the situation gave her an idea. She decided to make a "Needy Box" for her car.

THE STATS

Leading factors that contribute to homelessness: foreclosure, poverty, eroding work opportunities, decline in public assistance, and lack of affordable housing.

IN HIS NAME

In a perfect world, there would be no need for us to be prepared to help a homeless person. In a perfect world, we would never encounter someone who is cold and in need of a handout. But we don't live in a perfect world. We live in a world where drug addiction, unemployment, poverty, sickness, and alcoholism are all too common. As Christians, being prepared to help someone in need is part of living out our faith. Scripture warns us in James 2:2–4 not to treat the needy with reproach, but instead to give them proper respect:

For example, suppose someone comes into your meeting dressed in fancy clothes and expensive jewelry, and another comes in who is poor and dressed in dirty clothes. If you give special attention and a good seat to the rich person, but you say to the poor one, "You can stand over there, or else sit on the floor"—well, doesn't this discrimination show that your judgments are guided by evil motives?

While speaking to his disciples, Jesus said in Matthew 26:11, "You will always have the poor among you, but you will not always have me." There will always be those around us in need. That is just a reality of living in this world. But those of us who claim to be the hands and feet of the Savior of the world cannot treat the needy and the homeless as somehow lower or less worthy than ourselves. As Christians, we should always strive to see others through the eyes of Christ. Showing compassion to the needy was the heartbeat of Jesus' earthly ministry. Making a conscious decision to be ready to help those in need is one way to demonstrate our belief that Jesus died and rose again for each and every one of us, including the homeless.

A CUP OF COLD WATER

Making a Needy Box for your car is very simple. You can fill the box with anything you think a homeless person may need. Basic items like hats, scarves, gloves, snacks, and bottled water will get your Needy Box started. When you're finished, put the box in a handy place in your car (not the trunk) so that you can get to it when you see someone begging near a traffic light or street corner.

> *Gift cards to McDonald's or other restaurants are great items to have in your Needy Box.*

Preparing these boxes is a great opportunity to have your children help care for the needy. At our house, I buy items in bulk and I let my children divide them and pack the boxes. We have a box in each of our cars so that we are always prepared to help the homeless people we encounter. Being prepared is an important part of accepting Jesus' invitation to care for the needy. Our Savior encountered needy, hurting people throughout His ministry. And today, He still encounters needy, hurting people—through us, His children.

Abba, when your son walked this earth, He encountered needy, hurting, and desperate people in every place He went. Not once was He ever irritated or frustrated with the needs around Him. He just met them as He encountered them—one person at a time. Give me that kind of patient compassion, Abba, as I minister to the needy around me.

32. DONATE BUSINESS SUITS THAT CAN BE WORN FOR JOB INTERVIEWS.

My husband, Duane, has interviewed many people for several positions during his twenty-year career in engineering. He'll be the first to tell you that what a person wears to a job interview is extremely important. For an applicant, the first thirty to sixty seconds of an interview are crucial for making a good first impression. During that first minute, the person conducting the interview will make a mental note of whether or not the job candidate is dressed professionally.

Several years ago, Duane was interviewing a young man for a supervisor position. Quickly my husband noticed that this young man wasn't wearing socks. Now as crazy as that sounds, it stood out like a sore thumb. Here was a well-dressed job candidate in a nice suit and dress shoes but no socks. Duane just couldn't get past the man's hairy legs showing as he sat cross-legged across from him. During another interview, Duane had a well-dressed man come into the room for another supervisor position. Unfortunately, he had a wardrobe malfunction—his pants zipper was down and his white dress shirt was hanging out of it! Oh boy.

Needless to say, neither of these candidates got the job. Nothing they said

> Everybody can be great . . . because anybody can serve. You don't have to have a college degree to serve. You don't have to make your subject and verb agree to serve. You only need a heart full of grace. A soul generated by love.
>
> **MARTIN LUTHER KING JR.**

could erase the fact that they were not dressed professionally for the interview. For a hiring manager, first impressions are important. But when a person is unemployed or has depleted savings, finding a professional outfit is nearly impossible. Often people have the skills needed to get a job, they just need a professional suit or outfit for an interview. Simply by donating business attire, for both men and women, you can open a door of opportunity for them to get a new job, a better job, or a promotion that will greatly improve their quality of life.

IN HIS NAME

God has much to say about work in His Word. In Exodus 35:30–38 we read about those who worked with the skills God gave them to complete the tent of meeting, which served as the place of worship for God's people before a permanent temple was built during King Solomon's reign. Skilled craftsmen meticulously carried out every detail of the design of the tent of meeting. In Leviticus 19:13, God tells employers not to withhold the wages of a worker overnight. Deuteronomy 5:13–14 reminds us to work six days and rest on the seventh day. Proverbs 14:23 says, "Work brings profit, but mere talk leads to poverty!" In Proverbs 31:17, we read about the virtuous woman: "She is energetic and strong, a hard worker."

We all must work during our lifetimes. God uses our vocation as our personal ministries where we can be lights in our world. Whether it's being a homemaker, plumber, secretary, attorney, executive, nurse, teacher, pilot, or physician, we are called to a vocation. To help those who need work by donating a business suit or briefcase is a simple way to give someone the dignity needed to pursue a new job.

A CUP OF COLD WATER

Many charities give donated business clothing to those who need it. Often these charities and ministries also help with interview skills, résumé writing, and job placement. Creating opportunities for men and women to better themselves through employment is a priority for these charities.

Below are several places you can donate your gently used business suits. Some of them are Christian organizations, others are not, but they all give donated suits to men and women who are either looking for employment or are currently employed and in need of professional attire. Items that are typically needed for men and women are suits, dress shirts, blazers, shoes, belts, dress scarves, ties, overcoats, new black or brown socks, briefcases, portfolios, dress pants, watches, tie clips, and cuff links.

- Men's Warehouse Suit Drives: *www.menswearhouse.com/webapp/wcs/ stores/servlet/ContentAttachmentView_-1_10601_10051__10709_10684_ AbtNSDDonorInformation.html.* The retail store Men's Warehouse has suit drives each year during the month of August. A list of charities who utilize the donated suits is on their website.
- Dress for Success: *www.dressforsuccess.org.* Dress for Success has chapters in many cities around the United States. Find a chapter near you by visiting their website and clicking "Locations."

- Career Gear: *www.careergear.org*. Chapters are located in Houston, New York City, Baltimore, Jersey City, New Haven, San Antonio, and Miami.
- American Red Cross: *carecycleinc.com/wecollect*. Through their website, you can schedule a pickup time for your donated business clothing.

When you donate business attire, be sure to have the clothing cleaned beforehand. Also, put it neatly on a hanger. Whenever possible, put an entire outfit together. Having a belt on a pair of slacks or a blouse with a business skirt will make choosing an outfit easier.

> *Consider conducting workshops in your community where people can get help with résumé writing and job applications.*

If you want to take this idea further, consider having a "business clothing closet" at your church. People in the church can donate business clothing, and those in the community who need clothing can make appointments to visit the clothing closet and get what they need. Any help you can offer will be welcome during these tough economic times.

Giving a man or woman the gift of a business suit can not only make them look great on the outside, but it can give them the confidence they need on the inside to prepare for a job interview.

Abba, there are many items in my wardrobe that, if I am completely honest with myself, I will never wear again. As I look into my closet full of clothes, help me to decide what clothes, shoes, and accessories I can donate to someone who could use them for a job interview. Use each donated item to give someone new confidence and favor in their job search.

33. COLLECT COINS IN BABY BOTTLES FOR A CRISIS PREGNANCY CENTER.

Every Christian parent I know wants his or her children to grow up with a "giving" mind-set. We want to raise children who will be aware of the needs of the poor and not focus solely on themselves. But it's hard to raise selfless children in this "me-centered" culture. My greatest fear is that my seven kids will grow up and get caught in the American Dream, chasing after meaningless things like a big house, nice car, and designer clothes. What a waste of their lives.

> Come work for the Lord. The work is hard, the hours are long, and the pay is low, but the retirement benefits are out of this world.
>
> **ANONYMOUS**

Not long ago, a woman at my church told me that she prays every day that her kids will live close to her when they grow up. I cringed! What a terrible thing to pray for your children! I know that my prayer for my children—that they would change the world when they grow older, no matter where that takes them—is a dangerous prayer. Very dangerous. They may serve God in a country far away and never come home again. They may serve God in a closed country and be killed for professing their faith. I know all these things, but I pray the prayer anyway.

Ian, our nineteen year old, told me before his trip to South Africa a few years ago, "Mom, I may die on this trip. That's the worst thing that could happen to me. But Mom, I'd rather die at age fifteen knowing I'm on a mission with Christ than live to be a hundred and always wonder what would have happened if I had stepped out in faith to share Christ with the nations." Wow. That's a kid who knows that this world is not his home. Praise God! I'm so thankful that Ian's world doesn't center on him. He learned at an early age to focus on God's direction and plan for his life.

Teaching children to focus on Christ must be deliberate. Sitting idle as a parent, hoping that the youth pastor or the Sunday school leader will disciple our children is not good enough. Teaching our children the Bible, true discipleship, and how to care for the needy begins with parents at home. The good news is that it's never too late to start.

There are easy ways to teach children, even small children, to care for the needy and to focus on others instead of themselves. I have been a mom for nineteen years now and am in the thick of raising seven children, so I have been privileged to be a part of many ways to teach kids to help the less fortunate. A memorable way for our family was when we collected coins in baby bottles for a crisis pregnancy center.

The children, even my twins who were just three at the time, had so much fun putting coins in those bottles! Every night they would shake the baby bottles to see how much noise they would make. It took only a week to fill them. When the money our children collected was put with the money other children at our church collected, a sizable donation to our local pregnancy center was given. My teenagers still remember collecting coins in those baby bottles when they were little! It was a small way for them to begin to learn to care for others.

THE STATS

Studies have shown that 83% of children, especially those raised in Christian homes, accept Christ between the ages of 4 and 14.

IN HIS NAME

Proverbs 22:6 is a familiar verse for parents: "Direct your children onto the right path, and when they are older, they will not leave it." Finding ways to not only read Bible verses about helping the needy, but also giving our children opportunities to be the hands and feet of the Jesus they learn about is when faith becomes real to them.

My family has a little Bible storybook that I have read over and over to each of my children. It has the story of Ruth and Naomi (who were both widowed), the story of Esther (who was orphaned), the story of the ten lepers (who were isolated and contagiously ill), and the story of blind Bartimaeus (who cried out to Jesus for healing). As I continue to read that old storybook to my younger children, my older children often comment about how I used to read the stories to them over and over. They so loved to hear me read those stories from the Bible! But if I had remained a parent who simply read about what Jesus did for the orphan, the widow, the sick, and the dying, but never actually let them see me caring for the needy like Jesus did, then all of those stories would have been just words on a page.

As I care for the needy, and as I include my children in caring for the needy, then my children learn that they are to imitate Christ. They learn that Jesus is more than a great man from the Bible. They see that His love not only abounds for us, His children, but His love should flow in us and out of us onto the needy around us. And one of the best places to start teaching children about caring for the needy is right in our own communities.

A CUP OF COLD WATER

Beginning a drive like the Baby Bottle Coin Drive is simple, but it does require some planning. First, contact your local crisis pregnancy center to let them know about the drive. In my experience, they have always been thrilled to get the donation and want to know what they can do to help with the planning. Next, purchase—or have people donate—inexpensive plastic baby bottles. You can determine how many bottles to purchase based on the size and interest of the group that will be collecting the coins. For example, if your children's ministry is involved in the drive, then find out how many families are represented by children. Plan to give a child in each family a plastic bottle to fill. Make small notes to attach to each bottle explaining the coin drive. Don't forget to include a date to return the bottles.

> *One of the greatest lessons you can teach a child is*
> *to compassionately care for others with the love of Christ.*

A Baby Bottle Coin Drive can be done with children of any age. A moms' group or child's Sunday school class, children's choir, elementary school, day care, or play group could be approached for the drive. Each child is given a bottle to take home and fill with coins. Once the bottles are returned, exchange the coins for paper currency and give your donation to the pregnancy center. If you can, take a field trip to the center so the children can see the baby clothes, maternity clothes, strollers, bassinets, sonogram machines, and other items that their money will help purchase and maintain. What a great way to teach little ones to care for others!

It is very important to me, Abba, that my children learn to care for the needy. I want them to have Christ's compassion to serve the least of these. As I plan a coin drive for a crisis pregnancy center, let my children and every child who participates see that caring for the needy should be a natural, everyday part of our Christian faith.

34. ORGANIZE A CLOTHING MINISTRY.

Triplets. For most of us the mere word strikes us with awe and wonder when we think of how anyone could manage a house full of babies! The sleepless nights, the hundreds of diapers, the midnight feedings, the mountain of laundry—I get tired just thinking about the workload! It would stand to reason that having triplets would put a mom's personal ministry efforts on hold for at least a few years. And understandably so! But ministry doesn't always have to be put on hold just because you are a busy mom of little ones. Just ask Christa.

Christa not only has triplets, she also has an older daughter who was barely two years old when the triplets were born. Yes, you read that right— three newborns and a toddler. That's four in diapers. But God had an important mission for this busy mom of preschoolers. It all came about when Christa gathered some of her children's clothes for a secondhand clothing sale in her community. Having four little ones, Christa jumped at the opportunity to sell clothes her babies had outgrown. She organized the items, priced them, and took them to the community sale. But when the sale was over, Christa got a call to come and pick up her leftover clothing. Although some items did sell, she was disappointed that many items didn't.

While she was packing her minivan with the leftover dresses, shoes, coats, and jeans, a missionary friend who was home on furlough happened to pass by. When she realized that Christa had leftover clothes, the missionary asked if she could have some to take back to Mexico. She described how needy the children are in the area where she and her husband minister. As the missionary looked through Christa's leftover clothes, the Holy Spirit spoke to Christa's heart.

Christa knew her church supported many missionaries around the world. She also knew that if families in Mexico needed children's clothing, then families in other parts of the world must need clothing too. And not just other countries, but here in the States as well.

Christa began to dream big! She began dreaming of a clothing ministry where people in her church could donate gently used clothing and shoes. She could organize the donations so that missionaries on furlough could choose clothing to take back to the countries where they work. Foster families and adoptive families in the community could come and get clothing without cost for their children. It was indeed a big, God-sized dream! But isn't that how so many wonderful ministries and humanitarian missions start out—as big dreams? This was a dream that Christa knew could only happen if she completely trusted the Lord with every detail, stepped outside her comfort zone, and put the needs of others ahead of her fears.

> The greatest tragedy to befall a person is to have sight but lack vision.
>
> HELEN KELLER

IN HIS NAME

So many times, God-inspired dreams die at the "just dreaming" phase. Many people can't see past the dreams God has put in their spirit to the reality of what could be. For whatever reason, the big dream that starts as a tiny tickle in their spirit stays there and never manifests. Perhaps it's because of fear. Perhaps it's a lack of time or resources. But Christa knew something that we all need to remember. If God has placed a desire or a dream in your heart, then you need to run after it with all your might.

So many times taking the leap of faith is the hardest part. With Christa's big dream, she had a choice to make. She could give excuses—after all, she had four little ones to care for—or she could step out in faith and trust God for the rest. She chose to step out and trust the God who put this dream in her spirit. She's never looked back!

That was nearly two years ago and "Tabitha's Closet" (named after the widow in Acts 9 who made coats and other clothing for her widowed friends) has ministered to families all over the world and her community. Yes, Christa is still a busy mother of four little ones, but God has used her ministry, that started as just a dream in her spirit, to clothe countless needy children in Jesus' name.

THE STATS

An estimated 80% of people worldwide live on less than ten dollars a day.

A CUP OF COLD WATER

Starting a children's clothing ministry involves a few steps. First, you need to get the word out that you will be collecting gently used clothing and shoes. Decide ahead of time what type of clothing you will accept and what sizes. For example, Christa collected boys and girls clothing sizes newborn to 16. She also collected shoes, socks, coats, hats, gloves, and scarves. If you want to start out smaller, you could just collect infant and toddler clothing, and then increase the sizes you can take as your ministry grows. Christa listed several dates on a flyer of when church members could drop off their used clothing at her home.

After the clothing had been gathered, Christa then asked a few friends to help out by washing one or two bags of clothing. At their homes, friends washed and sorted items and brought the organized and clean clothing back to Christa. Next she sorted the clothing and shoes into big bins labeled with each size and gender. For example, she labeled one bin for infant boy's clothing sizes 0–6 months, and another bin for toddler girl's clothing sizes 3T—4T. Christa's biggest challenge was where to keep the bins. She considered a storage facility or an empty room at her church. She finally settled on housing the bins in an empty room in her basement.

> *Have people donate gently used suitcases for the missionaries to use when they take clothing back to the countries in which they serve.*

Several times a year, contact church members ahead of time to let them know that the clothing ministry will be open. If you open the clothing ministry for adoptive and foster families, be sure to contact your local Department of Children's Services so that they can tell area foster parents about the clothing giveaway. This is such a wonderful way to not only minister to missionaries, but also to reach out to foster families in your community.

Many children in the adoptive community as well as around the world have been recipients of the clothing from Tabitha's Closet. If Christa had not chosen to follow the idea she had, those children would not have been helped. God gives us ideas and opportunities to serve the needy around us. Following through on those ideas and opportunities can change the life of another person. Don't delay if God has given you an idea—even if it seems small.

Abba, from time to time I have ideas that may help needy people around me. But somehow the busyness of my life gets in the way of me following through on those ideas. Motivate me to follow my ideas and dreams and not to delay.

35. ORGANIZE A SEWING CLUB AND DONATE THE BLANKETS YOU MAKE.

A prized possession sits on the top shelf of my walk-in closet in a special box. It's a handmade quilt from my Grandmother Ward, and I wouldn't trade it for a million dollars. She made many quilts and blankets over the years, including one for each grandchild. We all highly value our quilts. It's not the colors that we admire so much. Some of the quilts have odd color combinations. It's not the design or the size of the quilts. Some are smaller than others. It's the fact that Grandmother made every stitch. She spent hours upon hours in her sunroom meticulously planning the quilts and sewing each stitch with great care and love. Grandmother designed nearly every quilt with a particular person in mind. For Grandmother, the best gifts were the ones that couldn't be bought in a store. The best gifts were made with time and with love, not bought with money. Now that she has passed away, how lovely it is to have one of her quilts to remember her by.

Grandmother had a quilting club that developed over the years with several friends from her church and community. All of the ladies loved quilting, so they came together periodically to enjoy each other's company and learn new techniques. One of my favorite quilts of Grandmother's had been inspired by a friend who explained a new way to sew a tiny pocket design and connect hundreds of them on a large quilt.

Although Grandmother's club made quilt gifts that were usually given to family

> Too many of us have a Christian vocabulary rather than a Christian experience. We think we are doing our duty when we're only talking about it.
>
> **CHARLES F. BANNING**

members and close friends, a group of quilters in Georgia makes quilts and blankets for some special little ones. These quilters are part of a sewing group chapter through a national organization called Project Linus, named after the Peanuts character Linus, who always carried a blanket everywhere he went. This special group of talented ladies gets together to make all types of blankets—afghans and quilts of every size, shape, and color. Then they give the blankets to children in hospitals and treatment centers around their town.

It makes me smile to think of the many thousands of children across the country who have received a special Project Linus blanket when they were sick in the hospital. Each blanket is as special and unique as the child who received it.

IN HIS NAME

Using our talents and giftedness to God's glory not only honors the One who gave us those talents, but it can bring people to the saving knowledge of Jesus Christ. Some Christians have the talent of singing. Some have the talent of baking. Some can coach baseball. Others can paint and draw. Still others may have a creative knack for sewing, while others have a special talent for fixing things. Whatever you enjoy doing and whatever your talent is, use it for the glory of God, friend! Just because your talent or giftedness may not be a "public" talent like playing the piano or preaching in front of others doesn't mean your talents are not vital to the kingdom of God. He has given you those talents to minister to others.

In 1 Kings 5–7 we read about the detailed plans that were used for building the temple of the Lord. The Bible explains that the craftsmen chosen for the work had been given special talents from God. These men used their great talents for the work of the Lord in building the temple. In a similar way, each of us has been given a talent. We may not think it's much that can be used for God's kingdom, but it is! Pray and ask God how you can use your talents and gifts to further His kingdom. You might be surprised how quickly God will put someone in your path who has a need for the very thing for which you are gifted!

A CUP OF COLD WATER

Starting a Project Linus chapter in your area will be a blessing to needy children right in your own community. First check the ministry's website, www .ProjectLinus.org, for an existing chapter in your area. If no chapter is nearby, then fill out the application on the website to apply to be a chapter coordinator. You simply need a love for sewing and a little computer knowledge for the job. Chapter coordinator requirements are listed on the website under the "Start a Chapter" link. New chapter applications are accepted in the months of March and August only.

THE STATS

Through the more than 365 chapters of Project Linus, over 3.8 million blankets have been given away.

If you have missed the application deadline, then consider creating a sewing club of your own. Within nearly every church or workplace you will find ladies of all ages who enjoy sewing and crafting. Organize a time when a small group of sewers can meet at the church or at someone's home. This meeting can be on a Saturday morning when each lady brings a breakfast item to share with the group, or it can be a Friday evening "ladies' night out." Every sewer can bring her materials or you can pool resources to create a group project.

> *In North Carolina, a group of women inmates at the Swannanoa Correctional Facility for Women have formed a knitting club. Through a partnership with area churches, their blankets are sent to needy orphans around the world.*

However you set up your sewing club, once your blankets have been completed, you can deliver them to babies and small children at local hospitals and cancer centers or you can give them to new babies within your church or community. Crisis maternity homes are another place these blankets could be used for ministry outreach. If possible, sew a tiny tag in each blanket that has a Scripture verse written on it.

As a group, be sure to pray over each blanket before delivering them. Pray that the child who is wrapped in that blanket will be wrapped in God's protection, security, and peace. Just think, your "blanket of prayers" may be the only Jesus some of the little ones experience. What a privilege to use talents and gifts of sewing and crafting that have been given by God, to touch the lives of hurting children and their families.

Abba, I've always enjoyed sewing and knitting. As I think about the idea of creating a sewing club to benefit little ones, bring to my mind others who also enjoy sewing. As we work together, give us sweet fellowship and also favor with the hospitals and maternity homes that have patients and clients who can benefit from the blankets we make.

36. GIVE A BABY SHOWER FOR A CRISIS PREGNANCY CENTER.

This was not what they had planned for their engagement. Eight months earlier on a warm afternoon at the beach, he had popped the question with a beautiful diamond engagement ring. Both in their last year of college, they were so excited to get married! Wedding plans were well under way. The train of her beautiful new beaded wedding gown would soon be altered for the big day. The bride-to-be had planned red and white long-stemmed roses for the bridesmaids to carry.

But those plans seemed a world away as she found herself sitting in the most unlikely of places for a young Christian college student—a crisis pregnancy center. She was waiting for the results of a pregnancy test. The seconds during the one-minute test seemed to tick by at a snail's pace. She knew the results could forever change the path of her life. As she waited, her heart beat like a drum inside her chest. It was too late for regrets, too late to erase the past, too late for self-condemnation. All she could do was wait. Finally, the volunteer holding her pregnancy test looked at her with eyes that revealed marked concern. She uttered four words that rocked the young twenty-year-old, soon-to-be bride's world—"It's positive. You're pregnant."

> Of all the things you must earn in life, God's unending affection is not one of them. You have it.
>
> MAX LUCADO

The girl's hands began to tremble. She swallowed hard as the room began to spin. She clutched the side of a table and closed her eyes tight to keep herself from passing out. The next ten minutes seemed like an out-of-body experience as her mind tried to comprehend the massive implications of the words she had just heard—*You're pregnant.* The words echoed in the caverns of her spirit.

The volunteers at the center knew exactly what to do. They had seen this scenario play out many times. They lovingly wrapped their arms around the girl. They offered support. Whatever the young girl needed, they were willing to give. They didn't scold or degrade. They didn't belittle or condemn. Instead, they offered to pray with her. They patiently let her talk through the thoughts and fears that now engulfed her senses like heavy, suffocating smoke.

In the days and weeks following the girl's visit to the pregnancy center, that suffocating smoke began to lift as God tenderly walked her and her fiancé through their wedding, their college graduation, and the birth of their beautiful child. What started as a "crisis pregnancy" ended up teaching the young couple that God is the almighty Author of second chances. He's the Redeemer of brokenness. He's the Restorer of contrite hearts. And I should know.

That girl was me.

IN HIS NAME

As I type this story, there is snow falling outside my window. Huge, white snowflakes are falling softly onto already snow-covered trees. The woods outside my home are pure white as showers of snow blanket everything in sight. What a picture of God's grace for me as I type about my experience nineteen years ago with a crisis pregnancy. As Christians, our sins always give opportunity for God's love, forgiveness, and grace to abound.

This incredible, tender-loving grace never ceases to amaze me. It literally has no end—no stopping place. His love and grace for us, His children, falls like pure white snow on all our transgressions and it covers them as if they were never there. I'll never fully understand it. The Bible says in Isaiah 1:18, "'Come now, let's settle this,' says the Lord. 'Though your sins are like scarlet, I will make them as white as snow. Though they are red like crimson, I will make them as white as wool.'"

For those walking through a crisis pregnancy, they need to know that God can make all things new. They need to know He can restore a broken life and can mend cracked vessels. He can take the mess of our life and turn it into something beautiful. Condemnation is not what these young girls in a crisis need. Pregnancy center workers across the nation know this. They speak God's love and His grace into the lives of the pregnant girls who come to them for help.

A CUP OF COLD WATER

A great way to support the ministry of a Christian crisis pregnancy center is to give the center a baby shower. Not only do these centers share the love of Christ with each girl who comes in for help, many of them have expanded their care to include prenatal counseling, sonography, parenting classes, temporary housing, adoption services, and mentoring services. A great number of them give baby supplies on a regular basis to their clients. If you have ever helped plan a friend's baby shower, then you have more than enough experience to plan a baby shower for a crisis pregnancy center.

Hosting a baby shower can replenish the shelves at a crisis center that gives supplies away regularly. Much like a traditional baby shower, start by sending invitations giving the date and time of the event and a brief explanation of the purpose of the shower. Be sure to include the center's name that will benefit from the gifts. The shower can take place at any location, but if you plan to have a large shower, you may want to use your church building. Check with your church office or pastor about the church's availability.

> *Focus on the Family maintains a website with several links to information on pro-life issues and life-affirming pregnancy resource centers. Visit www.focusonthefamily.com/about_us/pro-life.aspx.*

Next, ask the crisis pregnancy center in your area for specific needs they may have. Most centers need the following: diapers, baby wipes, car seats, cribs, crib bedding sets, crib mattresses, infant clothing, high chairs, bouncy seats, diaper bags, blankets, bottles, baby shampoos and lotions, maternity clothes, infant swings, infant formula, and safety items such as outlet covers. Items can be new or gently used.

In the past when I have hosted these events, I planned the shower during regular Wednesday night activity times at my church so that members could drop off their items anytime it was convenient for them.

Don't forget to have light refreshments as well as literature on hand from the crisis pregnancy center. With a little planning, you can bless a great ministry with gifts that they can use to touch many lives.

Abba, I forget what an important task those who work at pregnancy centers have in caring for women in crisis pregnancies. Their commitment to the unborn and the sanctity of life is to be praised and celebrated. As I plan to help a crisis pregnancy center by giving the center a baby shower, help me with each detail and bring others alongside me who can make the shower a success.

37. TAKE A MISSION TRIP TO AN IMPOVERISHED AREA WHERE CLOTHING AND SHOES ARE DESPERATELY NEEDED.

We were somewhere in the bush of Swaziland, in the heart of a small African nation where the HIV infection rate is thought to be as high as 40 percent. We had spent the last two weeks visiting orphan care points, AIDS hospitals, and ministry group homes. Today, on this last day, we were scheduled to attend Sunday worship at the church of a pastor we had met at a care point. We arrived late to the service and made our way through the small group of singing worshipers. Immediately I took notice of the worn, splintered wooden benches with no backs. The air in the cinder block church was stale and hot, but the Africans didn't seem to notice. I thought about my opulent megachurch back home in the States and its comfy pews and air-conditioning.

As we sang, the African children, many of them orphans, formed a line down the church aisle and walked to the front of the congregation. The pastor motioned for us to sit on the old benches as an older missionary couple helped to situate the children on a small wooden platform. The children's clothes were

> You can find Calcutta anywhere in the world. You only need two eyes to see. Everywhere in the world there are people that are not loved, people that are not wanted nor desired, people that no one will help, people that are pushed away or forgotten. And this is the greatest poverty.
>
> **MOTHER TERESA**

tattered and worn. Some wore only a dirty shirt with no pants. None of them wore shoes.

If these children had been singing in an American church, their appearance would have been shocking. But in Swaziland, it is a common, everyday sight to see little children in tattered, worn out clothes. In many parts of Africa, when a child is orphaned, there are no foster homes or children's group homes to care for them. They take care of themselves. Often a child as young as eight is the head of the household, taking care of several younger siblings because their parents have died of AIDS. The children who sang in church that morning were dirty with the dust from the African plain where they lived. Their hair was unkempt and matted. Most of their parents had died. They were "no one's children"—tossed from home to home in their village, given the villagers' leftover rotten vegetables to eat.

THE STATS

There are 2.2 billion children in the world. One billion of them live in poverty.

As the precious little children began to sing, my heart broke. The orphans stood in front of that small church, and the words they sang pierced my spirit in a way that no sermon, no Sunday school lesson, and no Bible study ever had or ever could. Without any accompanying music, the missionary led the little orphans in singing a song I had heard many times before, but it took on an entirely new meaning that day in Africa. They sang:

Seek ye first the kingdom of God
And His righteousness
And all these things shall be
Added unto you
Allelu, Alleluia

As they sang that chorus over and over with smiles on their faces, I felt as though I was the only one in the room. I wept seeing these children, who were orphaned because of AIDS through no fault of their own, singing about the kingdom of God and how everything would be added to those who seek Him first. I wept because I was angry at the disease that had taken their parents. I wept because I was frustrated at the American church for multibillion dollar building campaigns while these children were nearly naked. Didn't anyone care that these children lacked the basic need of clothing and shoes?

When our team returned to America, we had a choice to make. We could go about our normal lives and forget the needy children we had encountered, or we could let their faces stay at the forefront of our minds until we were moved with compassion to use our resources to change their plight. We could either "play church" on Sundays or we could get out of our comfy pews and "be the church" by helping the children God had put in our path.

We chose to rise up and be like Jesus to orphans.

IN HIS NAME

Clothing is a basic need of life. Many of us have closets full of clothes—and some items we will never wear. Before I visited Swaziland, I'm ashamed to say that there were days I would stand in my closet and actually say, "I have nothing to wear." After meeting those orphans who had only tattered and dirty clothes, that phrase will never cross my lips again.

The children of Swaziland taught me that true religion, as in James 1:27, is not about being comfortable in our "little worlds"—it's about helping others. James writes, "Pure and genuine religion in the sight of God the Father means caring for orphans and widows in their distress . . ." Pure religion is about stepping outside the church doors. It's about giving of ourselves. It's about being Christlike to the hurting. And it's about *being* the church Christ died for. James also writes, "But don't just listen to God's word. You must do what it says. Otherwise, you are only fooling yourselves" (1:22).

If God has given you the resources to have a closet with more than five outfits of clothing, consider yourself truly blessed.

A CUP OF COLD WATER

Taking a foreign mission trip will require preparation and planning (see appendix A). But it will also require spiritual preparation. To be immersed in extreme poverty can deeply change the way you view material possessions and cause you to focus more on things of eternal value.

Most of us have seen pictures of extreme poverty on television, but it seems so far away—so distant from our everyday lives. But when we experience poverty with all five senses on a mission trip, it's a realization like no other that poverty is the norm for billions of people around the world. Oftentimes on a mission trip, an urgency to move on behalf of the poor will emerge from a place of compassion that we may not have known existed in our spirit. That's the compassion of Christ rising in us, His body. And once that deep, Christ-filled compassion rises in you to care for someone who has no voice, no advocate, the foundational truth of Matthew 25:40 becomes real, tangible, and beautifully intoxicating: "I tell you the truth, when you did it to one of the least of these my brothers and sisters, you were doing it to me!"

> *Consider hosting a shoe drive at your church, place of business, or school. Be sure to ask for only new or gently used shoes.*

Every country, even the US, has pockets of people who lack proper clothing. Many relief organizations and ministries are working to change that:

Shoes for Orphan Souls: www.shoesfororphansouls.org. On this website you will find ideas on how to host a shoe collection, how to ship shoes to needy children, how to donate shoes, as well as information on how to distribute shoes on a mission trip with this ministry. Since 1999, over 2 million shoes and socks have been distributed around the globe through Shoes for Orphan Souls.

Buckner Missions: www.itsyourmission.com. Through Buckner Missions, you can not only donate shoes to orphans, you can help deliver shoes to orphans on a foreign mission trip.

Forgotten Children International: forgottenchildren.org. This ministry helps orphaned children in many areas of the world with various humanitarian efforts such as sponsorship and prayer. They also conduct ongoing clothing drives for oversees orphans and although they are located in Indiana, they welcome satellite collection sites. In 2009 alone, FCI clothed more than twenty thousand needy children in Ukraine and India.

For many children, getting a new pair of shoes is a luxury they have never experienced. A gift of a T-shirt or pair of boots may not stand out much to us, but you can be sure an orphan will be grateful.

Abba, there are so many options for foreign mission trips. I really have no excuse for not going, but if I'm completely honest, I think fear is holding me back. Help me to overcome my fears. Give me the strength and courage to sign up for a mission trip.

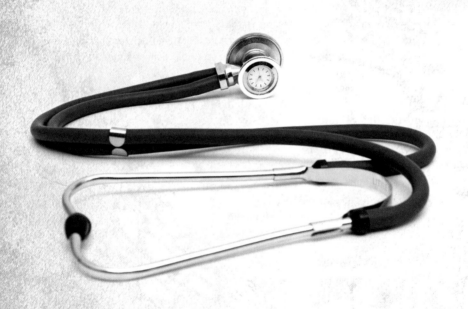

CARING FOR THE SICK

"I was sick and you looked after me."

38. TAKE FLOWERS REGULARLY TO A TERMINALLY ILL PATIENT.

I was just a little girl, but I still remember. I remember sitting in Ms. Lonie's living room by myself while my mother visited with her in the back bedroom. Each week it was the same routine. My mother had me pack a bag of coloring books and crayons before we got in the car. On the way to Ms. Lonie's house, she would stop to buy a handful of fresh-cut spring flowers. When we arrived at the house, we would ring the doorbell and the nurse would escort my mother to the back bedroom where Ms. Lonie rested.

> We make a living by what we get, but we make a life by what we give.
>
> **NORMAN MACEWAN**

I went with my mom to the back bedroom for a few visits, but I preferred to wait in the living room. I didn't like to visit with Ms. Lonie anymore. She looked so different from a few short months ago at church. Her terminal cancer had left her with no hair and a hollow face. Being a little girl, I didn't understand cancer and I felt safe waiting in the front of the house in the living room, where I could color in my coloring books and look at the paintings on the walls.

Ms. Lonie was an incredible artist. Her artwork literally covered the walls in her home. While I explored the old country roads and snowy landscapes in her paintings, I could hear Ms. Lonie and my mother talking in the back room. They talked about everything from Ms. Lonie's nursing care to church happenings to Ms. Lonie's artwork. I was young, but I knew my mother cared deeply for Ms. Lonie, and I could tell Ms. Lonie enjoyed my mother's visits—and she especially enjoyed the flowers my mother brought each week. Ms. Lonie would always say, "You brought me flowers again!"

When it was time for us to leave, the nurse would take the flowers and put them in water beside Ms. Lonie's bed. My mother would tell the nurse as we left, "I won't be sending flowers to the funeral. Instead, I'm bringing flowers each week when I visit. I want her to be able to enjoy them while she's still here." Ms. Lonie died a few weeks later, and when my mother attended the funeral, she saw many beautiful bouquets and sprays of colorful, fresh-cut flowers—but not one of them was from her. She had already taken beautiful flowers to Ms. Lonie for several weeks before her death. And she had the incredible privilege and personal satisfaction of knowing that Ms. Lonie had seen, touched, smelled, and enjoyed every single bouquet *before* she died.

> **THE STATS**
>
> An estimated 1,529,560 people in the US were diagnosed with cancer in 2010.
>
> Survival rates vary depending on the person and type of cancer.

IN HIS NAME

When I was a child, I didn't fully understand the magnitude of what my mother did for Ms. Lonie. I didn't understand how important it was for my mother to visit and minister regularly to Ms. Lonie during her illness. Now that I'm an adult, I realize that I learned much about human kindness and compassion from my mother. She was a nurse by trade, but her compassion went so much further than just nursing. Her compassion to touch the sick and the suffering shaped me into the person I am today. Ms. Lonie was not the only terminally ill person who my mother reached out to when I was growing up. There were many others.

When we care for the sick and the needy, we should keep in mind that others are watching—especially our children. They are being shaped by our compassionate responses to the hurting. The lesson my mother taught me by visiting Ms. Lonie and taking her flowers each week has lasted a lifetime for me. In fact, the painting that Ms. Lonie gave my mother just before her death still hangs on the wall in my mother's bedroom—and Ms. Lonie gave her the painting more than thirty years ago. The compassion my mother gave to her dying friend still hangs in the walls of my heart.

A CUP OF COLD WATER

It is important to support those who are facing illness—especially a terminal illness. Taking flowers to them regularly is a wonderful way to brighten their day. Giving flowers doesn't have to be expensive. If you have a flower garden, taking cut flowers that you tended yourself can mean more than an expensive bouquet from a florist. But if you don't have a flower garden, don't feel that you need to send a large arrangement of pricey cut flowers. A small bouquet of one, two, or three flowers is still a beautiful gesture for someone who is suffering.

If you visit a terminally ill patient, you should be mindful of the length of your stay. If you are not a family member, keep your visits very short to give the family their special time with their loved one. While you are there, tell the patient what you have always wanted to say, even if he or she is unconscious. Offer to listen and hear what the patient has to say. Avoid being judgmental, and prepare to hear a variety of emotions, including anger and frustration.

> *At the end of a person's life, even if he or she cannot respond to you, your words can encourage and affirm.*

Be sure to let the family know ahead of time that you won't be sending flowers to the funeral, but instead your gift of flowers to their loved one before he or she dies is how you have chosen to honor their loved one. My mother did this on several occasions for friends who had terminal illnesses, not just for Ms. Lonie. At the funerals of those friends, the families always told my mother how much her gift of flowers meant to their loved one—and also to them.

Abba, as I visit loved ones who are near death, help me to simply be comfortable as I talk with them and show them kindness in their last days. I pray that the flowers I bring, the conversations we engage in, and the friendship we share will be a worshipful and holy experience for us both.

39. HOST A HANDBAG PARTY TO BENEFIT WIDOWS.

When I walked into the dimly lit, one-room cinder block building in the African bush, the women were sitting on thin mats as they worked. The mats were the African women's only comfort against the hard and dusty concrete floor, but they didn't seem to notice as they threaded needles, cut patterns, and sifted through bags of colorful African cloth. Almost all of them were widows. Some of them were older, and their faces bore the signs of a hard life. Some were younger, and they had sleeping babies strapped on their backs.

AIDS had taken most of their husbands and as a result, their livelihood. But it had not taken their joy. As they sewed purses, they sang praise songs together—some in SiSwati, some in English. I marveled as I watched them work. They were quick with their fingers. The handbags they sewed were all unique. Some had button-down flaps and pockets in front. Some had long straps with burlap handles. Some were small with side pockets. All of them were colorful—made with authentic Swazi cloth bearing patterns that are uniquely African.

> Expect great things from God. Attempt great things for God.
>
> **WILLIAM CAREY**

These women meet once a week in the cinder block building to sew these purses. As each unique purse is finished, the woman adds one final touch—she writes her name on the tag attached to the purse's handle. The beautiful purses are then taken by an American missionary, Julie, and packaged for shipment to buyers in America. As the purses are sold and shipped, Julie makes sure the money from the sale of the handbags goes

CUP OF COLD WATER

back to the women who sewed the purses. This has become a way for these women to provide for their families, as most of them now run husbandless households.

Every purse is unique. Not one is exactly the same as another—just like the precious women who so lovingly make them. One such precious woman is Ruby. Ruby is eighty-one years old and is the primary Go-Go (caregiver) at a central care point in Swaziland. When I met Ruby, she was surrounded by needy Swazi children, most of them orphans. Ruby was cooking "pop" (ground corn maize in the consistency of porridge) in a big black kettle over an open fire. Her outdoor "kitchen" was nothing more than sticks held together with mud. The tin roof did nothing to block the wind that threatened to put out her kettle's flames. But the "kitchen" was all Ruby had. She stood over her pot of pop and stirred it with great care. She knew the pop she was cooking would be the only meal that some of the children would get all day.

Ruby and the other women who sewed purses once a week all gave of themselves in this way to the needy children at various care points. Each of them helped to care for the children of Swaziland who had been orphaned by AIDS. In Swaziland, orphaned children are cared for by the entire village at care points. The care point Ruby managed was one of many care points in Swaziland. Each woman gives of her own time, without pay, to sacrifice for these needy children who would likely starve if they didn't get their meal of pop each day.

THE STATS

In many parts of Africa, widowhood robs women of their status and places them in the margins of society where they suffer the most extreme forms of discrimination and stigma.

There is little research on the amount of widows in developing nations, although a 1991 census recorded 35 million widows in India alone.

I was so moved by the sacrifice that these women make on a daily basis. That is why on my trip back home to America, I was loaded down with a bulging bag full of Swazi purses made by these caring women!

IN HIS NAME

Widows and orphans are among the most vulnerable in our world today—especially in third world countries. And they always have been. That's why God was so clear in Old Testament law with how we are to care for them in their distress. God taught His people to leave provision for the widow among a harvest in Deuteronomy 24:19: "When you are harvesting your crops and forget to bring in a bundle of grain from your field, don't go back to get it. Leave it for the foreigners, orphans, and widows. Then the Lord your God will bless you in all you do."

Boaz obeyed this command. In biblical times, Boaz was a man of influence and power who made sure the poor were able to glean grain left behind by his workers during the harvest. He spoke kind words to one widow, Ruth, and made sure his harvesters dropped grain on purpose for her. The Bible says, "Ruth gathered barley there all day, and when she beat out the grain that evening, it filled an entire basket" (Ruth 2:17). She was able to provide for her needs and the needs of her widowed mother-in-law because Boaz opened his heart to widows and the poor.

If we are to accept Jesus' invitation to care for the needy, certainly the widow cannot be overlooked. Julie and other missionaries have made it easy for us to minister directly to a needy widow on the other side of the world.

A CUP OF COLD WATER

Handmade Swazi purses can be ordered and purchased online through a secure website, but another way to help these widows is to host an African handbag party. All of the details are listed at the website www.timbalicrafts.org. At the site, you can learn how the handbags are made, read about some of the women who make the unique bags, and see sample pictures of fabrics. Most handmade purses purchased through Timbali Crafts are priced less than twenty-five dollars.

To organize an African handbag party, order twenty or more bags from the website and receive them on consignment. Then use the site's downloadable promotional materials to send postcards to friends, family, and coworkers, or put posters in public places, like your church. After the party, simply send payment to the organization.

> *The women now use hand-cranked sewing machines to create Swazi handbags. On the website you can learn how to donate a sewing machine to this group of women.*

Other organizations also work in countries around the world and sell goods made by widows and other individuals living in impoverished areas:

- Bead for Life (Uganda): *www.beadforlife.org*
- Conosur Imports (Chile): *www.conosurimports.com*
- Corazon Scarves (Guatemala, Haiti): *www.corazonscarves.com*
- Far East Handicrafts (Nepal): *www.fareasthandicrafts.com*
- Singing Shaman Traders (Mexico): *www.singingshamantraders.com*

I'm so thrilled to know that since I first encountered the small group of women who sew the Swazi purses, the group has grown to nearly ninety women! Most of them were widowed due to AIDS and are now suffering daily with HIV. The missionary, Julie, regularly meets with these women for discipleship and hosts a retreat for them each year.

Empowering women and creating hope on the other side of the world just by purchasing a handbag—it really is *that* easy.

Abba, your Word is clear—we are to fight for the rights of widows. Widows in other parts of the world lack what they need for themselves and their families, and this is an injustice that I can do something about by hosting a party. I pray that as I plan and organize a party, I can raise awareness as well as monetary funds for suffering widows around the world.

40. TAKE MEALS TO A SICK PERSON AND HIS OR HER FAMILY.

Today, as I type, my heart is so heavy. I am grieving with my friends Cody and Maria. They face the most incomprehensible pain a parent can endure. Their little four-year-old girl, Susana, is dying. While Cody and Maria were on the mission field in Jacmel, Haiti, last year, their daughter Susana became lethargic and ill. She was flown to a children's hospital in Miami where the doctors found multiple tumors invading Susana's little body.

Immediately doctors began administering treatments to destroy the cancer. For nearly a year, Susana has been in and out of several hospitals and has bravely fought the battle for her life. And now, even after that long battle, Cody and Maria have learned that Susana's tumors are worse than ever. Hospice has been called in—Susana is dying.

Over the past year and now as Susana's health fades daily, I have watched Cody and Maria stand strong on the only thing that is truly stable in this life— Jesus Christ. Their faith has been tested. Their strength has been tried. But as they have walked through this fire, something amazing has happened. They have not been burned. As they have been dealt blow after pounding blow, they have gotten back up again. As they have been pressed under the weight of watching their little girl's health painfully deteriorate, they have not been crushed.

Their painful journey has been docu-mented in their mission's blog. You can

> God has given us two hands— one to receive with and the other to give with. We are not cisterns made for hoarding; we are channels made for giving.
>
> **BILLY GRAHAM**

LORIE NEWMAN

sense the raw emotion in Cody's writing as he and Maria walk in this dark valley. Here is an excerpt from the blog entry for February 7, 2011:

> Susana is not doing well at all. She has taken another turn. We just had a hospice nurse come to examine her because we weren't sure what was going on. She basically is now in the mode of sleeping all day. She has lost so much weight. She doesn't want to eat. It is so hard to see her go through this. The nurse said that she is in the transitional stage of dying. After this stage, her body will slip into a coma where she will not be responsive to anything, but she'll only be breathing . . . for a time. And then, in the blink of an eye, she will enter into glory and be made whole.
>
> So, we don't know how much longer we have with her. It could be days or it could be a few weeks. Oh how my heart hurts! How I wish the Lord would heal her at the last minute. How I wish that I could take her place. And yet, may the Lord's will be done knowing full well that He is good and that He will be glorified above all. Yes, friends, only with our hope rooted and fixed in Christ alone can we say such things while looking upon our frail little girl. God is enough. God is enough.

IN HIS NAME

What do you say to a friend who is going through such a trial? What can be done to help? How can we, as their brothers and sisters in Christ, ease their heartache? These were all questions my Bible study class asked when Susana was first diagnosed with cancer. We immediately went to our knees and interceded on behalf of this precious family. We have all committed to pray daily for Cody, Maria, Susana, and Susana's older sister, Isabela. And this precious family will be the first to tell you that it is prayer and the solid truth in God's living Word that have sustained them each day.

We all will go through trials in this life. Jesus said in John 16:33, "Here on earth you will have many trials and sorrows. But take heart, because I have overcome the world." Notice that Jesus didn't say *if* you have trouble. He said you *will* have trouble. Walking with each other as brothers and sisters in Christ is what being a part of the family of God is about. Leaning on each other during a crisis is a vital part of being a healthy family.

During Jesus' earthly ministry, He taught about how we, His children, are to love one another. It is that deep love for each other that Jesus said will show the world that we are truly His disciples (John 13:35). When a brother or sister in Christ is hurting or in need and we care for them with the unconditional love of God, we are showing the world that we are His ambassadors here on earth. Taking care of one another during a crisis is not only a privilege for us, but it also shows an unbelieving world what true disciples of Christ look like.

A CUP OF COLD WATER

Praying God's Word over Cody, Maria, Isabela, and Susana was the first priority for our Bible study class. But we wanted to do even more to support them on a practical level. We decided to take meals to their house each day.

Now, while providing meals is a wonderful way to bless a family facing a medical crisis, it's important to make sure it doesn't become a burden for the family. If each night the person who delivers the meal decides to stay and "visit," even if they are well meaning, that person can take away from family or rest time and also introduce potentially harmful germs into the home.

To avoid this situation, a large cooler was placed on Cody and Maria's porch so that anyone who wanted to bring a meal could do so without disturbing their family each evening. Another method to avoid disturbing the family is to use signals like open or closed window blinds. Open blinds indicate "this is a good time for a visit." Closed blinds mean "we are resting or spending time together with our loved one."

> *Having someone take care of everyday tasks can greatly lower stress levels of family members who are caring for an ill relative. Consider offering to help with child care, meals, household cleaning, or yard work.*

If someone you know is having surgery or having a baby, consider asking your small group, coworkers, or friends to bring frozen meals to one location. Then put them all in a cooler and let one person deliver them. Write encouraging notes to the recipient to let that person know you are thinking of him or her and praying for recovery. The recipient will be thrilled to receive the meals, and can rest without having to "visit" night after night when a meal is delivered. New moms may benefit from a "frozen casserole shower" even more than a traditional baby shower.

If you decide to minister to a family by taking them a meal, be sure to leave a note explaining exactly what the ingredients are and how they should prepare or warm the food. Making meals for a family experiencing a medical crisis or planned procedure can be such a blessing, and respecting their rest and family time by creative planning can make it a double blessing!

Abba, as I look around my church family, my workplace, and my neighborhood, show me those families that I can bless by taking them a meal. Help me to be the catalyst that moves the body of Christ into action for a hurting family. As I plan and coordinate meals, I pray that I can do so as a true servant. Help me to be a blessing while not expecting anything in return.

(Three days after I wrote this chapter, little four-year-old Susana breathed her last breath on this earth while her mom and dad held her tiny hands. Then she opened her eyes in the presence of Jesus. *Goodbye precious one—but only for a while. We'll all be together again soon.* To read more about Cody and Maria's journey through their daughter's cancer, visit www.howcantheyhear.org.)

41. OFFER A RIDE TO AN ELDERLY OR IMPOVERISHED PERSON.

The summertime heat in Georgia can be brutal. In fact, it can be deadly. During the heat wave of 2007, four people died during the month of August when the heat wave reached its peak. The first summer after my husband and I moved to Augusta, Georgia, it was over 100 degrees for twenty days straight with heat indexes near 115 degrees. Swimming at a lake or in a pool was the only outdoor activity that was safe during daytime hours that summer.

> I would like to buy $3 worth of God, please. Not enough to explode my soul or disturb my sleep, but just enough to equal a cup of warm milk or a snooze in the sunshine. I don't want enough of Him to make me love a black man [or any person of a different ethnicity] or pick beets with a migrant. I want ecstasy, not transformation; I want the warmth of the womb, not a new birth. I want about a pound of the Eternal in a paper sack. I'd like to buy $3 worth of God, please. [How much do you want?]
>
> **WILBUR REESE**

When we lived in Georgia, I tried to plan my weekly trips to the grocery store for early mornings so that my car wouldn't feel like an oven when I came out of the store. It was on one of those trips to the store that I saw her. She was a tiny, thin black woman who couldn't have been taller than 4' 11", and she was about fifty years of age. She was in the checkout line just ahead of me. She bought a few items and headed for the door. I continued through the checkout line with my two carts full of food (it takes a lot to feed my army of kids).

With five of my children in tow, we left the store, packed our car, and headed home. By this time it was mid-morning, and it was already 85 degrees.

Sweat poured from us and the air-conditioning in the car struggled to cool the stagnant, hot air. That's when I saw her again. She was walking home. Walking. In the heat. Carrying her groceries.

My kids even said, "Mom, there's the lady from the store! She must not have a car. We need to help her." I pulled the car over, got out, and offered to drive her home. I didn't know where she lived, but I knew it couldn't be far since she was trying to make it on foot. The sweet woman was so grateful. Her home was a good three miles from the grocery store. I couldn't believe she was walking such a distance in the summer heat.

She thanked me with a smile when we reached her house. I offered to help her with her bags, but she waved her hands with a big smile to let me know she could get them. It felt good to help her avoid walking in the heat. Little did I know that day would be the first time of many that I would see this sweet woman at the store and then drive her home.

Each week when I went to the store I prayed that God would let me see my "walking friend" so I could offer to drive her home. And sure enough, almost every week I had the privilege of helping this sweet woman to her house. I often spoke about Jesus in the car and asked her if she knew of Him. She always nodded her head "yes." Each week her words were few, but she always gave me the same smile of thanks when I offered to drive her home and when we arrived at her house. And that precious smile was "thank you" enough for me.

IN HIS NAME

While I don't normally pick up strangers who look like they need a ride, I do think that praying over how to use the car that God has given us to help someone else is a great way to accept Jesus' invitation to care for the needy. It would have been easy that hot summer day to look past the need of the woman walking home and just go about my day. It's easy to look the other way when someone is in need because, frankly, it can be time-consuming to help a needy person. It can be an interruption to our busy agenda. But Jesus always took the time to care for needs, even when He was busy.

Consider the story of Jairus's sick daughter in Mark 5:22–43. A frantic Jairus begged Jesus to come and heal his daughter. Jesus, on the way to Jairus's house, encountered another desperate person:

> A woman in the crowd had suffered for twelve years with constant bleeding. She had suffered a great deal from many doctors, and over the years she had spent everything she had to pay them, but she had gotten no better. In fact, she had gotten worse. She had heard about Jesus, so she came up behind him and touched his robe. For she thought to herself, "If I can just touch his robe, I will be healed." Immediately the bleeding stopped, and she could feel in her body that she had been healed of her terrible condition. (vv. 25–29)

Jesus stopped and spoke to the woman when He "felt" her touch. He could have ignored the woman who touched Him—after all, He was on His way to help a very important man's daughter. But He didn't look the other way. He didn't ignore the woman. He didn't see her need as an interruption to His busy agenda. Being a servant and loving people *was* His agenda. Shouldn't it be our agenda too?

A CUP OF COLD WATER

Many American families own at least one car. I assume that since you are reading this book, your name is on the title of a car. But not everyone has the luxury of owning a car, and those without a car still need to get to work, the grocery store, doctor appointments, and other necessary places.

Do you know someone who doesn't own a car or can't drive and may need help getting around? Perhaps someone at your workplace needs a ride to work in the morning, or maybe an elderly neighbor needs a ride to a medical appointment. A single mother who has transportation still may need someone to take her child to the dentist during the day because she can't leave work. Helping someone with a ride may seem so simple to those of us who do have a car, but to someone who doesn't drive, it can be a lifesaver.

> *Although many elderly adults can no longer drive a vehicle and have necessary and regular medical appointments, medical transportation is often not covered in health care insurance plans.*

There are ways to find a person in need of such services. A great resource is 211. In certain areas of the US, dialing 2-1-1 from a phone can connect you to ministries and resources in your area. To find out if your area is serviced by 211, go to http://211.org/ and plug in your city, state, or zip code.

Another website to visit is www.redcross.org. The American Red Cross chapter in your area may have information on volunteering with a medical transportation program. And if you have the time to give, your local Meals on Wheels chapter always needs drivers to deliver meals to shut-ins, and they welcome family volunteers. Visit www.mowaa.org for more information.

So many of us have busy schedules, agendas, and plans, but we can set our minds to be like Jesus to ensure that our busy schedules don't keep us from offering help to those in need.

Abba, let me remember that stopping to help a needy person is an opportunity to serve you instead of an inconvenience or interruption. I want helping others to be a welcome and regular part of my everyday agenda. So today, Abba, put someone in my path who needs help and give me the grace to see and meet their need with your compassion.

42. OFFER TO BE TESTED FOR HIV WITH SOMEONE WHO NEEDS TO BE TESTED.

When Zabilae and her husband fled their homeland of Sierra Leone with their young son, they found refuge in the United States. The civil unrest in their native land led to killing sprees and frequent gunfire exchanges in their village. Soon after Zabilae and her family found safety in the United States, her world was jolted once again when her husband died of AIDS. After his death, Zabilae found out she was HIV positive.

> Our lives begin to end the day we become silent about things that matter.
>
> **MARTIN LUTHER KING JR.**

Being a strong Christian, Zabilae found hope and acceptance at her new church where she joined a women's Bible study. That's where she and my sister-in-law, Tammy, met each other. The weekly Bible studies gave the women a chance to get to know one another, and it didn't take long for both of them to realize that although they were from opposite sides of the globe and two different cultures, they held in common what matters most. Both women had given their lives to Christ and both were learning to be the hands and feet of Jesus in their everyday lives.

At Christmastime, when Tammy realized that Zabilae and her son would be alone for the holidays, she insisted that they join her, my brother, and their two children for Christmas. Tammy wasn't sure Zabilae would agree to it, since each year they traveled four hours from Auburn, Alabama, to Augusta, Georgia, to be with family at Christmas. But to her surprise, Zabilae and her son agreed to spend a week in Georgia visiting our family! Tammy called all of us to tell us the news. Everyone was excited to have guests for the holidays, and I was especially thrilled that my adopted son, Daniel, would meet Zabilae and her son, since Daniel is also from Africa.

For the week of Christmas, Zabilae and her son joined our big, supersized, extended family for Christmas dinners and church services. Like always, we had more than enough holiday food, gifts, and over-the-top decorations. All the aunts, uncles, grandparents, cousins, and siblings did our best to make sure Zabilae and her son felt welcomed and loved. It was so special to share our Christmas with them that year.

On the long drive back home, Zabilae told Tammy what a great time she had had with our family. She couldn't thank Tammy enough for sharing her family's Christmas. Then she explained that sometimes when people, even Christians, find out that her husband died of AIDS and that she is HIV positive, they avoid her. But not Tammy. Tammy had not only found a sweet friend in Zabilae, she had also invited her to be part of her own family—even if it was only for a week.

It broke Tammy's heart to learn that Zabilae had experienced such rejection from people within the body of Christ. But what a blessing and high privilege it was for Tammy to know she had been used by God to bring the love of Christ to Zabilae and her son.

IN HIS NAME

When Jesus healed the sick, not once did He say, "Now, tell me, how did you get this illness?" He simply loved the sick and healed them with open arms of compassion. HIV/AIDS has such a stigma, even within the church. And it's not just in America. In sub-Saharan Africa, where an estimated 22.5 million people are HIV positive (2.3 million of them are children), people suffer with the disease in silence because they will be cast out and literally pushed away by villagers who don't fully understand the disease. Often when someone dies of AIDS in Africa, that person's family tells others that he or she died of pneumonia or tuberculosis.

All over the world, and even here in the United States, people are dying of AIDS and suffering alone with HIV. They are afraid. And worst of all, many times they are rejected by the church. What a shame. Aren't we as God's people called to raise a banner of forgiveness and hope in a Savior whose blood can cover any and all sins? When someone is dying, should it matter what he or she is dying from? Would we, as the church of Christ, treat someone differently who is dying of cancer?

There is currently no cure for HIV/AIDS. But there is a cure for broken hearts and lives. His name is Jesus. And His compassion for the sick and the dying knows no bounds.

A CUP OF COLD WATER

Today, although there is no known cure for HIV/AIDS, an HIV diagnosis is certainly much different than it used to be. With antiretroviral drug combinations, people who have been diagnosed positively with HIV are living much longer, healthier lives. It's imperative that those who think they may have been infected get tested as soon as possible so that they can begin the antiretroviral treatment. But, with the stigma still attached to AIDS, many people put off testing. They know they may be carriers, so they avoid testing to delay the probable diagnosis.

> *In Florida, a joint initiative between the African Methodist Episcopal Church and the state Department of Health has a goal to establish at least one AIDS testing site in a place of worship in every county.*

Being well informed is the key to handling the disease. Saddleback Church in California is leading the charge in Christian ministry for the testing, treatment, support, and counseling of those with HIV/AIDS. In fact, Rick Warren, the senior pastor of Saddleback, leads his congregation in testing by being tested himself—once during a church service.

The Centers for Disease Control and Prevention recommends regular HIV testing for everyone between the ages of thirteen and sixty-four. Ideally with a pastor leading the charge, a group from your church can go together to get tested for HIV. If you know someone who may be infected but is afraid to get tested, offer to be tested with them or invite them to be tested with the group. For a list of places that offer HIV testing, visit www.hivtest.org. The Saddleback website provides valuable information and a safe place for anyone to ask questions about HIV. Visit www.hivandthechurch.com to learn more.

Jesus never asked sick people how they got sick. He just had compassion on them. Should we, as the body of Christ, show any less compassion for a person who is living with HIV?

Abba, HIV/AIDS is something that I don't think much about because it doesn't affect me directly. Yet it's a very real disease for Christians and non-Christians alike. Abba, give me your compassion for those who are suffering with HIV and help me to lead the charge in my church to show your love to them in practical ways.

43. TAKE CARE BASKETS TO HOSPITAL WAITING ROOMS.

Bleak walls. Worn magazines. A television stuck on the news channel. Uncomfortable chairs. Exhausted and concerned family members constantly checking the clock on the wall. So many of us have been there—a hospital waiting room. For me it was 2:00 AM on a snowy night in January. Our then twelve-year-old son Marc had been sledding earlier that afternoon with his siblings. They trekked up the biggest neighborhood hill they could find and decided to see who could make it to the bottom the fastest.

Marc was in the lead when the disc sled he was on hit a rock under the snow. The sled flipped and Marc tumbled down the hill. As he fell, he twisted his lower leg and broke his tibia and fibula. My oldest son ran to get us, because it was obvious that Marc's left leg was broken. The bone was protruding and he was in a lot of pain. My husband and I called an ambulance, and as I rode to the hospital beside Marc, I remember thinking, *Thank you, God, it's just a broken leg. If he had hit his head, it could have been so much worse. We'll get to the hospital, they will set his broken bone, and we'll come home late tonight with some pain medication.*

> Live for the applause of nail-scarred hands.
>
> **MARK BATTERSON**

But it didn't work out that way. When we arrived at the emergency room, the doctors couldn't find a pulse in Marc's foot. There was little blood circulation in his lower leg, and an orthopedic surgeon was called in. The surgeon looked at me and said, "He has compound spiral fractures and has developed compartmental syndrome in his leg. Three surgeries will be required—one now, one later this week, and then a third one in six months. He will have to stay at the hospital at least eight days. This is a serious injury." Then he looked at the nurse and said, "Get him prepped for the surgery now." My heart dropped to the floor. Three surgeries? Eight days? For a broken leg? This was not supposed to happen.

So there my husband and I were at 2:00 AM in a hospital waiting room. I prayed. I cried a little. I prayed some more. I tried to keep my overwhelmed mind occupied by staring at the TV. It was no use. I really wanted a drink from the vending machine but I didn't have any change in my purse. We had left the house so fast—of course I didn't think to grab a snack or loose change. The other people in the room seemed just as anxious and tired as we were. The hands of the clock on the wall seemed frozen as we waited.

Finally the doctor came by. The surgery was over and Marc had been taken to a room where he would spend the next eight days. Seven months, one walker, two crutches, three surgeries, and eight weeks of physical therapy later, Marc made a full recovery. His accident and subsequent surgery was just one of hundreds of emergencies at that hospital. Every day hundreds of family members sit in that same hospital waiting room and others like it in every city in America. What a fertile place for an act of kindness!

> **THE STATS**
>
> Each year over 45 million surgeries are performed in US hospitals.
>
> With each of those 45 million procedures, at least one person sits in a hospital waiting room while their loved one is in surgery.

IN HIS NAME

In the days of Jesus' earthly ministry, we find many examples of His healing power in the lives of those suffering with various illnesses. But have you noticed that Jesus also ministered to those who were closest to the sick person? In John chapter 11, Jesus comforted sisters Mary and Martha just after the death of their brother, Lazarus. And in Luke 8, a synagogue leader's daughter died while Jesus was on the way to see her. Jesus tells the grieving father, "Don't be afraid. Just have faith, and she will be healed" (v. 50).

On another occasion, as Jesus and his disciples entered the village of Nain, they encountered a funeral procession. The young man who had died was the only son of a widow. The Bible says that Jesus' heart "overflowed with compassion" for the widow (Luke 7:13). He told her not to cry, and then walked to the coffin and touched it. "'Young man,' he said, 'get up.' Then the dead boy sat up and began to talk to those around him! And Jesus gave him back to his mother" (vv. 14–15).

Jesus understood then and He understands now the anguish that we face when a loved one is sick, suffering, or dying. Following Jesus' example by ministering to those who are closest to the sick and suffering is one way to imitate Christ in our everyday lives.

A CUP OF COLD WATER

Waiting for someone to come out of surgery is an anxious time for loved ones. A simple way to show the love of Christ to those waiting is to make care baskets for hospital waiting rooms. Showing kindness in such a tangible way can be a ray of hope in what may be a very dark day.

> *In one morning, a group can assemble and deliver several care baskets.*

Making and delivering care baskets is a project that you can do alone, or with your Bible study group, Sunday school class, youth group, or coworkers. In a large basket, put items that you think will be used by family members confined to a waiting room. Here are some suggestions:

- *Bottled water*
- *Sodas*
- *Packs of crackers*
- *Bags of chips*
- *Mints and gum*
- *Hard candies*
- *Notepads and pens*
- *Religious magazines or tracts*
- *Scripture cards*

Be sure to make a small sign for your basket explaining that items are free to take. You may need to replenish your baskets often. Always ask at the nurses' desk if you can place the care baskets in the waiting room before doing so. If you make an extra basket just for the nurses at their station, you are sure to get a resounding yes!

Taking a care basket to a hospital waiting room is something I can easily do, Abba. Please comfort those who take an item from a basket and give them peace as they wait for news of their loved one. Let them sense your love through the gifts. Use the Scripture cards in the baskets to minister personally to each person who sees them.

44. ROCK BABIES AT THE NICU OF YOUR LOCAL HOSPITAL.

Not many people notice what Julia does in the mornings. She makes her way through the automatic doors of the children's hospital near her home, takes the elevator to the third floor, and puts on a yellow hospital jumper over her clothes—just like she's done each day for nearly seven years. Her volunteer work isn't glamorous. No one pats her on the back or cheers her on. In fact, the small people she ministers to are often too sick to ever know the wonderful gift she gives them.

Julia is a volunteer baby cuddler. She comes to the hospital each morning and rocks the tiny babies in the Neonatal Intensive Care Unit. Some of them are drug addicted. Some were born weeks premature. Still others need special care due to illness or AIDS. Over the past seven years, Julia has seen hundreds of babies in the unit. She has held and rocked nearly every one of them. But the most wonderful part of what Julia does goes far beyond merely holding them.

As Julia rocks the hospital's smallest patients, she also sings hymns to them and prays for them. Each baby, by name. She told me recently that she prays that the ones who are drug addicted will withdraw from the drugs quickly and without complications. As they shake and tremor in her arms, she holds them close and softly sings. For the ones who are HIV positive, she prays that they will live a long life and that a cure will be found in their lifetime. For the ones who are sick, she prays for healing from their specific medical condition and for the doctors caring for them to have supernatural wisdom. For the ones who are alone because their mothers abandoned them at the hospital, she prays that they will never know they were unwanted when they were born. She prays that each baby will come to know the Lord at an early age and that they will realize their infinite worth in God's eyes. For every infant's parents, she prays for wisdom.

Not many people notice what Julia does each weekday morning in that rocking chair, but God notices. The little ones she rocks and prays for will never even remember Julia. But her loving care for those sweet babies is not given to receive accolades or thank-yous. Julia doesn't care about that. The prayers she offers on behalf of these little ones are her offerings to God. She counts it a great privilege to be serving Jesus each day in a wooden rocking chair.

IN HIS NAME

> There is nothing small in the service of God.
>
> **FRANCIS DE SALES**

The University of Wisconsin published a study in the National Academy of Sciences showing that cuddling in the infant stage is vital to a child's emotional well-being. Babies need interaction and stimulation from human physical touch. But aside from newborns' scientifically proven need of physical touch and cuddling, as Christians, we know that we are called to care for little ones because our Savior did in His earthly ministry.

In Mark 10, we read that people were bringing their little children to Jesus for Him to bless them. When the disciples tried to push them away, Jesus rebuked them and had the little ones come close to Him. Then the Bible is clear that Jesus took those sweet children in His arms and blessed them.

One day some parents brought their children to Jesus so he could touch and bless them. But the disciples scolded the parents for bothering him.

When Jesus saw what was happening, he was angry with his disciples. He said to them, "Let the children come to me. Don't stop them! For the Kingdom of God belongs to those who are like these children. I tell you the truth, anyone who doesn't receive the Kingdom of God like a child will never enter it." Then he took the children in his arms and placed his hands on their heads and blessed them. (vv. 13–16)

Long before any scientific testing was done to conclude that little ones need physical touch, our Savior provided our example as He took little children into His arms. I imagine those excitable little children playing and laughing as they climbed into Jesus' lap and how He probably made them giggle with glee as He blessed each one of them. What a precious example our Jesus gives us as to how we too are to take little ones into our arms and bless them.

THE STATS

Premature birth occurs in 8–10% of all pregnancies in the United States.

A premature baby is one who is born before 37 weeks of pregnancy.

A CUP OF COLD WATER

Nearly every major city has a hospital that encourages volunteers to rock babies in their Neonatal Intensive Care Unit. The volunteer programs began in the early 1990s when "crack babies" were being born to drug-addicted mothers. Their withdrawal symptoms were soothed by being held and rocked. Today, volunteers are not just utilized for drug-addicted infants. Many babies who are in the hospital for long-term care, such as babies with serious illnesses or premature babies, also need to be rocked and held.

· - · - ·—— —— — · · ——— ·——— ———— -·—— **CUP OF COLD WATER**

Rarely do nurses have time to both care for infants and hold them during their busy shifts. That's where the baby cuddler volunteers come in. In one hospital in Oklahoma, baby cuddlers put a sticker above the cribs of each baby they rock so that the parents know that their baby was rocked and cuddled that day. It is not possible for some parents to be at their baby's bedside all day during a long-term hospitalization, so the parents count it a real blessing to see that sticker and know their little one was held and cuddled.

> *To find a hospital close to you, visit the American Hospital Directory at http://www.ahd.com/freesearch.php.*

If you would like to volunteer to rock babies, you will likely have to take a class. Your instructor will teach you the hospital rules and regulations as well as how to hold, bottle-feed, pat, and soothe hospitalized, sick babies. To sign up for training, call the hospital and ask for the volunteer coordinator. Most hospitals offer the class free of charge. You may need to be tested for tuberculosis and pass a background check to qualify as a volunteer.

Baby cuddlers are also needed in orphanages, group homes, and specialized nurseries. What a privilege it will be to minister to these tiny ones who need to be held, rocked, and prayed for. As you take sweet little ones into your arms, hold them close and bless them—just like Jesus did.

Abba, as I read about your love for little children, I smile as I think about how their happy giggles must make you smile. Babies especially are so precious. It's hard to imagine what it must be like to be a parent with a tiny child in the hospital. As I hold, feed, and soothe hospitalized babies, help me to be a part of their healing just by the care I give.

45. TAKE "CHRISTMAS" TO A FAMILY AT THE HOSPITAL.

Being at the hospital for many days with a sick family member is physically and mentally taxing. When my son was hospitalized for over a week due to a sledding accident, I stayed at the hospital with him day and night as he endured two surgeries and painful physical therapy. After eight days I was so exhausted. My back hurt from sleeping on a tiny couch and I couldn't get enough sleep at night because of the beeping machines and monitors. But that little pediatric patient room became my home away from home. I even started wearing my big, fluffy, red bedroom slippers to the cafeteria.

Many parents spend far more time than eight days at medical facilities with their ill children. In fact, while I was at the children's hospital with my son, I met a woman who had been at the hospital with her daughter for many weeks. I had seen her a few times in the hallway, but just in passing. Then one day I walked to the nurses' station to get a drink, and when I came around the corner, I saw the mother in the back hallway. She was leaning against the wall and sobbing uncontrollably.

I could hear her little daughter screaming in a room down the hall as the nurses worked with her. The screams of her daughter were breaking the mother's heart. I stopped to console her, but I couldn't think of anything to say that would help. I wished that I had some deep, insightful words of wisdom, but I didn't. I gave her a hug and whispered in her ear, "God loves your little girl even more than you do." She

> Some say if only my fears and doubts will leave then I will get to work. But instead you should get to work and then your fears and doubts will leave.
>
> **DWIGHT L. MOODY**

CUP OF COLD WATER

thanked me through her tears, but I knew nothing I could say or do would take away the ache of hearing her daughter suffer.

So many people are just like this sweet mother. They are in hospitals day after day, week after week, as their loved ones receive treatments and undergo procedures. Hospital rooms become their temporary homes and not much outside the walls of the hospital matters any longer as their focus shifts to their loved one getting well. This is an excellent time to reach out to these people and offer support.

IN HIS NAME

When we make a conscious effort each day to ask God to use us to touch the sick, the poor, the suffering, and the needy, there is no limit to what God can do through our sacrifice.

Exodus tells of the offerings that were brought before the Lord for the building of the tent of meeting, a moveable place of worship for God's people during their time in the wilderness. Moses had asked the people to bring precious metals, cloth, leather, and wood to the craftsmen building the tent (35:4–9). Each morning, the Israelites brought their offerings toward the making of this great tent of meeting, where Exodus 40:34–35 tells us God himself would dwell. Before long, the people brought so many offerings, Moses had to restrain them! The men who were working on the tent told Moses they had more than enough material to do the work (36:5).

I've pondered this incident from Exodus whenever I feel a pull to help the hurting and the sick. Many times I've told the Lord that I just didn't think I could do what He was calling me to do. Stepping outside my little world can be uncomfortable—can I really do it? Helping the hurting can be messy work—can I really do it? Taking the time to touch someone's life is costly—can I really do it? Being a servant to the broken can be taxing—can I really do it? Getting outside the church sanctuary into the world of the hurting can be risky—can I really do it?

He always gives me the same answer: *Lorie, if you give me all of you each morning, I can assure you, it will be more than enough for me to accomplish through you what I've asked you to do.*

What would your life look like if you gave everything to God each morning? How would your life change if today you focused on someone else's needs instead of your own? I have a feeling that if we as God's people gave Him the offering of *all* of ourselves each day, it would be more than enough for God to care for the sick, the poor, and the hurting around us!

A CUP OF COLD WATER

Due to the nature of certain terminal illnesses, family members are likely to be exhausted, discouraged, and even distant from their family and friends as they deal with day-to-day emergencies. By giving a family a special Christmas dinner and small gifts, you can provide them with a reprieve from the stress of their loved one's illness and being away from home.

If you would like to reach out to a family who is experiencing the prolonged illness of a child or other family member, the first place to start is with the hospital's social worker. The social worker can direct you to a family that may need a break from the monotony of daily medical treatments. If you are already aware of a family, then the social worker can direct you to a room at the hospital where you can provide a home-cooked meal to help a patient and his or her family celebrate Christmas.

> *Many cities have houses for family members who live too far to travel home each night after being with their ill loved one. Consider providing "Christmas" for individuals staying at these houses.*

This can be done any time of year, but Christmastime is an especially nice time to honor a family by making them a meal and bringing presents for each family member. The social worker can help you with age-appropriate gift ideas. Ask the social worker if you can decorate the room at the hospital to make the dinner extra special for the family. Perhaps the social worker can even find out what dishes the family enjoys most. After many days or weeks of hospital cafeteria food, a homemade meal will be a welcome break!

In Exodus 36, Moses had to announce to God's people that their gifts were more than enough for the tent of meeting. As you consider practical ways to help the needy, such as giving the family of a hospitalized patient a Christmas celebration, know that when you offer your creativity, your ideas, your resources, your gifts, your talents, and your time—when you give *all of yourself*—it will be more than enough for God to use in meeting the needs around you.

Abba, what I have to give to the poor and needy seems so small. Others have more money than me. They have talents and abilities that seem to surpass mine. Yet you tell me that I am to bring all of me to your living altar each day. Remind me, Abba, when I so often forget, that when I bring all of me, it's more than enough for you.

46. USE YOUR HORSES OR DOGS AS THERAPEUTIC ANIMALS.

When one of my sons was hospitalized on the pediatric floor, boredom was something we both struggled with each day. Not only was Marc missing his siblings and friends, but he was also stuck in bed with not much to do but watch TV, play video games, and read books. Sounds like a dream to many kids—an entire week away from school and chores—but it was anything but fun for Marc. After about the third day, he was bored to tears.

That's when a volunteer came by and gave us a weekly schedule of events for patients in the pediatric ward. Marc was a preteen, and many of the events were for younger patients, such as a sing-along with Mr. Music Man, a finger painting extravaganza, and a magic show. Marc looked over the schedule with disappointment, but at the bottom of the schedule, one event caught his eye (and mine too!). On Saturday was an event called Paws with a Purpose. Marc and I looked at each other, and a smile came across his face that lit up that dull hospital room! I hadn't seen that sweet smile in days.

> Lukewarm people call "radical" what Jesus expected of all his followers.
>
> **FRANCIS CHAN**

We asked the volunteer exactly what Paws with a Purpose meant. She said once a month a group of people who help out at the humane society bring a few of the friendly dogs to the pediatric ward to play with the children. The children can pet them, throw a ball to them, and walk them on leashes around the hallways if the children are medically able. She also told us that volunteers bring dogs to the rooms of children who are very sick.

I could see the boredom flee from Marc's eyes, and he asked what seemed like a hundred questions about the dogs. He asked what kind of dogs came each month, what their names were, and where they lived during the week. Although Saturday was still several days away, Marc circled Paws with a Purpose on the event calendar and had me tape it to the cabinet door. Each morning he talked about how he couldn't wait to meet the dogs!

Before those dogs even stepped a paw onto the pediatric floor, they were already working a little therapy on my son. Just the anticipation of their visit brought him such joy. And they were such sweet dogs! Truly, the volunteers had chosen a wonderful way to share the animals in their care. There is much to be said for how the dogs' visits aid in the emotional healing of children at that hospital.

IN HIS NAME

THE STATS

57% of psychiatrists, 48% of psychologists, and 40% of family practice physicians reported recommending animals to provide unconditional affection and companionship, a focus or perspective on a daily basis, amusement, and a feeling of being needed.

Animals can be used therapeutically for children and adults with mental or physical disabilities, or those recovering from injury, illness, or even abuse. Unlike humans who oftentimes shy away from people with special mental or physical needs, pets show no partiality. They don't notice disabilities and they love unconditionally. Pets don't discriminate. They don't judge based on physical disabilities, and they look right past mental challenges.

Perhaps that is why animals are so useful in therapy—they simply give love. It seems we could take a lesson from therapeutic animals. Could you and I, even as Christ followers, honestly say we show no partiality, don't notice disabilities, don't discriminate, never judge based on physical disabilities, and look past mental challenges? Could you and I say we always love unconditionally? I try to do these things every day, but I'm not there yet! I'm a work in progress. It's no wonder the use of therapeutic animals is recommended by many physicians and psychologists.

A CUP OF COLD WATER

Are you an animal lover? Do you have a dog or a horse that is mild mannered and loves children? Dogs and horses are used frequently in therapy situations for special needs children and adults. Officially called "special needs therapy and service assistance animals," dogs and horses can make a child or special needs adult feel accepted and loved. This can open pathways of expression that they didn't have before meeting and caring for the animal. These special needs children and adults can benefit from the relationships built between them and the dog or horse.

To begin an official horse therapy farm may require licensing, education, and training. To get more information about using your horses for therapy, visit the North American Riding for the Handicapped Association website at www.narha.org.

If your family is interested in fostering and training a service dog, several organizations specialize in this area:

Florida: *www.guidedogs.org*
Michigan: *www.pawswithacause.org*

North Carolina: www.caninesforservice.org
Texas: www.myservicedog.com

If you simply have friendly dogs and would like to share them in a way that would help children, contact your humane society to see if there is already a program in place in your area.

> *To learn more about your state's humane society,*
> *visit www.humanesociety.org, click "About Us" and "In Your State,"*
> *and then choose your state from the map.*

If there is not such a program with the humane society, call a nearby hospital and ask to speak with the volunteer coordinator. Explain your desire to share your kid-friendly dogs with patients once a month. You can also contact family counseling centers, special needs day cares, adult care facilities, and special needs teachers at schools. All of the workers at these facilities should be familiar with and educated in the benefits of animal therapy.

Utilizing your animal in therapeutic situations can be the key that begins to unlock healing and comfort for a child or adult recovering from illness, injury, or abuse, as well as someone living with physical or mental challenges.

I do love animals, Abba. Thank you for the joy my animals bring to my life. I can understand why well-natured dogs and horses can be used therapeutically. As I research ways to utilize my animals for therapy, lead me to the organizations that can help me get started. Use my animals to bless others and bring healing to many broken lives.

47. FORM A SUPPORT GROUP AT YOUR CHURCH FOR PEOPLE INFECTED WITH OR AFFECTED BY HIV/AIDS.

I had just finished speaking to a group of women at a small church in rural North Carolina when I noticed an elderly woman standing in the back of the room as if she were waiting to talk to me. When the room cleared for a lunch break, the elderly woman approached me. Her face was downcast and she looked as though she'd been crying. With a soft voice she told me that the words I had spoken were so true in her life.

I had taught that morning about how so many times as Christians we wear masks to pretend that our life is perfect. We're afraid that others will not accept us for who we really are, so we put on a mask, or a "perfect face" to hide behind. I taught that transparency and confession are the keys to real relationships in the church. But this precious lady told me that what hit home with her was when I spoke of *why* we so often wear masks in church—because church people can be very judgmental toward anyone who struggles with sin.

She went on to tell me about how she had been hurt by words spoken in her Sunday school class a few weeks before. The class had discussed homosexuality that day. Rather than focus on how God hates the sin but loves the sinner and how Christians can show the love of Christ to homosexuals, the Sunday school class began to mock the homosexual community and ridicule them for "bringing HIV/AIDS onto themselves."

As the elderly woman told me this story, she paused and began to weep quietly. Through her tears she said, "My son is a homosexual. I fear he is HIV positive. I know the lifestyle he has chosen is wrong. But he's my son. And I love my son." She couldn't believe the hurtful stance that her Christian brothers and sisters had taken. Her very own church had become a place where she was not free to talk about the struggles within her family. She didn't feel free to tell her Christian friends how to pray for her and how to pray for her son. She was suffering alone.

As I drove home from that weekend conference, that sweet woman's words—"I love my son"—kept ringing in my ears. A righteous indignation rose up in me. It bothered me that this sister in Christ could not share her broken heart about her son with her own church family because she feared they would judge her and even reject her because her son may be HIV positive. So she suffered in silence. My heart hurt for her, and it hurt for the people in the church who are called to love as Jesus loved, but instead chose condemnation.

IN HIS NAME

In Philippians 1:27, Paul urges the believers at the church in Philippi to come together, united in Christ: "You must live in a manner worthy of the Good News about Christ, as citizens of heaven. Then, whether I come and see you again or only hear about you, I will know that you are standing side by side, fighting together for the Good News."

> I used to think that prayer should have the first place and teaching the second. I now feel it would be truer to give prayer the first, second, and third places and teaching the fourth.
>
> **JAMES O. FRASER**

Sometimes we take "live in a manner worthy of the Good News about Christ" to mean that sinners need to "clean up" before they can join us in our congregations. But this means we're expecting non-Christians to act like saved believers. We say, "Come as you are." But do we really mean it? The church is not a place for condemnation. It's a place for Christians to stand together, side by side—a place where grace and love should freely abound.

Thankfully the attitude in the church the woman attended is no longer the norm. There are many Bible-teaching churches across the country that would be a safe place for her to share her heart and get the prayer support she desperately desired. Having a support group within the body of Christ where she could share her concerns for her son, get information about HIV/AIDS, and find out how to best minister to her son would be a great help to her and others like her.

A CUP OF COLD WATER

Creating a support group for people affected by or infected with HIV/AIDS in your church is an important way to provide a safe place for them to share their needs. Don't think that you must have a large amount of people to start a group. Start with a small number of people who want to meet and share. Others may join when they see that your group is a thriving, productive place of grace and love.

> *Over 75% of adults and adolescents living with an AIDS diagnosis are men. These men are sons, brothers, friends, uncles, or coworkers, and their loved ones also need support.*

Saddleback Church in California has created an HIV/AIDS initiative, which can give more information on how to create a support system at your church, as well as other ways to minister to those suffering with HIV/AIDS in your community. The website has many valuable tools and a wealth of information: www.hivandthechurch.com.

Caring for the sick is close to the heart of God. While on earth, Jesus spent nearly one-third of His ministry healing the sick. Having a support group for those suffering with HIV/AIDS and those who love them can reduce the stigma associated with HIV and become a place of emotional healing and physical well-being.

Abba, I pray that my church will be a place where Christians stand united, where relationships are genuine and transparent, and where your love flows freely through us, your children. And let that unity, transparency, and love start with me. As your love flows through me, show me how to open my heart to people who may be suffering with HIV/AIDS as well as to their loved ones who may need a friend with whom they can share their struggles.

48. ORGANIZE A FREE MEDICAL CLINIC FOR YOUR COMMUNITY.

When my son Ian, at the age of fifteen, took a month-long mission trip with Adventures in Missions to Africa, I must admit it was the scariest thing I had experienced as a parent. Just knowing that my husband and I couldn't contact Ian for a solid month as he ministered with other teens on the other side of the world was almost more than my "mother's heart" could endure. But when he came home, and we saw the incredible work that the Lord had done in his life, I knew the trip was worth it. He would never be the same. Ian told story after story of how he'd seen the Holy Spirit work. One such story took place at the public hospital in Manzini.

Today, if we walked into a hospital in a third world country, we might not even realize that's where we were. "Hospitals" in third world countries are often dirty, dim, hot, and crowded, with multiple patients in a room. They look nothing like our clean, efficient, and comfortable hospitals in America. In the third world, overworked nurses and doctors cannot provide the level of care needed for the number of patients they see. It was in this type of hospital where Ian and a few other team members ministered and helped in the children's ward.

On the first day, Ian was drawn to a little boy who was in the hospital with an

> God is in the slums, in the cardboard boxes where the poor play house. God is in the silence of a mother who has infected her child with a virus that will end both their lives. God is in the cries heard under the rubble of war. God is in the debris of wasted opportunity and lives, and God is with us if we are with them.
>
> BONO, LEAD SINGER OF U2

infection in his jaw. His jaw was swollen to twice its normal size on one side of his face. Although he didn't seem to be in too much pain, the little boy was disheartened and bored with his surroundings when the team arrived. In the children's ward, there are no TVs. No games. No stuffed animals. No toys at all. And with constant noise, rest is hard to come by.

Ian knew the boy spoke SiSwati, not English, making communication challenging, so Ian tried to think of a way to entertain the little guy. Then Ian remembered he had a quarter in his pocket. He took out the quarter and spun it on the table. The little boy's eyes lit up! A smile crossed the opposite side of his swollen jaw and suddenly he and Ian were fast friends. When the boy would try to spin the quarter, it would fall to the floor. Ian showed him how to hold the quarter on its edge and flick the quarter to make it spin.

Ian said they spent the entire afternoon smiling, laughing, and spinning that quarter until it was time for the team to leave. With a newfound smile, the boy waved goodbye to Ian and the other team members. Ian told the boy he'd be back the next day so they could play together again. Although they didn't speak the same language, the little boy seemed to understand. They exchanged smiles and Ian left with his team.

The next morning, as the team got ready for another day at the children's ward, Ian made sure he put the quarter in his pocket. He was eager to start a new day of ministry and see his new friend. But when the team arrived, the little boy's bed was made and he was nowhere to be found. Ian was taken aback and assumed that the boy was moved to another bed, or perhaps he had gone home. Ian found an English-speaking nurse, pointed to the boy's empty bed, and asked where he was. Nonchalantly, she said, "Oh, he died last night." Ian was dumbfounded. The words the nurse so casually spoke echoed in his mind all day.

When Ian told me this story, I could see the deep hurt in his face. I think it took some time before Ian realized that God had let this boy's last hours on earth be spent playing with Ian because He knew that the boy needed joy in his life before he died. God placed Ian there in that hospital on just the right day. Ian never even knew the little boy's name. He didn't know the circumstances surrounding his condition. But it didn't matter. Ian and this sick little boy had shared a divine appointment in that hospital that Ian would never forget.

THE STATS

In sub-Saharan Africa, measles takes the life of a child nearly every minute of every day. An effective measles vaccine costs as little as one dollar per child.

About 2.5 million children die every year because they are not immunized.

IN HIS NAME

The majority of the people in the world do not have clean water, adequate food, or proper health care. In many third world countries, hospitals are places where you go to die, not to get well. They can be places of great despair and pain. There is a tremendous need for doctors, nurses, and other medical professionals to care for the sick in these places of our world. Many are dying needlessly—today over thirty thousand people will die from preventable diseases. And in many countries where AIDS abounds, these people are dying alone, afraid, and oftentimes rejected by their own people. They need to know that the healing power of Christ can touch them physically *and* spiritually. But how will they know with no one to tell them?

Third world nations are not the only places where people suffer from poor medical conditions. People in our own communities may suffer from a lack of proper medical care too. Perhaps they cannot afford insurance or have to pay high costs for medicines. Providing a free medical clinic in your community or abroad can be a great help to people who are unable to pay medical bills or are suffering in an area of the world where proper health care is difficult to attain.

A CUP OF COLD WATER

The first step in providing a free health clinic must be prayer. Planning and obtaining necessary equipment and supplies is vital, but first there must be a foundation of prayer—especially for overseas medical clinics where medicines and equipment will be going through customs and security checkpoints.

A full six months before the planned clinic, begin praying with a group. Items to regularly and fervently pray over include the following:

- *Volunteers to join your clinic team, especially doctors, nurses, dentists, and translators (if needed).*
- *Donations of proper medical equipment.*
- *Donations of medicines.*
- *The people who will attend the clinic—for their salvation and their health.*
- *No problems or delays with equipment, medicines, and supplies going through customs and security checkpoints.*
- *Unity among your team of workers—that your team will work together in Christian love for each other and the patients.*

The initial planning for a free medical clinic in your community will be the same for a clinic overseas. At least four months before your clinic, find a place to conduct your clinic. It's imperative for a foreign clinic that you work closely with missionaries in the nation. They will be in charge of finding a place for the clinic, arranging for tents (if needed), and letting the people they minister to know about the clinic. For a clinic in an impoverished area in your community, ask your pastor if your church building can be used or partner with a church that is willing to host the clinic. A community clinic is generally held on one Saturday, whereas a foreign clinic may last for several days.

For medical mission trips or a community clinic, generate interest in volunteering by making announcements at your church and in church bulletins. Health care providers of all types can be utilized in the clinic—doctors, nurses, nurses' aids, dentists, optometrists, pharmacists, pharmacy technicians, dental hygienists, and medical students. You can also contact health care providers in your community to see if they are interested in helping. Laypersons will also be needed for triage, child care, spiritual support, and other nonmedical positions. If you are organizing a clinic for the first time, consider starting small and increasing your clinic size each year as your team of volunteers grows.

> *Medicalmissions.org promotes long- and short-term medical mission trips to countries all over the world. At the site you can search for opportunities to serve by country, specialty, region, or profession.*

Once you have a team of interested medical persons and laypeople, you can plan the medical stations of your clinic. Ideally, a clinic would have at least one station for each aspect of care—eye exams, dental care, general practice, and pharmacy needs, as well as a triage station. If you have enough volunteers, you can also have stations for wellness services such as blood pressure checks and diabetes screenings.

Begin advertising to your community at least one month before your upcoming clinic. You can use flyers, newspaper stories or ads, local radio announcements, or online tools. You can even request a reporter do a segment on your local television station. Contacting public schools to let them know of the event can bring children and families to your clinic that may need medical care.

When the planning for stations is well under way, begin collecting needed supplies. These can be donated by hospitals and medical supply companies, and by laypersons in your church. Donations can include bandages of all shapes and sizes, vitamins, pediatric and adult electrolyte drinks, eyeglasses, topical ointments, and toothbrushes. For a foreign trip, it will be imperative for each member of the team to pack lightly so that supplies can be properly packed and taken overseas in suitcases. If you collect supplies well in advance of your trip, consider shipping some supplies to the missionaries ahead of time.

By the day of your free clinic, each person should know exactly what their job will be and how to do it. This will require regular meetings with your team. I suggest meeting each week during the month leading up to your clinic to assign jobs and sort medicines and supplies. Make sure each person is active in prayer as well, as this is a vital part of the clinic.

With fervent prayer, planning, and organization, a free medical clinic can not only be a blessing to impoverished people, it could save their lives—both physically and spiritually.

Abba, I know people could benefit from a free medical clinic, but I can't plan this alone. Please send me others who have a heart for providing medical care. As we plan, give us favor with the medical community in providing volunteers, equipment, medicines, funds, and prayer support that we will need to make the clinic a true blessing to those who need it.

MINISTERING TO THE PRISONER

"For I was in prison and you came to me."

49. WRITE NOTES OF ENCOURAGEMENT TO INMATES.

We had met only briefly. Dave, a distant relative on my father's side, had come with his wife to visit our family for a few days one summer when I was a teenager. At that time Dave was in his late fifties, and he and his wife traveled all the way from California to spend the week with our family in Georgia. As I recall, their visit was pleasant and uneventful. That's why ten years later I was surprised to learn that Dave was imprisoned in a California state prison. His conviction? Murder.

I was even more surprised when I began to receive letters in the mail from Dave. At first I didn't respond. I wasn't sure what to think of his notes. He never wrote about his conviction or his sentence, but instead about his "job" at the prison library and about his wife and daughter whom he missed so much. After a while, I felt sorry for Dave. He just seemed lonely for a friend. He had also been writing to my grandmother and my father. I suppose when you are alone, corresponding with people on the "outside" can take the edge off loneliness. I decided to write him back.

I'm so glad I did. We corresponded through letters for three years. Dave never forgot a birthday. He made homemade cards for my husband, my son (who was a preschooler at the time), and me. They were

> While women weep, as they do now, I'll fight; while children go hungry, as they do now, I'll fight; while men go to prison, in and out, in and out, as they do now, I'll fight; while there is a drunkard left, while there is a poor lost girl upon the streets, while there remains one dark soul without the light of God, I'll fight; I'll fight to the very end!
>
> **GENERAL WILLIAM BOOTH**

beautifully crafted with pictures that Dave had drawn. In our letters, we talked about everything from family and religion, to classic books and Bible stories.

I came to look forward to Dave's letters in the mail. Sometimes Dave talked about lockdown in the prison after a riot or a fight among prisoners. During those times, no one was allowed in the prison and no one was allowed out. The prisoners were not allowed out of their cells for days at a time. I would read about lockdown and wonder how anyone could stand being imprisoned in a tiny cell with no human interaction. I was glad Dave had paper and a pencil to write to me during those times of heightened security.

Dave wrote one of the last letters I received from him in a hospital room. He told me he had been having chest pains and had been taken to a hospital for care. He did get better, but a few months later the letters stopped coming altogether. I thought perhaps Dave was in the hospital again with no way to correspond with anyone. A few days later, my dad told me a prison chaplain had called him with the news that Dave had died of a heart attack. How sad. Dave died in prison. Alone. No family at his side. No pastor to pray with him. No one to comfort him in his last moments. No one.

IN HIS NAME

What a privilege God gave me for those three years to correspond with Dave. Whether he was guilty or innocent was not for me to decide. I never asked Dave about his murder conviction. It was a subject that both of us avoided. I decided that if he was truly guilty of murder, he had to answer for that, but I was the one who had to answer for whether or not I had used this God-given opportunity to be a friend to someone in prison.

In Matthew 25 when Jesus says, "I was in prison, and you visited me," He doesn't give us, as His followers, the option of deciding to minister to prisoners only if they've pleaded innocent. In my experience with women's prison ministry, some women came to Bible study groups or chapel services out of curiosity. Some even came out of boredom. But as they heard the gospel message, many of them accepted Christ and were changed. More than one prisoner has told me that if it wasn't for their prison sentence, and someone taking the time to minister to them in prison, then they may have never accepted Christ as their Savior.

For the last three years of Dave's life, I had a glimpse into his life as a prisoner. It changed my thinking about people in prison. Prisons are lonely places. And prisoners are often forgotten people. Many of them long for companionship, acceptance, and the love that only Christ can give. Consider sharing Christ's love by taking the time to touch a prisoner's life.

A CUP OF COLD WATER

Many wonderful ministries, such as International Network of Prison Ministries (prisonministry.net/LfW) and Write-Way Prison Ministries (www.writewaypm.org), can put you in touch with a prisoner who wants to correspond. You can also contact a prison in your area, ask for a prison chaplain, and speak to him or her about how to write to an inmate. At www.writeaprisoner.com, you can search for a prisoner pen pal through a state or federal search engine. At www.prisoneralert.com, you can click on "Write an encouraging letter" to reach a prisoner in a foreign country who is incarcerated due to his or her stand for Christ.

> *Visit www.bgcprisonministries.com to view several ways to help incarcerated men and women or their families.*

Here are some simple guidelines to follow when writing a prisoner:

- *Keep the focus of your letters on spiritual things.*
- *Men should write to men, women should write to women.*
- *Refrain from any correspondence about court cases, convictions, or other legal issues.*
- *Do not contact anyone on behalf of an inmate.*
- *Use a post office box as your return address—never your physical personal or business address.*

Your note of encouragement may be the only "Jesus" an inmate has ever experienced.

I have to admit, Abba, that prisoners are not people I often think of ministering to. Yet you tell us to remember them and visit them. Help me to remember that I, too, was a prisoner before I accepted your forgiveness. While my chains were not physical, I was still held captive and bound by my sin. Give me compassion for prisoners, Abba. Use me to speak encouragement into their lives.

50. PARTICIPATE IN ANGEL TREE.

When I was in elementary school, there was a girl in my grade that everyone knew. Being in a small school, we all played well together at recess and PE—all except this little girl. Her name was Marcie. Oh, it wasn't that we didn't want to play with Marcie. She was always invited into our games of jump rope and kickball, but Marcie would never play with us. She just kept to herself. I'm not sure I ever heard her say more than five words during our elementary years together.

> The poorest of the poor are those who feel that they are unloved.
>
> **MOTHER TERESA**

But being quiet wasn't the only unusual thing about Marcie. Every day of the year, Marcie wore a heavy brown coat that hung down to her knees. Even when it was hot outside, Marcie wore her coat. When the PE teacher had us run two miles, Marcie wore her coat. Even on the best day of the school year, Field Day, she wore her coat. Her long, unkempt black hair was always tucked inside the fuzzy matted collar of that coat.

I'll never forget one day at recess when our teacher had had enough. It was a hot spring day toward the end of the school year, and I suppose the teacher knew Marcie was sweltering in that long coat. She told some of us girls to chase Marcie on the playground, catch her, and force her to take off her winter coat. Wanting to be obedient to our teacher, the girls of our class planned our teacher-directed attack. Then, with a force that would scare any shy kid, we launched a full-blown, all-out chasing attack on Marcie. It felt wrong, but my best friend and I went along with the other girls anyway.

Before long, we cornered Marcie near the jungle gym. My friend and I stood at the back of the pack, breathless from running. The girls taunted Marcie and tore at her old brown coat. Marcie was in tears. I couldn't stand the injustice anymore, and as I was about to step between Marcie and her pursuers, my best friend beat me to it. She ripped through the crowd of girls, stood in front of Marcie, and screamed, "LEAVE HER ALONE!"

With that, the girls stepped away one by one. My friend put her arm around a sobbing little Marcie and we both tried to comfort her. But Marcie just jerked away and ran to be alone near the playground fence. I couldn't understand what could possibly make Marcie so sad that she couldn't accept friendship from anyone.

Years later, I learned that Marcie had a very bad home life. All through our elementary years, Marcie's mother had been in prison. She and her brothers lived with their uncle in a rundown house. Knowing what I know now, Marcie was likely being abused by an older brother, who later got into much trouble with the school system and the law. As I look back, it was no wonder poor Marcie seemed strange to us. She was living in an abusive home with no mother to protect her.

There are millions of children just like Marcie who have one or more parents incarcerated. But unlike Marcie's situation from thirty years ago, there are now thriving prison ministries that not only help the incarcerated parent, but also minister to the children who feel the weight of heavy shame associated with having a parent in prison.

IN HIS NAME

Many times prison ministries focus on the prisoner. And that is a wonderful thing! I know four people who turned their lives

THE STATS

Among the men held in prisons, 55% report having minor children.

An estimated 80,000 incarcerated women are mothers to approximately 200,000 minors.

around for Christ within the walls of a prison as a direct result of a Christian prison ministry. Praise God! But I'm also thankful for those prison ministries that focus on the children and other family members of incarcerated persons. When little ones hurt, they often don't know what to do with their feelings of rejection, shame, and guilt. They may withdraw and stop being social like Marcie or they may act out with violence, substance abuse, or bullying.

Focusing on the emotional and spiritual care of these children is a vitally important part of their healing. Children of incarcerated adults oftentimes feel embarrassed, angry, and ashamed because of their parents' situation. Teaching these children to forgive can give them the spiritual tools they need to grow in their faith and fulfill the purposes God has for their lives.

I have never met a parent who wanted his or her child to fail. For incarcerated parents, breaking the cycle of dysfunction in their families is a powerful gift.

A CUP OF COLD WATER

When adults are incarcerated, their families suffer—especially their children. In the United States an estimated 1.7 million children have a parent in prison. Angel Tree is a ministry that focuses on the physical, emotional, and spiritual needs of family members of prisoners. At Christmastime, Angel Tree invites organizations to hang paper angels on Christmas trees. The paper angels display the first names of children who have an incarcerated parent. Under the names are written items that the children may want or need for Christmas. Individuals take a paper angel from the Angel Tree, purchase the gift, and give that gift in the name of the imprisoned parent. Trees can be displayed in stores, at workplaces, or in your church.

> *During the year, when you find toys on clearance,*
> *consider purchasing one or two for Angel Tree.*

If you can't find an Angel Tree in your area, consider signing up your church to be an official "Angel Tree Church." This is an easy project for churches, whether small or large. The Angel Tree website details the process. First, complete a registration form online to become your church's point of contact, or Angel Tree coordinator. Sometime in the fall, Angel Tree coordinators receive the names of children who were signed up by their mom or dad in prison. Then coordinators display the name tags and gift suggestions in their church. Church members participate by purchasing, wrapping, and delivering a gift for each child on behalf on his or her incarcerated parent—and in the process, share the gospel.

The Angel Tree ministry works year-round to establish relationships in order to share Christ. One of their primary goals is family restoration. The Angel Tree website has information and links to the various programs that have been created as a response to the outpouring of gifts from the original Angel Tree Christmas ministry. Programs include InnerChange Freedom Initiative, Justice Freedom, Operation Starting Line, and Out4Life.

Visit AngelTree.org to find out how you and your church can bring this unique, multifaceted prison ministry to your community. Through the ministry, churches can show the love of Christ to the children of inmates who so often feel the weight of embarrassment, rejection, and abandonment while their mom or dad is imprisoned.

Abba, buying a Christmas gift in the name of an incarcerated person for his or her child is such an easy way for me to share your love with a prisoner. Take the small gift I buy and use it to begin the healing of a parent-child relationship.

51. PURCHASE HANDMADE JEWELRY FROM WOMEN RESCUED FROM HUMAN TRAFFICKING.

My friend Bret once told me about a time he went for a walk. It was a cool spring evening and the sun was beginning to set over the trees. Bret had walked nearly a mile past several houses in a nice neighborhood not far from his home when he heard something strange in the distance. At first he thought it might be a bird, but as he continued to walk, the sounds got louder. It wasn't a bird, but music. Beautiful, soothing music. But he couldn't figure out where it was coming from.

As Bret followed the sound of the sweet melody, he was taken aback when he finally found the source of the music. It was coming from a large bag of trash on the side of the road. He stood over the heap of trash and could hardly believe the lovely music that was playing from inside the trash bag. It was the most unlikely place to hear a beautiful sound—the trash.

> I have come to believe that the one thing people cannot bear is a sense of injustice. Poverty, cold, even hunger, are more bearable than injustice.
>
> **MILLICENT FENWICK**

I thought about Bret's discovery last week when I heard the testimony of a woman who had been helped at the Dream Center in California (dreamcenter.org). She had been imprisoned in an upper-class neighborhood by a pimp who had bought her from the woman's father when she was young. This pimp brainwashed her by putting her in a dark box in the basement of a house and made her a

CUP OF COLD WATER

victim of human sex trafficking. Now rescued from that tortured life, she found emotional healing and physical safety at the Dream Center.

In her testimony, she spoke of how she had always felt like a piece of property. Her "owner" had brainwashed her into feeling like she was just someone's discarded trash. But like the music that my friend Bret heard sweetly emanating from that bag of trash, something beautiful is coming from this woman's horrific situation. This precious woman's life is being restored. Much healing still needs to take place in her life, but deep inside her spirit, past the "trash" of the scars, the torture, and the abuse, sweet music is beginning to play because Jesus Christ infiltrated the deep crevices of her heart and gave her hope.

IN HIS NAME

THE STATS

There are 27 million people worldwide in modern-day slavery.

Every year one million children are exploited by the global commercial sex trade.

Thirty-two billion dollars are generated yearly by the human trafficking industry.

Each year, an estimated 800,000 people are trafficked internationally across borders, and an estimated 27 million people are enslaved worldwide. Of the millions of people forced into human trafficking, 80 percent are women and children. Many times, young women are lured into trafficking with the promise of a better life. Once they are taken, they are either forced to become prostitutes or to work as slaves.

Having lived much of my life in Georgia, I was shocked to learn that the major hub for human trafficking in the United States is Atlanta. Media Freedom International reports that many forced prostitutes—young women and even children—are housed in businesses such as spas, hair or nail salons, and massage parlors, and some may be housed in single-family dwellings in order to avoid suspicion. Change.org reports that approximately 500 girls are trafficked through Atlanta each month for sex, servicing 7,200 men. And according to the Atlanta Human Trafficking Project, instead of traveling to Thailand or another foreign country to have sex with a child, men are traveling to Atlanta. They are picked up by a pimp at the Hartsfield International Airport, taken to an undisclosed location where a child sex slave is held, and afterward taken back to the airport to travel home to their families—all in the same night.

The deep pain and emotional scars that women have from abuse, brainwashing, and abandonment can be healed only by Christ. He is the only one who can heal hurts that deep and scars that seemingly permanent. Fortunately He is in the restoration business. His specialty is taking "hurt" and turning it into "hope." We are reminded in Hebrews 13:5 that God has said, "I will never fail you. I will never forsake you" (see also Deuteronomy 31:6; 1 Chronicles 28:20). The word *forsake* means "to give up on." God will not give up on those He loves. His healing is real. His redemption is always sufficient. And His restoration is far-reaching.

Supporting Christian organizations and ministries that rescue these precious women and teach them that God will never fail them or forsake them is a worthy calling. With a 32 billion dollar profit each year and millions enslaved, human trafficking is an issue that the church cannot ignore.

A CUP OF COLD WATER

Manipulation, brainwashing, abuse, and drugs are common in the world of human trafficking. But many ministries are working to free women and children from this horrible life. Several of them promote the sale of jewelry made by these rescued women who have learned a new trade of creating beautiful rings, necklaces, earrings, and bracelets.

> **Visit humantrafficking.org for more information on human slavery and trafficking.**

I can't think of a lovelier item to proudly wear or give than a piece of jewelry made by a woman who has been rescued and redeemed from a life of slavery. Here are some of the ministries that work to free women and children from human trafficking through selling homemade goods:

- Hope Jewelry: *hopejewelry.org*
- Made by Survivors: *www.madebysurvivors.com*
- Nomi Network: *www.buyherbagnotherbody.com*
- Trade Justice Mission: *okoajewelry.org*
- U Count Campaign: *www.ucountcampaign.org* (click "Shop")

By purchasing products made by women rescued from human trafficking, you give them the dignity of earning money through a new trade and empower them to live a new life full of hope.

The horror of human trafficking and child sex exploitation is almost more than I can wrap my mind around, Abba. The problem seems so huge, so enormous, so out of control. It doesn't seem like anything I do will make a dent in the problem. But you call me to help "one," Abba. Helping just one person to escape human trafficking by buying a necklace is something I can do. Keep reminding me, Abba, that by helping just "one," I'm serving you.

52. PRAY FOR FOSTER CHILDREN BY NAME.

All over the church you could hear the murmur of prayers being offered up to God. That holy hush you hear when a congregation of God's people gathers in small groups to pray aloud is like a beautiful symphony. That night, some groups were praying on their knees, others were bowing their heads, but all of them were praying aloud for children by name. And not just any children—they were lifting to heaven the names of children in state foster care.

The orphan ministry at the church had made hundreds of leather bracelets with lettered beads. Each beaded bracelet bore the name of a child who was in state care. Statistically, we knew some of the children had been physically or sexually abused. Some had severe medical issues. Some were orphaned. All of them had experienced abandonment, neglect, loneliness, and heartbreak. They were now trapped in the foster care system.

That night, perhaps for the first time in their young lives, those children were being lifted before the throne of the Living God. We prayed that God's love would permeate every part of their lives. We prayed that angels would surround them with divine protection. Prayers were offered up for godly influences in their lives. We prayed for the children's teachers and coaches to have patience, wisdom, and sympathy. We also prayed for foster parents to share unconditional love and discipline with wisdom. It was a glorious night of

> No one has yet fully realized the wealth of sympathy, kindness, and generosity hidden in the soul of a child. The effort of every true education should be to unlock that treasure.
>
> **EMMA GOLDMAN**

intercession where prayers for stability, love, and healing in the lives of these precious ones were taken before the Lord.

I still remember the name on my bracelet—Ebony. I wore the bracelet for two weeks and prayed for her every day. I still pray for her each time the Lord brings her to mind. That special bracelet now sits in my jewelry box. Each time I see it, I'm reminded to pray for Ebony and all the children in state care. If we don't pray for them, who will?

IN HIS NAME

Foster care can be a lonely place. Some foster children have been moved from home to home and have never learned to trust or deeply love anyone. Some of them have experienced sexual and physical abuse too horrible to write in this book. Their hurts are deep and Satan wants them to think they are lost forever, that no one cares for them, that they are worthless, that their lives don't have purpose. But their lives do have purpose and meaning.

It seems like such an injustice for children to grow up apart from a loving family, yet God has a plan for each child in foster care. Their lives are of infinite worth to the Lord. For foster children who have been taken from their homes, abused, abandoned, beaten down, discouraged, mistreated, neglected, and frightened, it is so important that we pray that their hearts will be tender toward God. When we pray for them by name, we advocate for them, asking God to break the bonds of injustice. Psalm 68:6 reminds us that "God places the lonely in families; he sets the prisoners free and gives them joy." As we pray, the Lord hears every prayer and He will answer (Psalm 6:9).

A CUP OF COLD WATER

Foster children desperately need our prayers. All of them have had a hard life and through no fault of their own, they have experienced horrific heartache. Lifting their names to God is a great privilege. Encouraging others to pray for children in foster care by name is a worthwhile project.

The names of foster children in your state can be found at www.adoptuskids.org. Click on "Meet the Children," and then check your home state. Leave all other search categories blank to see the names of children who are available for adoption through the foster care system. If you would like to pray for the children in foster care in your county, you can call your local Department of Children's Services for a list. Last names are not available for the protection of the children.

> *Prayer changes lives. When you pray for a child in foster care,*
> *your prayers may be the catalyst that brings them to faith in the Lord.*

We made bracelets using small, letter-stamped plastic beads and thin leather cord that comes on spools. Both of these materials can be purchased at a craft store or online. To make the bracelets, cut the leather cord into twelve-inch strips. Use the beads to spell the name of a child and slide the beads onto the leather cord. Then thread both ends of the cord through a clear bead. Tie a knot on both ends of the cord. This will hold the beads in place and allow the bracelet to slide open easily to fit various wrist sizes.

It takes quite a while to make the bead bracelets for a large group. You may want to have a "bracelet making party" or put the materials in small bags for people to work on at home. If everyone pitches in, the bracelets can be made in a few days.

The bracelets can be given out to an entire church, an orphan ministry, an adult or children's Sunday school class, a Bible study group, or the attendees of a special event such as a women's or men's retreat. Ask each person to pray for the child and to wear the bracelet to remind them to pray. At my church, we attached small cards to the bracelets that say, "Please pray for the child whose name is on this bracelet. Pray that they will be adopted twice—once by a family and once by God. 'God places the lonely in families' (Psalm 68:6)."

These bracelets are a simple way to remind people to pray regularly for a desperately needy child who might otherwise never be lifted to the Lord.

Abba, you know that when I pray for a child in foster care by name, I may be the only person praying for a child you value so highly. Praying isn't glamorous. It's not in public view. No one else will ever know. It's a silent partnership for a child in crisis—a partnership between you and me to bring a precious child into safety, salvation, restoration, and healing.

53. PRAY FOR ORPHANS THROUGH-OUT THEIR ADOPTION PROCESS.

When Renee Swope and her husband began praying about adoption from Ethiopia, they were not planning on adopting an infant. In fact, because they already had two biological boys, ages eleven and fourteen, they were convinced that God wanted them to adopt two little girls between the ages of four and eight. Starting over again with a small infant wasn't even on their radar screen! But God had other plans.

Little baby Aster entered an Ethiopian orphanage malnourished and weak. As she received care and proper nutrition at the orphanage, her frail body grew stronger by the day. By the time Renee and her husband were matched with Aster a few weeks later, she had gained much needed weight and was a thriving and active little eight-month-old baby. Two months after their match, Renee and her husband got the call they had been waiting for—Aster was officially their daughter! They would soon board a plane to Ethiopia to bring her home. This is an excerpt from Renee's blog the day they found out Aster was theirs:

> God wants to equip us with a vision that sees higher, deeper, and broader than our physical realities.
>
> BETH MOORE

Aster is officially OUR LITTLE GIRL!

Yesterday we spent the whole day on the beach, enjoying the moment we were in and trusting God for all that He was accomplishing far, far away in Africa. Since Ethiopia is seven hours ahead of us, by the time we went to the beach it was the end of the day in Addis. During our picnic lunch we got the call! Susan from Adoption Advocates International called to tell us that Aster's adoption paperwork was approved yesterday in court. She is ours!

How sweet of God to have brought us to this place—not only spiritually but physically. That we were together on a beach where we have made so many family memories was the perfect setting! We will never forget the day, the time, and the place our lives changed forever. And there will be one more family memory when we travel to get her.

> **THE STATS**
>
> Ethiopia has one of the largest populations of orphans in the world: 13% of children throughout the country are missing one or both parents.
>
> Ethiopia has seen a steady increase in the number of children becoming orphaned because of parents dying of AIDS.

The day Aster arrived at the orphanage she was six months old and weighed only eight pounds. She was so thin, lethargic, and very malnourished. We saw this frail child as evidence of a loving mother who couldn't bear to see her baby die. I can only imagine her sorrow as she searched for help and sacrificially found for her baby the love and care she needed, that she as a mother could not provide.

Thank you, friends, for your prayers and your part in our little miracle. And thank you, my sweet Jesus, for your favor and grace. I am humbled by all that you have done, are doing, and will do!

Aster's homecoming a few weeks later was truly a glorious arrival! She is now thriving in her new family. To see an orphaned child enter a forever family is a wonder that never ceases to amaze me. Praying for children throughout the adoption process and transition into their new home is a special privilege that is dear to my heart. If you would like to read more about Renee's adoption journey, visit www.reneeswope.com.

IN HIS NAME

When we adopted our daughter Grace from Haiti, hundreds of Christians, some I had never met, prayed for us as we walked through the process to bring her home. After nearly two years of waiting, there were days I didn't think I could go through with it. I was ready to give up. But any time I got to that point, it never failed—someone would tell me that they were praying for me. A dear friend, Michele, was the first person I told about our plan to adopt and she prayed us through the entire two-year process. So many others wrote e-mails, called on the phone, and sent cards just to tell us they were praying.

When we finally brought Grace home, the entire church felt as though they had adopted her! They had all prayed with us nearly every step of the way. Our daughter had been loved through prayer before she ever stepped foot on American soil! What a gift my church family gave me just by praying. Isaiah 65:24 reminds us of how God hears and answers our prayers, "I will answer them before they even call to me. While they are still talking about their needs, I will go ahead and answer their prayers!"

A CUP OF COLD WATER

Because I've walked the adoption path myself, I consider it an honor to lift up other families in prayer as they travel their adoption journeys. I get e-mails and Facebook messages almost weekly from people who want more information on how to adopt. They have heard the call from God to adopt an orphan and now they need to know how to get started. I've had the privilege of praying for many of them from the beginning of their adoption journeys to the day they bring their little ones home. It's my great joy to pray them through the process.

> *If you know a couple who is adopting, send them a card to let them know you've been praying for their child's transition into their forever family.*

But what if we reverse that prayer process and also pray for the orphans who need families? What if we pray for a child by name that waits in an orphanage? To pray over a child's picture, asking God to send him or her a forever family, lets us participate in the adoption process, even if we don't adopt a child ourselves.

When a child comes into the care of an orphanage, children's home, or foster care system, often you can pray for him or her by name. Visit www .precious.org to view photos and descriptions of children around the world in need of homes. A great way to care for these precious little ones is to pray for them to be adopted into a Christian home. What a joy it will be to pray for a child to have a forever family, and then see those prayers answered as God leads a Christian family to adopt him or her. It's a thrilling experience to realize that a waiting child's profile has been removed because the child has found a forever family!

This is a great project for your children as well. As a family, you can pray for these precious orphans throughout the adoption process. Some specific things you can pray as you hold an orphan's picture:

- *Pray that they will grow physically healthy as they wait for their forever family. Many of them are severely malnourished.*
- *Pray for the family who will adopt them. Adoption can be an emotional roller coaster.*
- *Pray that all paperwork will be done efficiently and quickly so that they can be united with a family soon.*
- *Pray that they will never feel the effects of their abandonment.*
- *Pray that they will always find their identity in Christ and that they will never question their life's purpose.*

All praise to the Father of the fatherless who answers our prayers on behalf of orphaned children around the world!

Abba, you are the Father to every fatherless child, and you know each child by name. What a privilege to pray for these precious children as they await a forever family. You promise us in your Word that you hear our prayers and know our needs before we even lift up our prayers to your throne. These children need homes, Abba. Provide a Christian home for each of them so they can grow and thrive in the plans you have for them.

54. TEACH LITERACY TO THOSE WHO CANNOT READ OR ARE LEARNING ENGLISH AS A SECOND LANGUAGE.

When Ben was a young boy in the 1930s, his parents worked their family farm in northern Alabama. Back then, sons were expected to help with the farm when they were old enough. Typically the boys of that time would go to school for three or four years, enough to learn the basics of the "3 Rs" (reading, 'riting, and 'rithmetic), and then they would quit school to learn how to farm.

This was what happened to Ben and his brothers. Ben finished a few grades of schooling, and then came home to join his father on the farm. Ben had never been much for school anyway, and although he was pretty good with numbers, he had struggled with reading and writing. As time went by, Ben married and started a family of his own. He still farmed the family land, but as the American economy changed, making a living by farming was becoming harder and harder. Ben found a good job in a manufacturing plant in Chattanooga an hour's drive away. He worked at the plant during the week and on his farm in the evenings and on Saturdays.

> Make sure your life writes a story worth reading. Your story starts with God.
>
> **PRISCILLA SHIRER**

For many years Ben made the hour-long drive to Chattanooga for work. His bosses took notice of his great work in the plant and eventually promoted him to a position of training and overseeing other factory workers. Although Ben still couldn't read or write well, he managed to keep this a secret. Whenever he needed to fill out papers or read inventory notices, he took them home to his wife, who would read them for him. But one day, Ben's supervisor requested that he write down the training steps for workers under his supervision and Ben froze. He knew he couldn't read well enough or write well enough to fulfill this request.

That was the day Ben felt he had no choice. Rather than face the embarrassment of admitting his illiteracy, he took an early retirement. His family and friends thought the early retirement was a great idea so he could focus more on the farm. But they didn't know the truth of why Ben cut his work short at the plant. From that day on, Ben made sure his children knew the value of a good education. It was quite a day when his grandson, Duane, became the first person in Ben's family to graduate from college.

I remember that day well—I was standing beside Duane, my husband of six months, when he received his engineering degree.

THE STATS

On average, adults at the lowest levels of literacy:

are almost ten times more likely to be living below the poverty line

are more than three times as likely to receive food stamps

work only 18–19 weeks per year

IN HIS NAME

English is considered the language of business in the corporate world. Being proficient in reading and writing the English language is imperative for anyone wanting to succeed in their job. In the United States, 14 percent of the population doesn't read well enough to fill out a job application. Illiteracy keeps them, as one man who learned to read as an adult expressed, "locked up in the world." Learning to read and write well will free them from the bondage illiteracy creates in their lives.

God said in Isaiah 58:6, "The kind of fasting I want calls you to free those who are wrongly imprisoned." Teaching someone to read may seem like a small task to you and me, but to someone who is suffering with illiteracy, learning to read will release them from chains of bondage and set them free from daily oppression.

A CUP OF COLD WATER

Illiteracy affects people right here in the United States. This problem seems to be an issue for many older adults who, like Ben, simply never finished their schooling. So many times illiteracy hinders them in job and even social situations. Often people who suffer from illiteracy are too embarrassed to tell anyone or to get help to better their reading skills. Others such as immigrants, migrant workers, and their children, whose primary language is not English, are also affected.

> *You don't need a teaching certificate to teach someone to read. You just need a caring heart, a patient spirit, and a determination to help someone better his or her life.*

There are many ways to volunteer with literacy efforts. Hundreds of literacy organizations around the United States are in great need of volunteers to tutor adults in reading and writing, to answer questions on "literacy hotlines," to administer GED practice tests, to help with computer instruction, and to provide child care during adult classes. You will likely need to attend literacy training with the organization where you would like to volunteer.

Below is a list of literacy organizations. Many of them have chapters in multiple cities and some of them focus on teaching English as a second language. Some of them even teach literacy in impoverished nations, and you can volunteer to take a mission trip.

- Literacy Connections: *www.literacyconnections.com*
- Literacy Information and Communication System: *www.literacydirectory.org*
- Literacy Partners: *www.literacypartners.org/volunteers*
- Mondo Challenge (based in the UK): *www.mondochallenge.co.uk* (click "Volunteer Teaching")
- ProLiteracy: *literacyvolunteers.org*
- ProLiteracyEducation Network: *www.proliteracyednet.org*
- Wonderopolis: *www.wonderopolis.org*

Another avenue to explore is your public library. Many libraries provide literacy training and tutoring.

Adult illiteracy binds so many men and women. By volunteering with literacy organizations, you will help release those who need to learn to read and write proficiently.

Abba, wherever I look during the day, I see words—on billboards, street signs, documents, and books. It's hard to imagine being locked inside a world of illiteracy, yet so many people are. Guide me, Abba, as I volunteer to help someone learn to read and free that person from illiteracy.

55. PAINT OR DECORATE AN EMERGENCY FOSTER CARE PLACEMENT ROOM.

Many years ago when my husband and I took adoption classes through our local Department of Children's Services, our class met in a building that housed the offices of many social services in our county. These services included food stamps and Medicaid as well as foster care and adoption. The building was old with dull beige colored walls, mazelike hallways, and heavy steel doors. The dimly lit waiting room had outdated magazines and a walk-up window with thick glass separating the people in the waiting room from the workers in the back. Honestly, it reminded me of a prison office! All it needed were security checkpoints!

Each week, Duane and I arrived with the other couples who were taking the class. We had to wait in the lobby until we could be escorted to our classroom, which was at the end of a maze of offices. During one of the classes, the instructor took us on a quick tour of the facilities. She showed us a tiny room that was used as a temporary holding place for children taken from their homes in emergency situations until foster placement could be made. The room had beige walls like the rest of the building, a small desk and chair with a telephone, a little box of old toys, and a tiny cot for the child to rest.

> The real test of a saint is not one's willingness to preach the gospel, but one's willingness to do something like washing the disciples' feet—that is, being willing to do those things that seem unimportant in human estimation but count as everything to God.
>
> **OSWALD CHAMBERS**

LORIE NEWMAN

I tried to imagine what it would have been like for the hundreds of kids who had come through that room. How scared they must have been when the authorities came to their home and took them away from the only situation they had ever known. Even if these children have been abused or neglected, they are still forced to leave their toys, their clothes, their bed, and their pets. Then a stranger takes them to a dimly lit office building and through a maze of hallways with heavy steel doors and dull beige walls. Finally the child arrives in the emergency placement room while the social worker tries to find a foster home for them. What a scary situation for any child.

Many times social workers do the best they can with limited resources. With budget cuts, long hours, and little pay, I truly think social workers have one of the hardest jobs on the planet! They endure an immense workload and emotional stress and fatigue from having to work with abused children daily. I have such respect for what they do. One way to support your community's social workers and the children they serve is to turn a bare emergency foster care room into a small "kid's haven" with colorful walls, baskets of toys, and pictures or artwork that will comfort foster children awaiting emergency placement.

IN HIS NAME

When I think about a prisoner, I think of iron bars, heavy shackles, and jail cells. I certainly don't think of children in foster care. Yet, for so many children, they are in a place of captivity that they didn't ask for, a place they didn't choose, and a place they certainly don't deserve. Through no fault of their own, they are captive—they are wards of the state, taken from the only life they've ever known.

Although making the emergency foster care room a bright and inviting place will not make everything better for little ones, it may take away some of their fears. We help these children because we want them to experience our God who allows us to "go to bed without fear," to "lie down and sleep soundly" (Proverbs 3:24). When you take the time to spruce up an emergency foster placement room, with every stroke of paint you put on the walls, with every storybook you place on the shelf, and with every small toy you put into a toy basket, you can know that you will help to calm the fears of a child who is entering protective custody and also entering a world of new fears and anxieties.

A CUP OF COLD WATER

Nearly every county, whether large or small, has some type of social services department that works directly with foster children. They will likely welcome any work you are willing to donate. Contact your local office and ask if you can spruce up their emergency foster care placement room. It should take only one day to complete the room if you plan ahead of time, especially if you recruit a team of helpers.

> *To establish relationships with social workers, consider taking breakfast or lunch to the workers on a quarterly or monthly basis. Always leave a note with your meal telling the workers that you are praying for them.*

The walls of the room will likely need to be painted. A cool color such as light blue or light green will work best, as colors like bright yellows, reds, and oranges are not soothing colors for children. Hang colorful pictures on the wall or, better yet, if you know an artist, have him or her paint a mural on the walls of the room.

Toys serve as a distraction for children, so place a few nice baskets of new toys in the room. A basket of reading books will also be appropriate, as well as a basket of art supplies such as drawing paper, crayons, colored pencils, coloring books, markers, and modeling clay. Consider adding a bookshelf to the room or installing low shelves on which the baskets can rest.

This is a small project for a group to take on, but it will have a great impact on hundreds of children in your community who are in crisis situations. It will also serve to build a much needed bridge between social workers and the Christian community, letting workers know that Christians care about them and the children they serve. Partnering with social workers, even in small ways, will speak volumes about how the church cares for the "least of these."

Abba, the picture of a prisoner in my mind looks nothing like a child in foster care. Yet these precious children are in captivity, even if their prison doesn't have four walls. As I prepare to decorate an emergency foster care placement room, I pray that my efforts will build bridges between the Christian community and the social workers in my community. I also pray that every child who passes through the newly decorated room will experience calming peace instead of fear and anxiety.

56. PLAN A REGULAR CHURCH SERVICE FOR AN ASSISTED-LIVING FACILITY.

Have you ever thought you had been in the presence of an angel? There have been a few times in my life where I wondered if I had just encountered a real angel. But has anyone ever thought *you* were the angel? It happened to me and my friend Michelle when we were teenagers. It was Christmastime and we wanted to do something nice for the people who lived in an assisted-living home downtown. So we bought some supplies to make little candy cane reindeer. We spent one Saturday morning bending bright green pipe cleaners into antlers and gluing tiny wiggly reindeer eyes and red pom-pom noses to oversized candy canes. They turned out so cute!

That afternoon we took our cute reindeer candy canes to the assisted-living home and knocked on a few dozen doors. Each time the door opened, we offered a candy cane treat and said "Merry Christmas!" I've never seen such smiles! So many of those elderly men and women were thrilled to see us and loved the treats we brought them. But one woman in particular cried—literally cried—at our gesture of kindness. She called us both angels as she wiped her tears. My heart broke. I was only fourteen years old, but I knew it wasn't the candy cane that brought tears to her eyes. It was the fact that someone broke the silence of her day and cared enough to enter her lonely world.

> If you want to have the mind of Christ, you must see yourself as his servant on earth.
>
> **CHARLES STANLEY**

LORIE NEWMAN

Since that day, whenever I am able, I take advantage of opportunities to visit assisted-living homes. Just last month, my daughter's dance teacher organized a dance recital for the residents of a nursing home. It blessed me as much as it blessed the residents.

Many churches provide CDs and DVDs of their worship services to the residents of assisted-living homes, but why not bring a small worship service to the home instead? These worship services can be a blessing to men and women who can no longer attend church due to declining health.

IN HIS NAME

So many people are faced with the decision to put a relative in an assisted-living home, and making the decision is never easy. Nearly every week on the prayer list for my Bible study group is a new couple asking for prayer as they move a parent into an assisted-living or nursing home. It's not only a difficult decision for the adult children, but also a difficult transition for the elderly parent. Many of them know they need the care a home can provide, but it's difficult for them to move from independence to dependence on their caregivers.

Making sure that the residents of these facilities and those considered "shut-ins" are spiritually ministered to is very important. Although many of the residents are frail in health, they can still enjoy the music, the teaching, and especially the fellowship that a regular church service provides. Hebrews 10:25 reminds us of how important it is to meet together regularly as God's family: "Let us not neglect our meeting together, as some people do, but encourage one another, especially now that the day of his return is drawing near." For elderly persons who are no longer able to corporately worship with a church family, consider the blessing that will ensue if you create a worship experience for them right where they live.

A CUP OF COLD WATER

When planning a worship service for an assisted-living facility, you will need to take into account several considerations.

How often can you facilitate the service? Every week? Once a month? Once a quarter? This will depend on what the facility allows and what your volunteers can manage. Volunteers can sign up to help on a rotating basis, but there should always be one or two "core members" to organize each service.

What musical instruments will be used? Check to see if the facility has a piano and be sure to reserve it. If there are no instruments at the facility, bring a guitar or other instrument that can be easily transported. Remember that most older people enjoy hymns, so have hymns in the mix of your song choices.

When will the service take place? This will depend on the home's schedule, but the service may be more meaningful to the residents if done on a Sunday morning.

Is there a room at the facility that will easily accommodate a small group of worshipers? Reserve this room ahead of time and make sure there is a place large enough in the front for the leaders to stand.

THE STATS

There are approximately 1.5 million residents in nursing homes across the United States.

The average length of time residents receive care in a nursing facility is 835 days.

Are there enough volunteers for each part of the service? Volunteers may lead the music, share a special short message, or distribute communion elements for residents who choose to participate.

> ***You don't have to be a pastor, worship leader, or church staff member to facilitate a worship service at an assisted-living home.***

Having a corporate worship service for those who are no longer able to attend their home church will be a blessing to them, to their families, and to the Lord, who inhabits the praises of His people (Psalm 22:3).

So many sweet, godly men and women now live in assisted-living homes, Abba. Even from my very own church, people who used to be active in our congregation now don't have the mobility to continue attending church. As I plan a worship service for them, help me to remember that they are still valuable members of your family. As I choose and plan the aspects of the service, guide me in wisdom toward the music and messages that will uplift their spirits.

57. START AN ORPHAN MINISTRY AT YOUR CHURCH.

The morning we left the orphanage in the mountains of Petionville, Haiti, the air was cool and crisp. Fog had settled on the two-story toddler house where we had been staying with our new adopted daughter, Grace. It was January 2004, exactly two years since we started the process to bring her home. When we had first seen her picture, she had been just one year old. Now she was three, and we were absolutely in love with her, even though we had met her face-to-face a mere two days before at the United States consulate in Port-au-Prince. It was hard to believe we were finally going home with our new daughter.

When the Haitian driver arrived to take us to the airport, the little children from the toddler house came out on the porch to say goodbye to Grace. They all wore their pajamas and some of them trembled in the cool morning air. I had to laugh as one of the smallest boy's teeth began to chatter in the early morning cold. I tried to take pictures, but the fog made it impossible to get good shots of the crowd of precious orphans that had gathered on the front porch. After we said our goodbyes, my husband and I piled into an old SUV with our new little girl.

> There are three stages in the work of God: impossible; difficult; done.
>
> **J. HUDSON TAYLOR**

As I got settled with Grace beside me, she did something that took me by surprise. She climbed up on the back of the seat and put her tiny hands on the back window to look outside. After a long look at her friends on the porch, she waved goodbye to the only family she'd ever known. My heart broke. It wasn't Grace's gesture that hurt my heart so deeply. It was the looks on the faces of the orphans left behind that cut me to my core. Their brown eyes seemed to say, *When will it be my turn? When will my Mommy and Daddy come to take me home? When will someone call me "baby" and give me a forever family?*

I wept as I watched the faces of those little ones fade away in the distance. For weeks afterward, their faces were at the forefront of my mind. I began to ask the Lord what He would have me do. There had to be *something* I could do to be a voice for those children and other orphans like them around the world, but I was unsure of where to start.

I prayed for several weeks before it became clear that there *was* something I could do, and I needed to start right where I was—in my very own church. With the help of many prayerful church members who also had a heart for the orphaned, within one year our church had a thriving ministry for orphans.

THE STATS

According to 2009 UNICEF statistics, there are an estimated

340,000 orphans in Liberia, West Africa

150,000 orphans in Honduras

31,000 orphans in India

630,000 orphans in Cambodia

IN HIS NAME

When God first put orphan ministry on my heart, I was surprised to find that many churches did not have any involvement with orphans at all. It's clear in the Bible that God's heart is with the orphan. Psalm 82:1–4 reads, "God presides over heaven's court; he pronounces judgment on the heavenly beings: 'How long will you hand down unjust decisions by favoring the wicked? Give justice to the poor and the orphan; uphold the rights of the oppressed and the destitute. Rescue the poor and helpless; deliver them from the grasp of evil people.'" God cares about orphans and widows.

As Christians, we are God's plan to care for fatherless children. There is no "plan B." We, the blood-bought church of Christ, are His plan. It's our responsibility to care for them. Each of the 145 million estimated orphans in the world is desperately loved by God. Each has a plan and purpose designed by God for his or her life. But many times, orphans have been forgotten by the church. That must change. We must be a voice for those who have no voice.

A CUP OF COLD WATER

Starting an orphan ministry requires at least six steps.

Step 1: Personal prayer. I've had many people ask me how to start an orphan ministry, and my answer always seems to surprise them. I tell them they must start with prayer. Before they take one step toward ministry, they must set a foundation of prayer. If God is leading you to begin a ministry to orphans at your church, start praying now and ask the Lord to open doors for your ministry.

Step 2: Meet with your pastor. Although this step is important, this is *not* the meeting where you need to unload all of your glorious, God-sized dreams for a dynamic orphan ministry on your pastor. Trust me, your pastor hears ministry ideas from lots of well-meaning people that never get off the ground. Sometimes people will even approach their pastor with a great need they have seen, and then expect the poor pastor to start a program or support a ministry right then and there!

So, with this in mind, schedule a meeting with your pastor and express very clearly your desire to help orphans. Simply tell him that God is stirring within your heart a need to help orphans. Make it clear that you are not asking him to do anything, except perhaps discerning God's leading with you. Ask him to pray with you for a set time as you pray about where your desire to help orphans may lead. I recommend praying for six months. This will take the pressure off your pastor while letting him know that you are serious about a prayerful foundation.

> *Each orphan ministry will look different depending on the specific area of orphan care a church is led to focus on: global orphan care, foster care, or adoption.*

Step 3: Meet regularly with seed families. By seed families, I mean other people who also want to see something done at your church for orphans. Meet monthly to pray. Resist the temptation to talk about ideas or goals, but simply pray. After several months of prayer, begin to talk about ideas that the Lord has given each person. Aim high! Discuss what your ministry would look like if resources were infinite.

Step 4: Meet with anyone interested in helping with this new ministry. Now that a foundation of prayer has been set, invite other people to help while still keeping the focus on prayer. Decide if your ministry will focus on foster care, adoption, international orphan care, or a combination.

Step 5: Meet once again with your pastor. At this point, meet again with your pastor. Tell him about the prayer meetings you've been having with other church members and let him know some of the ideas God has given you.

Step 6: Begin to plan and implement your ideas as the Lord leads. Some ideas for your orphan ministry may include the following:

· *Hosting an Orphan Sunday, where the entire service is dedicated to orphan advocacy.*

- *Teaching church members about the plight of orphans.*
- *Purchasing adoption resources for your church library.*
- *Raising awareness about respite and foster care.*
- *Beginning an adoption fund to help offset adoption expenses for families choosing to bring an orphan into their family.*
- *Hosting foster care/adoption classes in your church through your community's social services department.*
- *Taking mission trips to orphanages.*
- *Encouraging orphan sponsorships.*

Remember, every orphan ministry looks different in every church. For more information on how to start an orphan ministry, visit hopefororphans.org.

Abba, in many churches, we have ministries for children, women, men, and college students. But oftentimes our churches lack a ministry for orphan care. As I lay a foundation of prayer for a new or expanded ministry just for orphans, give me open doors to talk with my pastor and other families in my church who can help me. Then give us God-sized dreams as we think of ways to care for orphans in our community and around the world.

58. TEACH LIFE SKILLS TO FOSTER CHILDREN WHO ARE AGING OUT OF THE SYSTEM.

Although my mother was a hardworking nurse for many years, she was also a meticulous homemaker. She had our home running like a well-oiled machine. She cleaned our house on Thursday, did the grocery shopping on Friday, and washed laundry on Saturday. My mother taught me how to organize my time, run a shipshape household, and find bargains in every store.

I have fond memories of her also teaching me how to sew, cook, and launder my own clothes. When I was in the eighth grade, she took me to the fabric store, taught me how to choose a pattern, and walked me through how to use the pattern to sew a simple pillow. We cut out the cloth, pinned it at the seams, and then sat at the sewing machine together to stitch the pillow. I was so proud of that little lacy pillow! Now that I have a family of nine, I have taken so many of my mother's skills into adulthood with me. What a gift she gave me in modeling how to be a Proverbs 31 woman!

When I got my first job at age sixteen, I had no idea how to file income taxes the next year. I was appalled that a sixteen-year-old had to file anything with the government, but my dad assured me that it had to be done. He sat me down in his office and patiently walked me through each step of the tax forms. He also taught me to balance my checkbook and fill out the paperwork for my first car.

Both of my parents did their best to make sure I was ready to enter an adult world full of taxes, banks, bills, and home management. But isn't that what parents do? They raise up their children to live independently—to leave the comfortable nest of home and make responsible lives for themselves.

Can you imagine leaving home at the age of eighteen with absolutely no life skills? But that's exactly what happens to thousands of teenagers each year as they age out of the foster care system. So many of them don't know how to cook healthy meals, clean a bathroom properly, balance a checkbook, or sew on a button. This is not because they don't want to learn. They simply haven't had anyone to teach them these important life skills.

IN HIS NAME

When we think of what Jesus did on earth, we so often think of Him healing the leper, giving sight to the blind, turning water into wine, and raising the dead to life. Our Savior did these things, but sometimes we forget that though He performed miracles and was fully God, He was also fully human.

> Few will have the greatness to bend history itself; but each of us can work to change a small portion of events, and in the total of all those acts will be written the history of this generation.
>
> ROBERT F. KENNEDY

We read in Matthew 13:55 and Mark 6:3 that Jesus was a carpenter by trade. His father Joseph probably spent many hours teaching young Jesus how to measure, carve, and shape wood. We also read in John 21:9–13 that when the disciples saw Jesus on the shore of Galilee after their long night of fishing, He had cooked fish for them. Together they enjoyed breakfast by the sea, compliments of the King of kings. (Can you imagine how good that fish must have tasted?)

Clearly, when our Lord walked this earth, He wasn't a helpless man who couldn't handle life tasks. Our Lord knew how to fish! He knew how to use a hammer and a chisel! He knew how to cook! Yes, He was fully God. But He was fully man as well, and He understands that we live in a world of bills, careers, and home management. Teaching life skills to young people who have not had the opportunity to learn them will bless them daily as they use their acquired skills throughout their lives.

A CUP OF COLD WATER

Teaching life skills to teenagers who are about to age out of the state foster care system is a good group project. First, contact your Department of Children's Services or a foster care group home to ask if you can host a "Life Skills Day" for the teenagers. In the state where I live, social workers actively seek groups who will host a Life Skills Day for their foster children.

After you have permission to host a day of instruction for the teens in foster care, have volunteers in your church or Bible study group agree to host a class. For example, some members of your church may be able to teach a basic cooking class. Others can teach a class on basic car maintenance. Still others may be able to teach basic sewing—mending and sewing on buttons.

> *If you don't want to organize a group of volunteers,*
> *consider volunteering by yourself to share a life skill as*
> *a one-on-one tutor for a teenage foster child.*

Once you have your volunteers, organize your Life Skills Day around the services that the members can teach. For one full day, teach the classes at a foster care group home or at your church. Foster teens can rotate through the classes in one- to two-hour increments. Here is a list of possible classes that you can suggest when recruiting volunteers:

- Checking account basics: How to start and balance a checking account.
- Sewing: How to mend, hem, and sew on a button. (Keep this class simple.)
- Basic nutrition: How to choose healthy foods.
- Cooking: How to cook basic meals.
- Personal wellness: How to give yourself a manicure or pedicure, take care of skin and hair, etc.
- Exercising: How to establish a manageable exercise routine.
- Personal organization: How to budget, pay bills on time, use a personal calendar, file important documents, etc.
- Basic cleaning: How to sort laundry, iron, mop, and dust.
- Shopping on a budget: How to shop for bargains by clipping coupons, shopping for sale items, using thrift stores, etc.
- Job skills: How to write a résumé, fill out applications, and interview for a job.

By the end of the day, the teens will have had several classes of life skills that they will use for the rest of their lives. Your gift of helping older foster children learn skills they need to succeed will also help them face life's everyday challenges. And the time and energy you invest in them will show them how much they are valued and loved, which is a gift greater than any life skill.

Abba, it's easy to assume that all teenage children are equipped with the life skills they need to succeed in life. But it's simply not true for all foster children. They need people like me to teach them the basics. Even more than that, Abba, they need to know the Christian community cares for them as they start their life on their own. Use me and use others in my church to teach them the skills they need and to teach them about you through our time with them.

59. PRAY FOR IMPRISONED AND PERSECUTED CHRISTIANS AROUND THE WORLD.

I remember the date well: September 22, 2010. That night my husband and I met friends from our Bible study group for dinner. We had a great time sharing prayer requests and praises, encouraging each other with Scripture, and catching up on the details of each other's lives. I didn't realize it at the time, but on that very same day, September 22, 2010, while I enjoyed an evening of friendship with other Christian couples, a thirty-four-year-old Christian pastor on the other side of the world named Youcef Nadarkhani received his criminal sentence in an Iranian courtroom. His punishment? Death. His crime? Apostasy and the evangelism of Muslims to Christianity.

Today this Christian pastor, husband, and father of two small boys sits in a prison cell awaiting his death. He had been arrested one year prior to his sentencing for protesting a government policy that required children in his town of Rasht to study the Quran in school. After his arrest, officials tried to convert Youcef back to Islam using various methods, including medication. Youcef has not renounced his faith in Jesus Christ, and contacts say he is standing firm and strong in his Christian faith even though he is facing certain death.

It wasn't until I read Youcef's story at PrisonerAlert.com that I realized how much

> Princes, kings, and other rulers of the world have used all their strength and cunning against the Church, yet it continues to endure and hold its own.
>
> **JOHN FOXE (1517–1587)**

I take my religious freedoms for granted. We are so blessed here in America. We can walk freely into sanctuaries with our Bibles in hand. We can lift our hands and sing praise songs at the top of our lungs. In other parts of the world, Christians are forced to worship in secret each week. They hide their Bibles in the cracks of walls and sing praises and hymns in quiet whispers with no instruments accompanying them.

As I thought back to the events of my September 22 and how they compared to the events of Youcef Nadarkhani's September 22, I understood that I have a responsibility to pray for Youcef and other Christian brothers and sisters around the world who are imprisoned for believing in Christ and sharing their faith in Jesus.

IN HIS NAME

For Christians in other countries, sharing the gospel with people who desperately need Jesus can be a life or death situation. Christians can be imprisoned, tortured, or killed for sharing Christ. A pastor friend of mine has visited an underground church in China several times. When he e-mails me and others who are praying for him while he is there, he always talks in code, typing sentences like, "I've been talking to Father about you." And, "We've had several meetings here and I've enjoyed them immensely, meeting many new people." I know he is letting us know that he has been praying for us and that the underground church is still growing. This "code" protects the church from anyone who may want to harm her. (I still get "holy goose bumps" when I hear his stories of everyone in a small underground house church squeezing into a bathroom to watch a new believer get baptized in a bathtub!)

Praying for the people who share Christ despite the danger to themselves and their families is a privilege. They are witnessing for Christ in countries that are closed to us. The apostle Paul tells us in Romans 10:13 that everyone who calls on the name of the Lord will be saved, but he goes on to say in verse 14, "How can they call on him to save them unless they believe in him? And how can they believe in him if they have never heard about him? And how can they hear about him unless someone tells them?" Let us lift up our brothers and sisters in prayer as they share the gospel and seek to further the cause of Christ. They are truly on the front lines for His name's sake!

A CUP OF COLD WATER

While we can't travel to closed nations to free our brothers and sisters in Christ from their chains, we do have a powerful weapon against evil—prayer. Prayer is vitally important. A great resource as you begin praying for the persecuted church is Persecution.com. On this site you will find the stories of imprisoned Christians like Youcef Nadarkhani who have been arrested for their Christian beliefs.

> *Although prayer is the most important way to help persecuted Christians, you can also help by sending Bibles, writing letters of encouragement, and becoming an advocate.*

When you pray for imprisoned believers, pray for their release, for their families, for their attorneys, and most of all for Christ to be glorified in their situation. If you supply your e-mail address, Persecution.com will send you a weekly prayer newsletter so that you can be aware of persecuted and imprisoned believers around the world and pray specifically for their needs.

Christian persecution is real. Christian martyrdom is real. It still happens in our world today. But prayer is also real. And its power on behalf of the persecuted church is evident in our world today. One day soon, every knee will bow and every tongue will confess that Jesus Christ is Lord. But for now, as we live in this world where evil abounds, let us raise our voices and shake the gates of hell with our battle cry on behalf of our persecuted brothers and sisters in Christ!

Abba, each Sunday morning when I walk into my nice, climate-controlled church with my Bible and sing praises and hymns at the top of my voice, remind me that brothers and sisters in Christ in other nations are worshiping you in secret for fear of imprisonment or even death. Send your mighty angels to protect them, Abba, and give them opportunities to share the gospel with boldness to the lost people around them.

60. ORGANIZE A HANDYMAN MINISTRY.

It started as a small, yet God-inspired idea in the back of Frank Page's spirit. It just wouldn't go away. The idea sprung up from the many single mothers he had encountered at his church. As senior pastor, Frank had counseled many singles who had experienced divorce and were now struggling not only with the spiritual aspects of their separation, such as abandonment, guilt, and isolation, but with the financial effects as well. Many single mothers were working multiple jobs to put food on the table, and the stress of raising their children while working long hours left them mentally and physically fatigued.

While Frank's idea wouldn't alleviate their work situations, it would help lessen the stress of getting to that job. His idea was to give single mothers in the church and the surrounding community a free oil change for their cars. And by free, he really meant free! Absolutely no donations would be accepted.

> God hasn't called us to be God. He's called us to be ourselves.
>
> **MARK BATTERSON**

When Frank presented his idea to his staff, the deacons, and other church members, several of the men agreed to help. So, one Saturday, the men turned the church parking lot into an auto service. They placed a huge sign in front of the church one week before the event to advertise to the community. The sign read in big, bold, red letters, "This Saturday—Free Single Moms' Oil Change. Absolutely No Donations Will Be Accepted."

At first, I suppose it sounded too good to be true! Only a few moms came. But as word spread, single mothers from all over the area brought their cars to have them serviced at the church. They got their oil changed and enjoyed hot coffee, juice, and pastries inside the church while they waited.

This service has now been given free of charge quarterly for over ten years. At the last oil change event, the church serviced over ninety women's cars by utilizing twenty stations with two to three volunteers at each station. Many single mothers bring their cars to the event each time they see the sign go up in the churchyard. Some have come to the church on Sundays for worship and accepted Christ as a result of the free service.

Later, the church started a full "handyman" ministry for single mothers, widows, and wives of deployed soldiers. For those women in our churches and communities who do not have a man around the house, often repairs to vehicles and homes remain undone. That's where a handyman ministry can be such a blessing to them.

THE STATS

There are 11.6 million single parents in the United States.

9.9 million of them are single mothers.

About 37% of families headed by a single mother are living below poverty level.

IN HIS NAME

Just think—the ministry started with one man's simple idea. What if he had said no? What if he had dismissed the idea and refused to be bothered with the work that it would involve? He certainly had that choice. God-inspired ideas typically begin as "spiritual tickles" in our minds and spirits. It's almost as if God whispers to see if we're willing to listen. When He does, we have a choice—we can ignore it, or we can ponder it and ask God to reveal more of the idea if it's truly from Him.

King David had one of these "spiritual tickles." In 1 Chronicles 28:2, we read that King David had the idea to build a temple for the Lord. David rose to his feet and said, "My brothers and my people! It was my desire to build a temple where the Ark of the Lord's covenant, God's footstool, could rest permanently. I made the necessary preparations for building it."

David could have ignored the idea. But he didn't. He took detailed notes as the Lord provided him with the plans. Those plans were passed down to his son Solomon, who later built the beautiful temple where God's people worshiped and brought sacrifices for generations. And it all started with an idea that God put in David's head and heart.

Do you have an idea that would be beneficial to God's people like Frank Page did? Don't ignore it. Don't dismiss it because you don't think you have the resources, the time, or the wisdom to pursue that idea. If it's truly from the Lord, He will equip you where He's called you. Is there any limit to what God can do with a man or woman who is willing to take even a small step outside their comfortable world to help someone else in need?

A CUP OF COLD WATER

To host an oil change event for single moms, you will need to gather several volunteers with experience in servicing cars. To cover expenses, you can ask church members to donate motor oil prior to the event. As your ministry grows, consider adding this event's funding as a line item in your church's outreach or community ministries budget.

Since women will need to wait for their cars, consider providing a place where they can have refreshments. It would also help to provide a place for children to play, such as a supervised playground or playroom. This part of the event should have female volunteers, as they will be interacting one-on-one with the single mothers. Make sure the women who volunteer in the refreshment area can make the single mothers feel at home by making conversation and giving them information on the church. They should be ready to share their own testimonies and the plan of salvation.

> *If your church is not ready to start a large handyman ministry, then start small. Find a needy widow in your church and put your skills to work!*

As your church's ministry to single mothers grows, you may want to start repairing the homes of single women, widows, elderly persons, and wives of deployed soldiers. Make an announcement to your church congregation or Bible study group asking for volunteers one Saturday a month or one Saturday per quarter. Getting volunteers will be the easy part.

The hard part will be to get the single moms and widows to ask for help. Many may be embarrassed by how bad they have let things get in their homes. One single mom had no money to fix a leaking toilet, so she and her children stopped using that toilet altogether and began using the second bathroom instead. It had been nearly a year, and she still hadn't had the toilet repaired. When a man from the church came to her house, she was embarrassed for someone to find out how long the toilet had needed repair, but was grateful to the man who fixed it with one simple part in about ten minutes. This is the type of repair that your group will likely encounter.

Having the women and elderly persons sign up ahead of time, as well as having them give a brief description of the repairs that are needed, will help greatly. If your ministry is large enough to go beyond your church body's needs, then you may have to rely on word of mouth to get your ministry started within the community.

Have your volunteers meet together for prayer at the church before you go out in teams to make the necessary repairs. (Keep in mind that a man should never go alone to a single woman's house.) Ask volunteers to bring a wide range of tools, including tools for yard work.

Meeting the needs of single mothers, widows, elderly persons, and wives of deployed soldiers in our own congregations is foundational to a healthy, well-functioning church. Making sure that basic repairs and home maintenance are taken care of is an easy way for the body of Christ to care for these vulnerable people.

Abba, knowing that I have the tools and the time to give to people who need help with their cars and homes makes me realize that I have no excuse. You have called me to serve, Abba, and you taught us how to serve through your son, Jesus. Now as I serve in a handyman ministry, give me your compassion as I minister to people who need practical help.

CONCLUSION

"Dear brothers and sisters, I plead with you to give your bodies to God. Let them be a living and holy sacrifice—the kind he will accept. When you think of what he has done for you, is this too much to ask?" (Romans 12:1).

We are called to be living, breathing sacrifices for our God. Just like the burnt offerings of the Old Testament, when God required every part of the sacrificed animal to be burned on the altar, God calls us today to put every part of ourselves on the altar as a living offering. *Everything*—our failures, our triumphs, our gifts, our talents, our time, our resources. And just like the fire under the burnt offering would consume every part of that animal, when we place everything on the altar—nothing set aside, nothing taken out—the fire of the Holy Spirit will begin to consume our lives and He will use everything! And our lives will become a sweet aroma to our God!

When we give our lives completely each day on the altar, God will turn us into people who look more and more like Christ. And a person who looks like Christ is a person whose heart aches for the oppressed, the orphans, the downtrodden, the widows, the poor, and the needy.

When you step outside of the church walls to begin to *be* the church that Christ died for, you will soon learn that faith is a real place. It is a place where peace quietly rains over your soul like a cool summer rain shower on a hot day. It is a place where an overwhelming desire to serve the Lord envelops your spirit like a thick cloud until you are so full of the Holy Spirit you can hardly breathe. It is a place of warmth where you can bask in the legacy of the saints who have been right where you are. It is a place of sacred holiness where your spirit freely and willingly bows down in submission and your voice sings praises of true joy even in the midst of trials. It is a place of true friendship where you can walk beside the God of the universe and call Him Abba. And it is a place where God can use you—a place where the Master Potter reshapes and reworks broken vessels into beautiful masterpieces.

Becoming Christlike in caring for the needy will challenge you and, at times, it may force you to lay down everything you have. It may take all of your resources, all of your money, all of your time . . . it may very well take everything.

But, friend, isn't that what Jesus Christ did for you? He gave everything He had to ransom you and set you free. And after all, one day soon everything of earthly value will fade from view. Only what you have done for Christ will remain. It really is that simple.

MISSION TRIP CHECKLIST

ONCE YOU'RE ACCEPTED

° *Contact your pastor and Bible study group* to let them know you are
  planning to take a mission trip. Tell them the dates and the country.
  Ask them to pray for you as you begin the process of preparing for your trip.
° *Start compiling a list of potential supporters* and begin gathering
  their addresses.
° *Apply for or renew your passport.* If you already have a passport, check to
  be sure it is valid for at least three months past your travel dates. If it is
  not, it will need to be renewed. Go to the US Department of State web
  page travel.state.gov/passport/renew/renew_833.html for details and
  restrictions on renewing by mail.

  If you do not have a passport, you should apply for one as soon
  as possible. It usually takes 4–6 weeks to have a passport processed.
  For a fee, this process can be expedited. A passport can be obtained by
  contacting your post office or going online to travel.state.gov/passport/get/
  get_4855.html. For most post offices, an appointment is needed.

  Two pictures of yourself are needed to process your passport. If you
  would like to take your own picture, follow the Department of State regulations found at travel.state.gov/passport/pptphotoreq/pptphotoreq_5333
  .html. Sometimes your passport photo can be taken during your appointment for a fee of approximately fifteen dollars. If you need to use this

service, verify that your post office takes passport photos when you set up your appointment.

For adults and children sixteen years of age and older, the fee for passports is currently $110. Be prepared to make two separate payments at your appointment—one for the passport fee ($85) and one for the acceptance fee ($25). Use of cash and debit/credit cards to pay the application fee is prohibited, so if you don't use checks, you'll need to buy a money order. Cash, check, money order, or credit/debit cards are acceptable forms of payment for the acceptance fee. For an updated list of fees, visit travel.state.gov/passport/fees/fees_837.html.

You will need to bring your birth certificate and driver's license to your appointment. Additional documents such as marriage license may also be needed, so ask the passport officer what you need to bring when you make your appointment or visit www.usps.com/shop/apply-for-a-passport.htm. The passport forms you need to have filled out for your appointment are online at travel.state.gov/passport/forms/forms_847.html.

12–14 WEEKS BEFORE YOU LEAVE

Now that you have committed to a mission trip, it's time to raise support from friends and family. Here are some fund-raising tips.

° *Pray.* Commit your support to the Lord and ask Him to help you raise every dollar you will need on your mission trip.
° *Finalize your list of supporters.* Supporters can include coworkers, church friends, Bible study groups, neighbors, fellow students, professors or

teachers, employers, and family members. Try to think of one hundred people. A strong relationship with a person isn't always necessary before putting that person on your list. Many Christians cannot travel on a mission trip, but it is their joy to support you prayerfully and financially. They are grateful for the opportunity to partner with you in ministry.

° *When you write the letter, be personal.* The key to raising support is to be personal. Give details about what God is doing in your life, what your trip is all about, and why you feel called to go. Even though this is a personal letter, be sure to make it professional looking. A sample support letter is included in appendix B.

° *Keep it short.* Try to keep your letter to one page. Write, rewrite, and streamline. Be brief and to the point, and don't try to impress with eloquence or spirituality. Just be yourself in your writing.

° *Be specific about your financial needs.* Be sure to let your potential supporters know that no gift is too small and you need prayer support as much as you need financial support for your trip.

° *Be excited.* Let your excitement for the mission trip and the needs in the country exude from your words.

° *Give the ministry address.* Include the ministry's address in the body of your letter and let your potential supporters know their contributions are tax deductible. Remind them that if funds are sent directly to you, donors cannot get a tax deduction. Instead, have them make checks out to the ministry. If they send their checks directly to the ministry, have them include a note with your name on it so the money is credited to your fund and the ministry can keep accounting records accurate.

° *Handwrite a note.* To give each letter a personal touch, add a quick, handwritten note to the bottom of your letter. It can be as simple as, "Hey,

Jim and Beth—please pray for me as I get ready for my mission trip to Liberia." Or, "Hi, Pat and Carol—I know you both are prayer warriors, and I thank you in advance for praying for me as I travel to Mexico. I can't wait to see what God does in my life." Or, "Hey, Jeremy and Kim—Hope you guys are doing well. Let me know how I can pray for you too."

° *Add a picture of yourself or your family.* This gives your letter another personal touch.
° *Enclose a separate prayer reminder.* Making small magnets, bookmarks, or prayer cards (small note cards detailing your prayer requests) are a great way to help your supporters remember to pray for you.
° *Include a small, self-addressed envelope.* Address the envelope to yourself or the ministry. This will make it more convenient for your supporters to send their checks.
° *Mail your support letters.* Don't forget to double-check your spelling and grammar before you send it out.

8–12 WEEKS BEFORE YOU LEAVE

° *Make a foreign travel appointment with your family doctor or public health travel clinic.* You should schedule your appointment for 4–6 weeks before your trip.
° *Create a prayer team of five to ten people who will pray and/or fast for you and the specific needs you have for your trip.* This small team should be composed of close friends or family members whom you trust to cover you and your mission team in prayer—before, during, and after your trip. It's a good idea to e-mail your team a specific list of prayer items.

4–6 WEEKS BEFORE YOU LEAVE

° *Attend your foreign travel appointment.* The ministry you are traveling with can give you specifics on vaccinations required for the country you are visiting. You can also go to wwwnc.cdc.gov/travel/ to see exactly what the Centers for Disease Control and Prevention recommends for the country you will be visiting. This is the website used by doctors to determine which vaccinations to give you.

Some countries in Africa or Asia may require you to get vaccinated against yellow fever. They will not let you into the country unless you have the vaccination. Once you are inoculated, you will be given a yellow card. It's best to staple the card to the inside back page of your passport.

You may need a prescription for antimalarial drugs. Again, the Centers for Disease Control website mentioned above will let you know if antimalarial medicine is recommended for the area you will be visiting. Ask your nurse or doctor for instructions on how to take the medication.

At your foreign travel appointment, the nurse or doctor will advise you of any other recommended shots, such as typhoid, tetanus, or polio. These shots may be recommended but not required for travel. Also, as a precaution, your nurse or doctor may prescribe an antibiotic for you to take on the trip.

Be sure to bring your immunization history (shot record) and travel itinerary to your appointment. The fees for vaccinations for foreign travel average about $60 per immunization. Some insurance companies cover these costs.

CUP OF COLD WATER

4 WEEKS BEFORE YOU LEAVE

° *Apply for a travel visa.* Some ministries may apply for the visa for you, while other ministries will instruct you on how to do this yourself. Some countries do not require a visa. Check with your ministry to be sure. Visit http://travel.state.gov/visa/ for more information.

1–2 WEEKS BEFORE YOU LEAVE

° *Begin packing.* Of course, necessary items will vary greatly depending on the country you are traveling to, but here is a general list to keep handy.
  - *Your driver's license, passport, and yellow card.* Also, keep one copy of each in your suitcase and leave copies with a family member at home.
  - *Medications in original containers.* Prescriptions must have your name on them.
  - *Comfortable clothes for ministry.* Your clothing will vary depending on what country you will be visiting. Some countries require ladies to wear long skirts. Others require men to wear collared shirts. Modesty is the key. If in doubt, leave it at home. You may want to take one set of dress clothes for a church service.
  - *Comfortable shoes*
  - *Modest swimsuit*
  - *Sunscreen*
  - *Light rain jacket*
  - *Camera*
  - *Sunglasses*

- *Backpack*
- *Baby wipes or disposable facial cleansing cloths* (to freshen up with)
- *Flashlight* with extra batteries
- *Hand sanitizer* (in a personal size to keep with you)
- *Snacks*
- *Bible, pen, notebook*
- *Electric converters* (you can purchase these at most electronic or travel stores)

SAMPLE SUPPORT LETTER

Dear Ben and Kendra,

I can't tell you how excited I am about what God is doing in my life right now. I have the privilege to join a small group of students and adults who are taking a mission trip to Liberia, Africa, this summer. I'd like to ask you to prayerfully consider supporting me as I venture out to share God's Word on this trip with the people in Liberia. I know it will be a life-changing experience for me and my fellow team members. Our team will be busy! We'll be ministering to orphans and encouraging the young people who are part of the community of Congo Town.

Here's where you come in. *I need to raise $3,500 for my mission trip.* I have enclosed a preaddressed envelope, which will make it convenient for you if you decide to join my support team. Please make checks payable to [ministry name]. In turn, the ministry organization will send you a contribution receipt. They request that you send all donations by [date].

[Ministry name] is registered with the Internal Revenue Service as a 501c(3) nonprofit organization. Donors will receive receipts for their gifts with the understanding that the disbursement of those gifts lies completely at the discretion of the ministry organization and that gifts are nonrefundable and nontransferable, per IRS regulations. Gifts may be tax deductible. Please place a note in your return envelope with my name on it to ensure I am credited for your donation.

I also need of a group of people who will pray for me. I'm really trusting God to do far more than I could ask or imagine. Please join me in praying for the same thing. If you have any questions about my trip, you can contact me directly at [phone number] or [e-mail address].

Thanks in advance for partnering with me. I simply cannot do this without your support!

In His grip, [Your name]

Appendix C

ADOPTION AGENCIES

AAC Adoption and Family Network
www.aacadoption.com; 970-532-3576
AAC is an adoption agency based in Colorado. AAC specializes in international adoption from Korea and China.

Adoption Advocates International
www.adoptionadvocates.org; 360-452-4777
Adoption Advocates International (AAI) is a humanitarian and adoption agency specializing in international adoptions from Ethiopia, China, Thailand, and Ghana. They are located in Washington State.

Adoption Associates, Inc.
www.adoptionassociates.net;
800-677-2367; 800-677-2367
Adoption Associates, Inc. (AAI) is an adoption agency located in Michigan, specializing in both domestic and international adoptions.

AdoptUSKids
adoptuskids.org; 888-200-4005
AdoptUSKids is a photo-listing database of adoptable children in the United States foster care system.

All God's Children International
www.allgodschildren.org; 800-214-6719
All God's Children International is an adoption and orphan care ministry with programs in Ethiopia, China, Taiwan, Rwanda, Bulgaria, India, Nepal, and Ukraine.

America World Adoption Association
www.awaa.org; 888-ONE-CHILD
America World Adoption (AWAA) is an adoption agency specializing in adoptions from Brazil, China, Ethiopia, Honduras, India, Russia, Rwanda, and Ukraine. Although their headquarters is located in Virginia, they have offices in more than twenty-five states.

Associated Services for International Adoption
www.asiadopt.org; 503-224-1860
Associated Services for International Adoption (ASIA) is an Oregon-based

international adoption agency that places children from China, Taiwan, and Haiti.

The Barker Foundation
www.barkerfoundation.org; 301-335-2141

The Barker Foundation is a comprehensive adoption center focusing on pregnancy services, international adoption services, domestic adoption placements, counseling, and education. They operate in the Washington DC, Virginia, and Maryland areas.

Bethany Christian Services
www.bethany.org; 800-BETHANY

Bethany has offices in 103 locations across the United States, and specializes in domestic and international adoptions. They also have ministries dealing with infertility, foster care, and post-adoption.

Children's Hope International
adopt.childrenshope.net; 888-899-2349

Children's Hope International is an adoption agency based in Missouri with international adoption programs in Ethiopia, China, Russia, Colombia, Bulgaria, Ukraine, and Kazakhstan.

China Adoption with Love, Inc.
www.cawli.org; 800-888-9812

China Adoption with Love, Inc. (CAWLI) is a child placement agency specializing in Chinese adoptions. They are located in Massachusetts, although they can place children in all fifty states.

Chinese Children Adoption International
chinesechildren.org; 303-850-9998

Chinese Children Adoption International (CCAI) places children from China and also gives charitable support and cultural education to adoptive families.

Christian World Adoption
www.cwa.org; 888-97ADOPT

Christian World Adoption (CWA) offers international adoption placements. China, Russia, Ukraine, and Ethiopia are among the countries where they have adoption programs. CWA is one of the largest adoption agencies in the United States.

Chrysalis House, Inc.

www.chrysalishouse.com; 559-229-9862

Chrysalis House, Inc., is a California-based adoption agency that places children domestically and internationally. They offer infant, foster care, sibling groups, international, and special needs adoption services.

Dillon International

dillonadopt.com; 918-749-4600

Dillon International is an adoption agency offering services in several countries, including Haiti, China, and Korea. They also have a pilot program in Ghana.

Faith International Adoptions

faithadopt.org/FIA; 253-383-1928

Faith International Adoptions (FIA) is an international adoption agency that works in several nations, including China, India, and Ghana. They also provide relief work for impoverished children overseas.

Families Thru International Adoption

ftia.org; 812-479-9900

Bulgaria, China, and Russia are among the countries where the international adoption agency Families Thru International Adoption has programs. They are based in Indiana.

Great Wall China Adoption

www.gwca.org; 888-GW-FAMILY

Great Wall is not only an international adoption agency specializing in Chinese adoptions, but they also have charity missions for impoverished children. They have regional offices throughout the United States.

Hand in Hand International Adoptions

www.hihiadopt.org/china.htm; 520-745-1322

Hand in Hand is an international adoption agency that works with parents desiring to adopt from China, Haiti, Russia, Ukraine, and the Philippines. They have offices in Arizona, Colorado, Florida, Indiana, and Minnesota.

A Helping Hand Adoption Agency

www.worldadoptions.org; 800-525-0871

A Helping Hand Adoption Agency is based in Kentucky and specializes in adoptions from China, Ukraine, Kazakhstan, Panama, Nicaragua, and Russia.

Holt International
www.holtinternational.org; 541-687-2202

Holt is not only an international adoption agency, but it also specializes in child welfare programs. Holt was founded over fifty years ago and is still a world leader in adoption.

International Family Services
ifservices.org; 281-992-4677

Over four thousand orphaned children have found their forever homes since International Family Services (IFS) began in the early 1900s. IFS has programs in several nations, and they also have many domestic adoption programs.

La Vida International
lavida.org; 610-688-8008

La Vida International is an adoption agency based in Pennsylvania. They have programs in Nepal, Colombia, and China. La Vida also offers humanitarian aid.

Lifeline Children's Services
lifelineadoption.org; 205-967-0811

Lifeline is an adoption agency that works in domestic adoptions, as well as international adoptions in twelve countries. Lifeline has offices in Georgia, Alabama, and Washington.

Little Miracles International
www.littlemiracles.org; 806-351-1100

Little Miracles offers humanitarian aid, as well as adoption programs in more than nine countries, including DR Congo, Russia, and Mexico.

Living Hope Adoption Agency
www.livinghopeadoption.org; 888-886-8086

Living Hope Adoption Agency, based in Pennsylvania, can provide all adoption services for adoptions in China, Honduras, and Taiwan.

Nightlight Christian Adoptions
www.nightlight.org; 864-268-0570

In addition to international and domestic adoption programs, they also specialize in embryo adoption.

Sunny Ridge Family Center

www.sunnyridge.org; 630-754-4500

Based in Illinois, Sunny Ridge Family Center provides numerous adoption programs, including embryo, international, domestic, African-American, and special needs.

Villa Hope Adoption

www.villahope.org; 205-870-7359

Costa Rica, China, Peru, and El Salvador are among the countries where Villa Hope has international adoption programs. They can provide home study services for residents of Alabama.

Wasatch International Adoptions

www.wiaa.org; 801-334-8683

Wasatch International Adoptions (WIA) is an adoption agency with international programs in over eight nations. The Utah-based agency also specializes in birth-mother and second-chance adoption programs.

Wide Horizons for Children

www.whfc.org; 781-894-5330

Wide Horizons for Children (WHFC) provides pregnancy services, humanitarian aid, domestic and international adoption services, sponsorship, and post-adoption services.

World Association for Children and Parents

wacap.org; 800-732-1887

World Association for Children and Parents (WACAP) is an agency that offers both domestic and international adoption options for families. Their international programs include India, China, and Taiwan.

SOURCES

Introduction

United Nations Development Program, "2007 Human Development Report," http://hdr.undp .org/en/reports/global/hdr2007-2008/.

United Nations Development Program, "2006 Human Development Report," http://hdr.undp .org/en/reports/global/hdr2006/.

Martin Ravallion, Shaohua Chen, Prem Sangraula, "Dollar a Day Revisited," May 1, 2008, http://econ.worldbank.org/external/default/main?pagePK=64165259&piPK=64165421 &theSitePK=469372&menuPK=64216926&entityID=000158349_20080902095754.

Bread for the World, "Global Hunger," http://www.bread.org/hunger/global/.

CBC News, "925 Million People Undernourished: UN," September 14, 2010, http://www.cbc .ca/news/world/story/2010/09/14/united-nations-food-hunger.html.

US Department of State, "Trafficking in Persons Report," June 3, 2005, http://www.state .gov/g/tip/rls/tiprpt/2005/46606.htm.

UNICEF, "Maternal and Newborn Health," http://www.unicef.org/sowc09/docs/SOWC09-FullReport-EN.pdf.

Chapter 1

UNICEF, "Eradicate Extreme Poverty and Hunger," http://www.unicef.org/mdg/poverty.html.

Feeding America, "Mission and Values," http://feedingamerica.org/how-we-fight-hunger/ mission-and-values.aspx.

Chapter 2

Ronald McDonald House Charities, "What We Do," http://rmhc.org/what-we-do/ronald -mcdonald-house/.

Chapter 3

AARP, "Hunger in Your Community," http://drivetoendhunger.org/hunger-in-the-united-states/#.

Feeding America, "Hunger in America," http://feedingamerica.org/hunger-in-america/hunger-facts.aspx.

Your Neighborhood Produce, "A Modern Day Produce Co-op in Your Neighborhood," http://yourneighborhoodproduce.net/.

Angel Food Ministries, "Frequently Asked Questions," http://www.angelfoodministries.com/frequently_asked_questions.asp.

Chapter 4

US Census Bureau, "Single Parent Households Showed Little Variation since 1994, Census Bureau Reports," March 27, 2007, http://www.census.gov/newsroom/releases/archives/families_households/cb07-46.html.

US Census Bureau, "Custodial Mothers and Fathers and Their Child Support, 2007," November 2009, http://www.census.gov/prod/2009pubs/p60-237.pdf.

Chapter 5

Feeding America, "Rural Areas—Hunger Facts," http://feedingamerica.org/hunger-in-america/hunger-facts/rural-hunger.aspx.

Carmen DeNavas-Walt, Bernadette D. Proctor, Jessica Smith, "Income, Poverty, and Health Insurance Coverage in the United States 2009," US Census Bureau, September 2010, http://www.census.gov/prod/2010pubs/p60-238.pdf.

Associated Press, "Poll: Americans Consider Pets Part of the Family," June 23, 2009, http://www.msnbc.msn.com/id/31505216/ns/health-pet_health/t/poll-americans-consider-pets-part-family/.

American Pet Products Association, "Industry Statistics and Trends," http://www.americanpetproducts.org/press_industrytrends.asp.

Chapter 6

Feeding America, "Hunger in America—Key Findings," http://feedingamerica.org/hunger-in-america/hunger-studies/hunger-study-2010/key-findings.aspx.

Feeding America, "Hunger in America—Test Your Hunger Knowledge," http://feedingamerica.org/hunger-in-america/hunger-facts/quiz.aspx.

Chapter 7

Harvest Ministry, "Startling Orphan Statistics," March 1, 2011, http://harvestministry.org/orphan-stats.

Compassion International, "Rescue Babies and Mothers," http://www.compassion.com/help-babies.htm.

Chapter 8

Alicia Coleman-Jensen, Mark Nord, Margaret Andrews, Steven Carlson, "Household Food Security in the United States 2010," United States Department of Agriculture, September 2011, http://www.ers.usda.gov/Publications/err125/.

US Department of Agriculture Economic Research Service, "Food Security in the United States: Key Statistics and Graphics," http://www.ers.usda.gov/Briefing/FoodSecurity/stats_graphs.htm.

Feeding America, "Hunger and Poverty Statistics," http://feedingamerica.org/faces-of-hunger/hunger-101/hunger-and-poverty-statistics.aspx.

Bread for the World, "U.S. Hunger," http://www.bread.org/hunger/us/.

Chapter 9

National Coalition for the Homeless, "Why Are People Homeless?" July 2009, http://www.nationalhomeless.org/factsheets/why.html.

"Preventing Homelessness in America," http://solutionsforamerica.org/thrivingneigh/homelessness.html.

Chapter 10

Bureau of Labor Statistics, "American Time Use Survey Summary," United States Department of Labor, http://www.bls.gov/news.release/atus.nr0.htm.

Jackie Brown, "Our Communities," *Cook and Play,* http://cookandplay.webs.com/ourcommunity.htm.

Chapter 11

World Health Organization, "10 Facts on Sanitation," March 2011, http://www.who.int/features/factfiles/sanitation/en/.

World Health Organization, "Facts and Figures on Water Quality and Health," http://www.who.int/water_sanitation_health/facts_figures/en/index.html.

The Water Project, "Why Water?" http://thewaterproject.org/why_water.asp.

Chapter 12

Oracle Think Quest Education Foundation, "An End to the Hunger—Hope for the Future," http://library.thinkquest.org/C002291/high/present/stats.htm.

World Health Organization, "World Health Statistics Report," May 2008, http://www.who.int/whosis/whostat/2008/en/index.html.

Chapter 13

Cindy Sanders, "Why Vacation Bible School Is Still Relevant, Still Reaching," *Church Executive,* January 3, 2011, http://churchexecutive.com/archives/why-vacation-bible-school-is-still-relevant-still-reaching.

Chapter 14

The Centre for Addiction and Mental Health, "The Causes of Depression—Current Theories," http://www.camh.net/About_Addiction_Mental_Health/Mental_Health_Information/ Depressive_Illness/depressive_ill_causes.html.

Bob Murray and Alicia Fortinberry, "Depression Facts and Statistics," *Uplift Program,* January 15, 2005, http://www.upliftprogram.com/depression_stats.html.

Jonathan Lavine, "What's in a Smile?" *The Dr. Oz Show,* February 1, 2010, http://www.doctor oz.com/blog/jonathan-b-levine-dmd/what-s-smile.

Chapter 15

World Crafts, "Countries," http://worldcraftsvillage.com/countries.asp.

World Crafts, "Artisans," http://worldcraftsvillage.com/artisans.asp.

Chapter 16

"Statistics on Single Parenting in the United States," http://singleparenting.net/single -mothers-statistics.html.

Chapter 17

Judy Foreman, "Staying Happy May Lead to Staying Healthy," *Boston Globe,* September 29, 1992.

Chapter 18

Barry Kosmin and Ariela Keysar, "ARIS 2008 Report Highlights," American Religious Identification Survey, http://www.americanreligionsurvey-aris.org/reports/highlights.html.

Chapter 19

Child Welfare Information Gateway, "Foster Care Statistics 2009," http://www.childwelfare .gov/pubs/factsheets/foster.pdf.

Chapter 20

Kenneth Woodward, "Is God Listening?" *Newsweek,* March 30, 1997, http://www.thedaily beast.com/newsweek/1997/03/30/is-god-listening.html.

Beliefnet, "US News and Beliefnet Prayer Survey Results," http://www.beliefnet.com/Faiths/ Faith-Tools/Meditation/2004/12/U-S-News-Beliefnet-Prayer-Survey-Results.aspx.

Chapter 21

National Coalition for the Homeless, "Who Is Homeless?" July 2009, http://www.national homeless.org/factsheets/who.html.

National Coalition for the Homeless, "Homeless Families with Children," July 2009, http://www.nationalhomeless.org/factsheets/families.html.

Chapter 22

American Medical Student Association, "Health Care Delivery: Rural vs. Urban Communities," http://www.amsa.org/AMSA/Libraries/Committee_Docs/ruralurban.sflb.ashx.

Chapter 23

"Extreme Poverty in Africa," *Cozay: Through Their Eyes,* http://cozay.com/.

Chapter 24

Child Welfare Information Gateway, "Foster Care Statistics 2009," http://www.childwelfare .gov/pubs/factsheets/foster.pdf.

American Adoptions, "State Adoptions Cost," http://www.americanadoptions.com/adopt/ state_adoption_costs.

AdoptUSKids, http://www.adoptuskids.org/.

Chapter 25

UNICEF, "Orphan Estimates," *Child Info,* http://www.childinfo.org/hiv_aids_orphanestimates.php.

Associated Press, "US Population Hits 300 Million Mark," October 17, 2006, *MSNBC,*
http://geography.about.com/od/obtainpopulationdata/a/uspopulation.htm.

Chapter 26

National Coalition Against Domestic Violence, "Domestic Violence Facts," http://www.ncadv
.org/files/DomesticViolenceFactSheet(National).pdf.

Centers for Disease Control and Prevention, "Violence Prevention: Injury Center,"
http://www.cdc.gov/ViolencePrevention/index.html.

Mukti Khanna, Nirbhay N. Singh, Mary Nemil, Al Best, and Cynthia R. Ellis, "Homeless
Women and Their Families: Characteristics, Life Circumstances, and Needs." *Journal of
Child and Family Studies,* http://www.springerlink.com/content/r208786101021640/.

Chapter 27

United States Conference of Mayors, "Hunger and Homelessness Survey," December 2008,
http://www.usmayors.org/pressreleases/documents/hungerhomelessnessreport_
121208.pdf.

Chapter 28

Donald Hernandez, "Double Jeopardy," The Annie E. Casey Foundation, April 2011,
http://www.aecf.org/~/media/Pubs/Topics/Education/Other/ DoubleJeopardyHowThird
GradeReadingSkillsandPovery/DoubleJeopardyReport040511FINAL.pdf.

Chapter 29

National Retail Federation, "Back to School Sales Expected to Be Flat as Parents Practice
Restraint," July 21, 2011, http://www.nrf.com/modules. php?name=News&op=viewlive
&sp_id=1157.

Chapter 30

Ipsos, "Despite Recession 6 in 10 Adults Have Given in Charity This Year: 8 in 10 Plan to
Give Over the Holidays," December 21, 2010, http://www.ipsos-na.com/news-polls/
pressrelease.aspx?id=5085.

Chapter 31

National Coalition for the Homeless, "Why Are People Homeless?" July 2009 http://www.nationalhomeless.org/factsheets/why.html.

Chapter 32

Alexander Kjerulf, "Top 10 Reasons Why Happiness at Work Is the Ultimate Productivity Booster," *Chief Happiness Officer,* March 27, 2007, http://positivesharing.com/2007/03/top-10-reasons-why-happiness-at-work-is-the-ultimate-productivity-booster/.

Paul Elsass, "Tips on Having a Successful Job Interview," *Livestrong.com,* August 12, 2010, http://www.livestrong.com/article/203285-tips-on-having-a-successful-job-interview/.

Chapter 33

Dan Brewster, "The 4/14 Window: Child Mission and Ministry Strategies,"*Compassion,* August 2005, http://www.compassion.com/multimedia/The%204_14%20Window.pdf.

Chapter 34

Shoahua Chen and Martin Ravallion, "The Developing World Is Poorer than We Thought but No Less Successful in the Fight Against Poverty," World Bank, August 26, 2008, http://siteresources.worldbank.org/JAPANINJAPANESEEXT/Resources/515497-1201490097949/080827_The_Developing_World_is_Poorer_than_we_Thought.pdf.

Anup Shah, "Poverty Facts and Stats," *Global Issues,* http://www.globalissues.org/article/26/poverty-facts-and-stats.

Chapter 35

Project Linus, "Vital Statistics," http://projectlinus.org/.

Chapter 36

Centers for Disease Control and Prevention, "Abortion Surveillance—United States 2000" Morbidity and Mortality Weekly Report, November 28, 2003, http://www.cdc.gov/mmwr/PDF/SS/SS5212.pdf.

The National Campaign to Prevent Teen and Unplanned Pregnancy, "14 and Younger, The Sexual Behavior of Young Adolescents," http://www.thenationalcampaign.org/resources/pdf/pubs/14summary.pdf.

Chapter 37

UNICEF, "Children Living in Poverty," http://www.unicef.org/sowc05/english/poverty.html.

Chapter 38

Janet Clark, "Visiting a Terminally Ill Patient," *Examiner,* May 15, 2009, http://www.examiner.com/relationship-in-des-moines/visiting-a-terminally-ill-patient.

Lynndee Marooney, "How to Give Support to Terminally Ill Patients," *Health,* October 2, 2010, http://www.ehow.com/how_7271071_give-terminally-ill-cancer-patients.html.

American Cancer Society, "Cancer Facts and Figures 2010," http://www.cancer.org/acs/groups/content/@epidemiologysurveilance/documents/document/acspc-026238.pdf.

Chapter 39

Encyclopedia of Death and Dying, "Widows in Third World Nations," http://www.deathreference.com/Vi-Z/Widows-in-Third-World-Nations.html.

Chapter 40

People Against Childhood Cancer, "Childhood Cancer," http://curechildhoodcancer.ning.com/page/childhood-cancer-1.

Chapter 41

National Oceanic and Atmospheric Administration, "August 2007 Heat Wave," http://www.ncdc.noaa.gov/special-reports/2007-aug-heat-event.html.

"Medical Transportation Study on the Needs of the Elderly," http://www.njfoundationforaging.org/NJFA_MTSExecsummary.pdf.

US Department of Labor, "Consumer Expenditures in 2009," May 2011, http://www.bls.gov/cex/csxann09.pdf.

Chapter 42

Centers for Disease Control and Prevention, "Diagnosis of HIV Infection and AIDS in the United States and Dependent Areas, 2009" http://www.cdc.gov/hiv/surveillance/resources/reports/2009report/index.htm.

We Make the Change, "Initiatives," http://www.wemakethechange.com/initiatives/faith-based-initiative/.

UNAIDS, "Global Report," http://www.unaids.org/globalreport/Global_report.htm.

Chapter 43

Centers for Disease Control, "National Hospital Discharge Survey: 2007," National Health Statistics Reports, October 26, 2010, http://www.cdc.gov/nchs/data/nhsr/nhsr029.pdf.

Chapter 44

"Premature Babies," *MedlinePlus,* http://www.nlm.nih.gov/medlineplus/premature babies.html.

Quint V. Boenker Preemie Survival Foundation, "Premature Birth Statistics," http://www.preemiesurvival.org/info/index.html.

Chapter 45

Centers for Disease Control, "National Hospital Discharge Survey: 2007," National Health Statistics Reports, October 26, 2010, http://www.cdc.gov/nchs/data/nhsr/nhsr029.pdf.

Chapter 46

"Animal Assisted Therapy," *Gomestic,* January 27, 2007, http://gomestic.com/pets/animal-assisted-therapy/.

Chapter 47

Centers for Disease Control and Prevention, "Diagnosis of HIV Infection and AIDS in the United States and Dependent Areas, 2009" http://www.cdc.gov/hiv/surveillance/resources/reports/2009report/index.htm.

Chapter 48

World Health Organization, "Global Immunization Data," December 2010, http://www.who.int/immunization_monitoring/Global_Immunization_Data.pdf.

Measles Initiative, "The Solution," http://www.measlesinitiative.org/portal/site/mi/menuitem.49e6575162334463c1062b10133f78a0/?vgnextoid=e79ed78aa7ca3210VgnVCM10000089f0870aRCRD&vgnextfmt=default.

World Health Organization/UNICEF, "WHO/UNICEF Joint Statement on Strategies to Reduce Measles Mortality Worldwide," http://www.measlesinitiative.org/mi-files/Reports/Policy/Position%20Papers/Joint%20Statement%20on%20Strategies%20to%20Reduce%20Measles%20Mortality.pdf.

Chapter 49

Associated Press, "US Report: 2.2 Now in Prisons, Jails," *MSNBC.com,* May 21, 2006, http://www.msnbc.msn.com/id/12901873/ns/us_news-crime_and_courts/t/us-report-million-now-prisons-jails/.

Council of State Governments Justice Center, "Report of the Reentry Policy Council—Charting the Safe and Successful Return of Prisoners to the Community," http://www.reentrypolicy.org/the_problem.

Chapter 50

Child Evangelism Fellowship, "Reaching the Children of Inmates," http://www.cefonline.com/index.php?option=com_content&view=article&id=706:reaching-the-children-of-inmates&catid=68:prison-ministries&Itemid=100101.

Lauren Glaze and Laura Maruschak, "Parents in Prison and Their Minor Children," United States Department of Justice Statistics, August 2008, http://bjs.ojp.usdoj.gov/content/pub/pdf/pptmc.pdf.

Chapter 51

"Slavery in Our Days," *Newsweek,* March 8, 2008, http://www.thedailybeast.com/newsweek/2008/03/08/slavery-in-our-times.html.

Angela Longerbeam, "Putting Faces to the Statistics: Child Sex Trafficking in Atlanta," *Change.org,* June 11,2010, http://news.change.org/stories/putting-faces-to-the-statistics-child-sex-trafficking-in-atlanta.

International Labor Organization, "A Global Alliance Against Forced Labor," http://www.ilo.org/dyn/declaris/DECLARATIONWEB.DOWNLOAD_BLOB?Var_DocumentID=5059.

US Department of State, "Trafficking in Persons Report," June 3, 2005, http://www.state.gov/g/tip/rls/tiprpt/2005/46606.htm.

"More Than 12 Million Are Trapped in Forced Labor Worldwide—International Labor Organization Releases New Major Study on Forced Labor," http://www.worldhunger.org/articles/05/global/forced_labor_ilo.htm.

Global Fund for Children, "Child Trafficking and Prostitution," 2002, http://www.globalfundforchildren.org/pdfs/GFC_childtraffic_prost.pdf.

Russell Goldman, "Modern Day Slavery in America," *ABC News,* March 26, 2007, http://abcnews.go.com/US/story?id=2981327&page=1.

Chapter 52

Child Welfare Information Gateway, "Foster Care Statistics 2009," http://www.childwelfare.gov/pubs/factsheets/foster.pdf.

Chapter 53

Indrias Getachew, "Ethiopia Steady Increase in Street Children Orphaned by AIDS," UNICEF, January 20, 2006, http://www.unicef.org/infobycountry/ethiopia_30783.html.

Chapter 54

"Illiteracy, the Downfall of American Society," July 13, 2011, http://education-portal.com/articles/Illiteracy_The_Downfall_of_American_Society.html.

"ProLiteracy Annual Report 2009–2010," http://www.proliteracy.org/Downloads/ProLiteracy_Annual-Report09-10.pdf.

Chapter 55

Child Welfare Information Gateway, "Foster Care Statistics 2009," http://www.childwelfare.gov/pubs/factsheets/foster.pdf.

Chapter 56

Centers of Disease Control, "Nursing Home Facilities, 2009," http://www.cdc.gov/nchs/data/nnhsd/nursinghomefacilities2006.pdf.

Chapter 57

UNICEF, "Liberia Statistics," http://www.unicef.org/infobycountry/liberia_statistics.html.

UNICEF, "Honduras Statistics," http://www.unicef.org/infobycountry/honduras_statistics.html.

UNICEF, "India Statistics," http://www.unicef.org/infobycountry/india_statistics.html.

UNICEF, "Cambodia Statistics," http://www.unicef.org/infobycountry/cambodia_statistics.html.

Chapter 58

The Children's Aid Society, "Aging Out of Foster Care," February 8, 2005, http://www.childrensaidsociety.org/issues/aging-out-foster-care.

Chapter 59

Pierre Tristam, "Christians of the Middle East: Country by Country Facts," *Middle East Issues,* November 16, 2010, http://middleeast.about.com/od/middleeast101/a/christians-middleeast.htm.

Cindy Grayson, "Christian Persecution Statistics," *Christian Persecution Examiner,* July 27, 2010, http://www.examiner.com/christian-persecution-in-national/christian-persecution -statistics.

Chapter 60

US Census Bureau, "America's Families and Living Arrangements," http://www.census.gov/ population/www/socdemo/hh-fam/cps2009.html.

Department for Professional Employees, "Professional Women Vital Statistics, Fact Sheet 2010," http://www.pay-equity.org/PDFs/ProfWomen.pdf.

NOTE TO THE READER

The publisher invites you to share your response to the message of this book by writing Discovery House Publishers, P.O. Box 3566, Grand Rapids, MI 49501, U.S.A. For information about other Discovery House books, music, videos, or DVDs, contact us at the same address or call 1-800-653-8333. Find us on the Internet at http://www.dhp.org/ or send e-mail to books@dhp.org.

ABOUT THE AUTHOR

Lorie Newman is a national speaker, author, and busy homeschooling mother of seven children. Her professional background and degree is in education. Lorie also enjoys freelance writing and speaking at Christian retreats and ministry events.

Lorie has been published in *Hearts at Home* and *Proverbs 31 Woman* magazines, as well as the *FamilyLife Today* blog. Her article "I'm Done Playing Church" in the online mission magazine Wrecked.org is the e-zine's most read article. *A Cup of Cold Water in His Name* is her first book.

Lorie has taught Bible studies and led prayer groups for more than fifteen years. She is the founder of an orphan ministry that enables over 250  impoverished African orphans to receive food, clothing, and education through a partnership with Children's HopeChest. Lorie has coordinated ministry events with FamilyLife's Hope for Orphans and Interfaith Hospitality Network, and leads mission trips with groups of women speakers to teach, train, and minister to the women of impoverished nations. Because of her work, Lorie has been a guest on Moody Broadcasting Network's *Midday Live Connection* during their "Women Making a Difference" series.

Lorie, her husband, Duane, and their seven children—including twins and two children who were internationally adopted from Haiti and Liberia—make their home in the southeastern United States.

For more information on booking Lorie to speak at your church or event, visit her website at LorieNewman.com.